REACTION

THE NEW COMBINES INVESTIGATION ACT

REACTION

THE NEW COMBINES INVESTIGATION ACT

Contributors include:

Reuven Brenner
L. Philippe de Grandpré
Steven Globerman
J. William Rowley
Donald N. Thompson
Edwin G. West

Edited by Walter Block

THE FRASER
INSTITUTE

Canadian Cataloguing in Publication Data

Main entry under title:
Reaction: the new Combines Investigation Act

Bibliography: p.
ISBN 0-88975-083-1

1. Canada. Combines Investigation Act – Addresses,
essays, lectures. 2. Antitrust law – Canada – Addresses,
essays, lectures. 3. Restraint of trade – Canada –
Addresses, essays, lectures. 4. Competition, Unfair –
Canada – Addresses, essays, lectures. I. Brenner,
Reuven. II. Block, Walter, 1941 – III. Fraser Institute
(Vancouver, B.C.)
KE1639.5.R42 1986   343.71'072   C86-091206-X

61 383

Printed in Canada

CONTENTS

Chapter Six
The "Errors" in Atlantic Sugar et al.V.R.   95
Colin Irving

Introduction

On December 17, 1985, Federal Consumer and Corporate Affairs Minister Michel Côté tabled in the House of Commons a bill to amend Canada's present competition law.

Although Mr. Côté claimed that the new legislation will "protect the marketplace" and "give consumers the widest selection of goods at the lowest possible price," this is extremely unlikely. A Combines Investigation Act which interferes with our system of competitive enterprise will instead stifle business rivalry, and lead to economic inefficiency. This, in turn, will reduce the welfare of the Canadian consumer.

The main drawback in Mr. Côté's initiative is that it is predicated on an untenable and outmoded economic theory. This is the view that business concentration and rivalrous competition are incompatible. It, in turn, stems from the textbook model of "perfect competition," which declares ideal a scenario in which firms are small and numerous, goods are homogeneous and unchanging, information is costless and profits are always zero.

But in the real world which Canada for better or worse inhabits, these conditions are irrelevant to rivalrous business struggle. In the marketplace, large scale enterprises, even gigantic ones, are not exempt from competition. They, too, can fail if they cease to satisfy consumer demands for quality, low price, efficiency, new products, good service and reliability.

Some improvement

Thus, it is erroneous to equate industrial concentration — whether achieved through merger, corporate take-over, or attracting customers from competitors — with failure to compete. To the credit of the new amendments, high concentration, large size, great market share and dominant position are no longer *per se* illegal. There is still a presumption, however, that these criteria are indications of, or evidence for, non-competitiveness. But there is no necessary relationship between scale of operation, no matter how large, and lack of competitive behaviour.

On the contrary, competition and concentration of achievement go hand in hand in most human endeavours. This is the rule, not the exception. Given that talents and abilities are unequally spread around among the population, and given that full and rigorous competition takes place, it should occasion no surprise that there should sometimes be only a few ''winners,'' ''survivors,'' or eminent persons associated with each activity. This is true in all areas of human endeavour, sports, politics, the arts — and business as well.

In sports, those who think that competition can occur only if numerous competitors take part, fail to appreciate what takes place in a boxing ring. In politics, those who think this believe that the continued success of one party implies monopoly, or non-competitiveness. They cannot understand the difference between the situation in Alberta and Albania — both of which have had a single government for several decades, ''supported,'' as the case may be, by overwhelming majorities. But we all know full well that quite vigourous competition can indeed take place in a boxing ring, or between two, three or four teams, as in a track or swimming meet. It is patently obvious that rigorous political rivalry exists in Alberta, not Albania, even though only one party is successful in each case. It is only regarding business where unequal results are seen as evidence of non-competitiveness. Far from an indication of lack of competition, however, inequality of retrospective results is perfectly compatible with rivalrous struggle. And this goes for business as well as these other fields.

There is all the difference in the world between a company that attains a (temporary) monopoly position through service to the consumer (new product, lower price, better service, etc.) and one that is given a permanent monopoly position through the coercive power of the state. The pre-eminent example in the latter category is the Post Office. It owes its monopoly not to its superior competitive activity, but to the law of the land which threatens those who would deliver first class mail privately with stiff fines and even jail sentences.

Implicit assumptions

Mr. Côté's Bill C-91 implicitly assumes that since the marketplace is imperfectly competitive, government can improve matters by compelling firms to compete. To be sure, the free enterprise system is indeed imperfect (and what institution composed of flesh and blood human beings is without flaw?). But it by no means follows that government can promote competitive markets. For it, too, consists of imperfect people.

Nor are their mistakes automatically kept to a minimum by a profit and loss system such as operates in the private sector.

Anti-combines legislation, moreover, is basically arbitrary. If a firm charges more than its competitors, it is subject to charges of "exploiting," or "profiteering"; if it charges the same amount, it can be seen as "colluding"; and if its prices are below those of the rest of the industry, its actions may be interpreted as "predation," or "cut-throat competition." Since there is no fourth alternative, all business concerns, without exception, are potentially liable to be accused of lawlessness. This is truly a "Catch-22" situation.

Since Mr. Côté's amendments to present combines legislation ignore these crucial points, they cannot protect the marketplace or promote competition. In penalizing firms for large scale or "dominant" market position, the Act will tend to retard, not enhance, competition. What enterprise will seek to out-compete all of its rivals if the prize is a trip to the competition tribunal?

However, the Minister has expressed himself as willing to consult extensively with consumers, business and other private-sector interests before final passage of this legislative enactment. The tabled bill, then, can best be interpreted as a "first draft" of the law which will ultimately govern Canada's competition policy, and not as a final, immutable statement, cast in concrete. In this spirit, and in the belief that the Ministry of Consumer and Corporate Affairs consists of responsible public servants who are amenable to reasoned discourse, the Fraser Institute is publishing this critique of Mr. Côté's competition law amendments.

This book, *Reaction: The New Combines Investigation Act,* features the analysis of twelve nationally renowned economists and legal scholars. The economic theory underlying the new bill is highlighted, its legal implications are explored, and the historical, empirical and statistical record is brought to bear on the problem of promoting a truly competitive business environment in Canada. This is third in a series of Fraser Institute explorations of this subject. The other two are *Competition versus Monopoly: Combines Policy in Perspective* by Donald Armstrong, and *A Response to the Framework Document for Amending the Combines Investigation Act,* by Walter Block. Both were published in 1982.

Legal commentary

As might be expected, the assessment of Bill C-91 offered by our legal scholars is measured and judicious. It is nonetheless exhaustive and thorough. If there is one constant refrain running through all six contributions in this section of the book, it is that while the present amendments may be an improvement in some ways over combines bills tabled in the past, this latest venture into competition policy is still unsatisfactory on numerous grounds. Criticisms include the following:

- It fails to reflect fully the realities and necessities of today's world economy (Macdonald);
- Markets are not fragile, as some professional worriers about the marketplace fear, but vital, as actors in the marketplace well know (Rowley);
- There is no doubt that any business entity which could be classified as a monopolist has to be very careful in fighting the competitive battle since constraints are placed on it which do not attach to its rivals (Flavell);
- Only a true Court should pass upon the subject matters entrusted by the Bill to the Competition Tribunal, which does not pass the Constitutional test (de Grandpré);
- The Crown did not have a legitimate conspiracy case against the sugar refineries, and adjusting the law to enhance the prosecution side is certainly unwarranted (Armstrong);
- An action taken by an individual company on its own, and without collusion, ought not to be potentially illegal depending upon whether or not others correctly discern its purpose and act in the same way (Irving).

We turn now to a summary of the evaluation of Bill C-91 offered by our battery of legal commentators.

William A. Macdonald

In the lead-off batter's position is William A. Macdonald, who offers a legal overview. One major complaint that arises from his analysis is that Canada and the U.S. have virtually swapped perspectives on combines policy since 1971. At that time, this country had a "minimalist" competition law, confined largely to reining in the extremes of allegedly anti-competitive behaviour. The Americans, in contrast, had a "maximalist" regime, based on a "simplistic" belief that competition could be "fine-tuned" by the public sector. But now, just as the events of the last few decades have brought an about-face south of our border, Canada, even with a Conservative government, has embraced a policy of greater government intervention. Says Macdonald "Incredible as it may seem, while the Americans were becoming more realistic during the past fifteen years, Canadians, partly insulated by a misguided sense of wealth based on resources, were becoming less so."

So much for the philosophy of Bill C-91. What of the specifics? Here, too, our author is critical. First, there are unresolved constitutional problems, regarding the "validity of granting a civil cause of action in a manner not clearly ancillary to validly enacted criminal or civil law." Then there are the difficulties with the competition tribunal, whose permission for certain mergers and other transactions must be received. On the positive side, it will now be possible to appeal its decisions. However, the whole idea indicates a regrettable faith in the ability of "so-called economic experts to second guess market processes and outcomes." There are other shortcomings as well, regarding access to computer records and extra-territoriality.

Further, the bill goes awry on merger policy, says McMillan-Binch's Macdonald. Rather than looking at the state of competition after an acquisition, C-91 probes into its effect on the number of firms, and their market share. That this is unwise is shown by the breweries and department store cases. At the time of these mergers, monopoly and undue market power were widely feared. But "today, it would be hard to point to any reduction in competition" in these fields.

But all is not lost, in Macdonald's view. Mr. Côté's amendments are to be applauded in several aspects. The search and seizure powers have been reduced. This will have positive repercussions for business-government cordiality and trust. Another source of adversarial relations, the Restrictive Trade Practices Commission, has been wisely removed. The new provision pertaining to civil abuse of dominant position is acceptable, as is the efficiency defence in merger suits.

Mr. Macdonald concludes his analysis with words that ought to be required reading for every politician and editorialist concerned with competition policy in Canada. States he: *"Market forces, sometimes slowly but nonetheless surely, sometimes and increasingly with incredible speed, erode the position of the inefficient. No company, no worker, no industry and no country has escaped from this reality. But this is not reflected in the merger provisions of Bill C-91. It is, however, recognized increasingly in the United States."*

J. William Rowley

Batting in second position is J. William Rowley, also of McMillan-Binch, who focuses a similar philosophical outlook on the question of merger.   He begins by denying the claim that the present law is nothing but a paper tiger. Despite the fact that "there has yet to be a conviction in a contested case which has been sustained on appeal," the Crown, as a result of *Irving*, can successfully prosecute, he notes. All it need do is satisfy the double test of lessened competition and public detriment.

To be sure, improper mergers are possible under free enterprise. But as those "professional worriers" who see the marketplace as "fragile" fail to reckon, the competitive system itself comes with a ready-made, self-correcting mechanism: in the absence of government bailouts, "those who make mistakes by and large pay for them through the working of the market." And most important for combines policy, we cannot blithely assume that a bureaucratic third party can "have a better view of the merger consequences than the parties themselves," states Rowley.

Our analyst, moreover, is highly critical of several elements of the merger provisions. Under the substantive test of C-91, government need no longer prove public detriment (which cannot in any case be deduced solely from market share). Instead, it need only show the *likelihood* of a substantial reduction in competition, a far less daunting task. This, according to Rowley, "sets too low a threshold for merger review and prohibition."

In his view, the bill's move away from structuralism (defining competition solely in terms of concentration ratios) is a very welcome one. However, in practice, it would not be difficult for the tribunal to evade such protections. "It is far too easy for an adjudicative body to say that its decision was not based on any one aspect of the evidence alone," he states.

But Rowley's assessments are not completely negative. He welcomes, for example, the new bill's merger definition, its joint venture sections, the elimination of criminality, and C-91's simplified and rationalized efficiency defence. He credits the consultative process for the removal of market share thresholds and the reverse onus provisions. But the bottom line is still the substantive test — which has failed to conform with the economic realities of Canada, in his opinion.

The chapter concludes with a diagrammatic formulation of sections 80-96 which outlines the prenotification procedures. No one who hopes to fully come to grips with the welter of legal requirements imposed by C-91 can afford to neglect this presentation.

C.J. Michael Flavell

C.J. Michael Flavell begins his analysis of the monopoly provisions of the bill by comparing them to the law as presently constituted. Under existing combines legislation, it is made clear, a successful prosecution for monopolization must prove both "bigness" and "badness." Nor, as *Irv-*

ing has shown, may one deduce the latter from the former; on the contrary, each is independent of the other. Along the way, in his survey-explication of how present law works, Mr. Flavell has occasion to touch upon such cases as *Eddy Match*, *Anthes*, *Irving*, *ERCO*, *Canada Safeway*, and *Canadian General Electric Company*.

Our author then summarizes the main elements of C-91, and points to what might be considered a shortcoming: the element of arbitrariness which surrounds the concept of controlling a market. How, for example, should the match market be defined? Does it comprise wooden matches alone, or does it include paper or cardboard matches, and mechanical lighter devices as well? The more narrowly defined is the product, the easier it is to "control" the market and thus be found guilty of "monopolization."

And the same holds true for geography. If the relevant market is a small town, thousands of firms in Canada can be seen as "anti-competitive"; each is a "monopolist" in its own domain. If the relevant market is the entire country, or better yet, the whole world, then no firm may be seen in this light. Tribunals may of course make determinations in this regard, but the point is that no such definition has any more economic justification than any other.

Section 51 proscribes a long list of activities — if engaged in with "predatory intent." This includes squeezing, acquisition of a supplier or customer, freight equalization, fighting brands, preemption of scarce resources, purchases to prevent price decreases, incompatible product specifications, freezing out.

Flavell, an attorney with Courtois, Clarkson, Parsons & Tetrault, notes wryly that this would appear to "curtail even defensive moves." A firm accused of "controlling," or "monopolizing" would have to, in effect, walk on eggs; it would be precluded from using techniques open to its competitors.

Nor is he particularly happy with the status of the efficiency defence. The problem is that it is exceedingly difficult to distinguish between market dominance achieved through "anti-competitive practices," on the one hand, and superior economic activity, on the other. Says Flavell, "Bill C-91 makes no attempt to resolve this dilemma." As well, he is highly critical of its provisions regarding the statute of limitations, and its unwise attack on joint monopolization, oligopolistic industries, and conscious parallelism.

L. Philippe de Grandpré

Batting in the clean-up spot is L. Philippe de Grandpré, weighing in with an analysis of the legal powers conferred by the new legislation. He begins by considering the precise legal and constitutional justification for combines law in Canada, and discusses under this heading the Criminal Law power, the Peace, Order and Good Government provision, and the Trade and Commerce clause.

Mr. de Grandpré credits Bill C-91 for correcting the constitutional defects associated with the Restrictive Trade Practices Commission's search and seizure mandate, and for thus bringing the amendments into conformity with the findings in *Southam*. But it is with regard to its replacement, the Competition Tribunal, that he reserves his most serious misgivings. In de Grandpré's view, "the substance of this committee's jurisdiction is to do and to undo contracts, to refuse to recognize contractual relationships or to impose such relationships." But this has all the earmarks of a court — without the usual constitutional, legal, or judicial safeguards that protect this institution. Nor does the fact that its decisions would be subject to oversight by the Federal Court of Appeal "validate the exercise of Judicial power by an administrative tribunal," concludes this legal scholar from Lafleur, Brown, de Grandpré.

Donald Armstong

Batting in fifth spot is Professor Donald Armstrong, who discusses the Sugar Case. This is "Exhibit A" in the brief compiled by the Ministry of Consumer and Corporate Affairs in order to show that the present Combines Investigation Act ought to be strengthened.

Since it failed to obtain a conviction in this open-and-shut case, contends the Ministry, it could scarcely stop any abuse of competitive markets. On the contrary, maintains Armstrong, "What the Sugar Case demonstrates is that under existing law companies can be punished with long and expensive trials, and can come perilously close to being fined for behaviour that is innocent of any criminal or economic wrong doing."

The McGill University professor begins his study with an overview of the trial process, an account of the activities of the three main players (Redpath, St. Lawrence, and Atlantic), a long and detailed characterization of the specialized market characteristics of sugar (expert buyers and sellers, homogeneous product), and a description of the competitive options available to them. These include, at the two extremes, super aggressive price cutting and price wars, or explicit price and market sharing agreements; the middle ground would feature independent behaviour, with the realization that, faced with the same, or very similar endowments and opportunities, this

could well be interpreted as "conscious parallelism," or "tacit agreements."
Armstrong's plaintive plea is "that the law having declared the Scylla
of predation and the Charybdis of collusion to be illegal, *it must not now
declare to be illegal that narrow band of water in between.* If it does, it
will deny to us the made-in-Canada products that must be produced by
homogeneous oligopolies."
The author of this chapter is clearly in the behavioural, not the structuralist camp. He therefore assigns little intrinsic weight to the importance
of market share as evidence of rivalistic competition. However, his empirical and statistical findings cast great doubt on the contention of the Crown
that the proportions of sales accounted for by the big three sugar giants
were fixed over time.

Colin Irving

Colin Irving's contribution is directed at two new paragraphs which are
to be added to Section 32 of the present law by Bill C-91. The first passage
provides that the Court may infer conspiracy from circumstantial evidence.
But as such an inference is already well established in law practice, we must
seek elsewhere for the real significance of these amendments, he notes.
According to Phillips & Vineberg's Irving, this is to be found in an attempt by the Crown to overturn one of the findings in the *Atlantic Sugar*
case. He refers to the view articulated by Mr. Justice Pigeon that no conspiracy may be deduced from Redpath's decision to end its price cutting
tactics, even if it did so in the expectation that its competitors would correctly interpret this behaviour, and follow suit. Says our analyst, "If the
amendment is successful in overturning the conclusion of the Supreme Court
on this issue it will have produced a profound and disturbing change in Canadian concepts of conspiracy."
As well, Mr. Irving objects to paragraph (1.3) of Section 32 on the ground
that it is an attempt to eliminate a "double intent" requirement (the "undueness" of any lessening of competition) that simply does not exist, thanks
to *Atlantic Sugar*. Even though unnecessary, fears Irving, this provision
"may well have eliminated the onus of proving any criminal intent."

Economic Commentary

If the evaluations of Bill C-91 made by our legal scholars were by and large
negative, this is no less true of our group of economic experts. Their
criticisms range widely, and include the following:

- The recent amendments do not represent a substantial step forward toward promoting free and fair competition. Rather, they continue a tradition of substituting the judgment of government-appointed ''experts'' for the judgment of the marketplace. Whether Canadians would be better off without the entire Combines Act is at least a debatable question (Globerman);

- The Act's first goal of encouraging competition, efficiency and adaptability, may be inconsistent with its second, ensuring that small and medium-sized enterprises have an equitable opportunity to participate in the Canadian economy (the Brenners);

- While it is true that increased competition may confer the benefits of low prices, increased variety and quantity of goods and services on consumers, it is a mistake to believe that legislation to restrict freedom of competition, by whatever means firms consider efficient, is the best way to achieve this goal (Ahiakpor);

- The Bill gives no suggestion as to how superior economic performance is to be measured, thus creating considerable uncertainty in the application of the law (Thompson);

- A competition policy that limits firm size will have an adverse effect on the national economy. This has led even economists such as Thurow to change their minds about the efficacy of government's use of competition laws to restrain firm size (Lecraw);

- It may well be that a new Competition Act which sharpens the teeth of the Canadian system will result in a *reduction* in efficiency, despite the claims of its advocates to the contrary (West).

We now consider the assessment of our economists in some detail.

Steven Globerman

Steven Globerman addresses himself to the question, What kind of behaviour can we reasonably expect from the operation of a competition tribunal? Lacking any direct evidence as of yet, the Simon Fraser University professor does the next best thing; he looks at the operation of similar bodies in this country, such as Investment Canada, and its predecessor, the Foreign Investment Review Agency.

Unfortunately for the economic well-being of the average Canadian citizen, Globerman's research indicates it is unlikely that the competition tribunal will function in the public interest.

He finds that although F.I.R.A. approved the overwhelming majority of mergers proposed to it, the bureaucrats in charge were apparently sensitive to the political priorities of government. Instead of sticking to its mandate of ''net benefit to Canada,'' this organization allowed itself to be diverted by lobbying efforts, economic nationalist influences, and partisanship. ''This experience,'' says Globerman, ''suggests how difficult it is to separate economic decision-making in the public sector from political imperatives.'' In addition to this empirical examination, Chapter VII also provides a theoretical cost-benefit analysis of mergers. Professor Globerman considers several arguments that have been advanced in favour of government oversight and review. Included are the views that

- the major motivation, and accomplishment, of mergers is an accretion of market power;
- if a newcomer did not enter a market by acquiring an extant firm, it would have entered *de novo,* and more competitors would exist as a result;
- highly concentrated markets are self-perpetuating, in that investors are less likely to lend to new entrants to such industries;
- mergers create barriers to entry, since they enable resulting firms to extract lower prices from suppliers, which leaves new entrants at a competitive disadvantage.

In each case, Globerman rejects these positions as untenable in the face of the evidence.

Gabrielle and Reuven Brenner

Professors Gabrielle and Reuven Brenner direct their attack on Bill C-91 at the most basic part of the edifice, the foundation. Their charge amounts to no less than a claim that these amendments are fundamentally flawed, in that they fail to come to grips with the idea of competition itself, the supposed goal of the entire enterprise.

That great philosopher Yogi Berra is reported to have coined the aphorism, ''If you don't know where you're going, you ain't gonna get there.'' If so, this certainly applies to the present endeavours, according to the Brenners.

As they explain, there is not one but rather two definitions of competition. According to the misleading academic and textbook version, competition refers to a situation where an indefinitely large number of firms sell a homogeneous product, where all relevant market information is known, ''where all innovations have long been made, all demands have long been anticipated, and where differences in entrepreneurial and managerial talents play no role." Hence, the "suspicion of relatively large enterprises," and of path-breaking innovations which do not neatly dove-tail with extant technology.

The second definition is more in keeping with ordinary parlance and the common-sense understanding of businessmen and most ordinary Canadian citizens. In this view, competition is a rivalrous and continuous process, with a "conscious driving against other business firms for patronage of buyers." Here, far from generating suspicion, large size and innovation are seen, if anything, as evidence of success in the competitive struggle to satisfy the ever-changing desires of consumers.

The core problem with the new combines bill, state the Professors Brenner, is a "fatal equivocation." In some passages, it is the first version of competition that is urged; in others, it is the second.

The difficulty is that the authors of C-91 have failed to distinguish between the two. This, unfortunately, has imparted a certain schizophrenia to the whole endeavour. In order to ameliorate this confusing situation, the husband and wife team of economists from the University of Montreal urge that the framers adopt the more reasonable (rivalrous) definition. Then, the Act can take as its purpose "to maintain and encourage competition in Canada" in *this* sense.

What public policy recommendations flow from this seemingly innocuous and sensible redefinition of terms? They are numerous, and they imply a radical departure for competition law. For one thing, "no reference should be made to the size of enterprises. Businesses may be small or medium-sized because that scope fits the talents of their decision-makers. In order to encourage competition, one must look at the *behaviour* of enterprises, rather than their size."

And how might the authorities implement this insight? One possibility is to look at the comparable rate of innovations, i.e., the percentage of company revenues which flow from products not in existence 5, 10 or 15 years ago. Such a behavioural test could have been applied to the I.B.M. or Kodak cases with far more relevance than the structural (concentration ratio) data actually employed. However, the Brenners concede that this necessary but not sufficient criterion "will not always be easy to use" in all industries. Certainly, innovation cannot be limited to the actual product in all cases (how can sugar or salt be innovated?). Rather, it must apply to service, reliability, packaging, location, informational services (such as marketing and advertising) and to all other dimensions of consumer satisfaction, including pricing policy.

In addition to their incisive work on the meaning of competition, the Brenners also show how a series of competitive behaviours have been misinterpreted as predatory or collusive. Examples include "squeezing," "consignment and commission," "fighting brands," "below cost pricing," "incompatible product specifications," and "delivered pricing." Particularly obnoxious in this regard was the whip-saw applied to I.B.M. Not only was it castigated for "withholding information," it was also attacked for "premature announcements." The co-authors of this chapter trenchantly describe this as "Damned if you do, damned if you don't."

The Brenners are also concerned about the treatment of circumstantial evidence. In C-91, it can serve as evidence of guilt — a great departure from usual practice. As well, they point to the "perversity" of the Combines Investigation Act, which allows for the legal retardation of efficient and innovating firms by those who cannot keep up in the competitive struggle.

James Ahiakpor

Before launching into a critical evaluation of C-91, Professor James Ahiakpor is careful to note that this bill is a product of the best intentions: to promote fairness, efficiency, competitiveness and consumer satisfaction. However, good intentions do not always make good public policy.

Like the Brenners, but independently of them, Ahiakpor notes the bill's misunderstanding of its own central concept of competition. He sees this as the fundamental flaw in the amendments. Since the St. Mary's University economist's brief was to trace the effect of C-91 on consumer's welfare, he links this failure to appreciate the nuances of competition with its inability to protect the Canadian shopper. For example, the bill proscribes as "anti-competitive" acts whose effects may harm the financial interests of other firms in the industry. And yet, notes Ahiakpor, the result of the fierce competition which has this effect, and is therefore prohibited, is often to reduce prices faced by the consumer. To further compound the irony, our author shows that C-91 is fully cognizant of this phenomenon. But this indicates not that Mr. Côté's Ministry is completely unaware of the implications of rivalrous competition, only that it cannot fully distinguish this notion from the textbook model of perfect competition.

Perhaps the most crucial point made by the Nova Scotian economist concerns the importance of artificial (legal) barriers to entry. This is so important because the necessary and sufficient condition of competition in the rivalrous sense is that there be free and unimpeded access to all industry for all new entrants. If there were one thing that a public policy could do to effectively promote competition, it would be to sweep away into the dust bin of history all non-market obstructions. And yet irony of ironies, it is the government, the self-styled agency of competition promotion, which erects legal road blocks to would-be enterpreneurs.

The entry barrier that Ahiakpor focuses on is tariffs and quotas. Says the Ghanaian-born economist: "Great good would be done for consumers by allowing into this country as many Japanese cars, foreign-made clothes and shoes as Canadians would like to purchase. This would far better serve consumer interests than competition laws affecting the automobile, clothing and shoe industries."

But these are only some of the main points of a fascinating Chapter 9. Professor Ahiakpor also discusses why tribunals cannot be expected to have the information assumed available to them by C-91, why the Consumers Association of Canada did not protest this bill on behalf of its membership, and how the additional red tape granted by this bill to the bureaucrats will likely impact negatively on this country's consumers. His work is punctuated throughout by pithy and incisive quotations from the classical economists such as Adam Smith, John Stuart Mill and George Marshall (who well knew the meaning of competition). This historical touch adds an attractive dimension to his analysis and reminds us that the debate about such endeavours as C-91 is not of recent origin.

Donald Thompson

Professor Donald Thompson is perhaps the least critical of the economic commentators toward the new bill. To be sure, he agrees with his colleagues in this volume that reliance on concentration ratios and other aspects of the structuralist perspective are not conducive to sensible public policy. However, he finds that "the new dominant position provision employs a behavioural rather than a structural test of illegality, focusing on anti-competitive conduct rather than the notion of monopoly."

Much of his commentary is descriptive, and predictive, rather than evaluatory. Under this rubric he discusses how the new Act might affect abuse of dominance, the superior performance defence, merger, divestiture, conscious parallelism, explicit collusion, basing-point pricing, information exchange, augmented price leadership, and price protection agreements.

In his concluding assessment of the new legislation, the York University Professor sees C-91 as "a considerable improvement over the monopoly provisions found in Section 33 of the Combines Investigation Act."

Donald Lecraw

Professor Donald Lecraw briefly reviews the structuralist paradigm which "forms the theoretical basis for many of the sections of Bill C-91," and which justifies its treatment of mergers, specialization agreements, and abuse of dominant position, etc. But he then subjects this textbook model of perfect competition to a scathing and exhaustive critique.

According to the University of Western Ontario economist, these are the main flaws in the model:

- Increased evidence has been uncovered that large firm size in many industries is necessary for efficient operations. I.e. there are economies of scale which include very large plant and firm sizes, and mergers are often undertaken to achieve these economies of scale rather than to enhance market power.
- Industry structure as it affects performance has been found to be far more complicated than was described in the original formulation and testing of the paradigm. Attempts to change industry structure directed solely or even primarily against concentration have not had the results envisioned. In fact, there have been many unforeseen, and even perverse, consequences.
- There has been increased awareness and concern over the competitive position of national firms in a globally competitive world trade, production and investment environment. In the face of large national and multinational enterprises abroad, highly mobile capital and technology, and falling tariff and non-tariff barriers to trade, there has been a re-ordering of anti-combines policy.

Another high point in this chapter is its historical account of the "saga" of anti-combines legislation in Canada. This begins in the 1960s, when the federal government funded several research efforts in the field. It continued with the (so-called) Interim Report on Competition Policy (1969), Bill C-256 (1971), the Stage I Amendments (1975), the Skeoch and McDonald Report (1976), the Stage II Bill C-13 (1977), the Proposals for Amending the Combines Investigation Act: A Framework for Discussion (1981), Bill C-29 (1983), and, finally, Bill C-91 in December 1985.

Edwin West

While several other contributors to this volume have briefly alluded to U.S.

experience with antitrust legislation as a pattern for our own efforts in this field, Professor Edwin West has devoted his entire chapter to this end.

He, too, is highly critical of the structuralist model of perfect competition which is the bedrock of Canadian combines policy. He cites studies of both profits and efficiency to cast doubt on the textbook-inspired thesis that industrial concentration can best be explained in terms of collusion. As an alternative perspective, one which is more relevant to the real world, the Carleton University economist reiterates the notion that competition is a process of business rivalry. In this view, "excess" profits would be seen not as evidence of "imperfect competition," or "predation," but rather as an inducement, reward, and spur toward efficiency for creating new products, and introducing them more quickly, the better to satisfy consumers. And the same holds true for other market practices vilified by the interventionists such as tie-in sales, vertical integration, and resale price maintenance.

Numerous observers of Bill C-91 have raised doubts about the competition tribunal, its function, its make-up, its justification.

But West raises tribunal criticism to the level of a new art form. Cynically, he notes, "these bureaucracies strive for high budgets and look for the maximum amount of work to do. To this end, government enforcers are apt to undertake sheer numbers of cases regardless of their social benefit."

Not only is it *now* unwise to legislatively prohibit tie-in sales, collusion, price fixing, information exchanges and delivered pricing (as long as government erects no entry barriers) but this was true as well in the 19th century when the Sherman Act was passed. At that time, states West, "the trusts caused output to expand faster than the rest of the economy. As a result, their prices were *falling*. This was not only recognized by Congressional opponents of the trusts, but it was the subject of their complaint that falling prices drove less efficient 'honest men' out of business."

It is for these reasons that virtually the entire economics profession has become disenchanted with competition legislation. This reappraisal, moreover, covers the entire political spectrum from left (John Kenneth Galbraith, Lester Thurow, Robert Reich) to right (Yale Brozen, Harold Demsetz, Dominick Armentano), to say nothing of the present author, Edwin West.

Conclusion

Although acknowledging that Bill C-91 is in many ways an improvement over its predecessors, the scholars in this volume have expressed major reservations about Mr. Côté's amendments to the Combines Investigation

Act. The analysis suggests that if the Federal Ministry of Consumer and Corporate Affairs has the true long-term interests of the Canadian people at heart — and we have every reason to suppose that this is so — it must seriously reconsider major portions of this program.

Indeed, as this book goes to press, there are indications that governments everywhere are retreating from the philosophy of interventionism. The U.S. is undergoing a radical alteration in its antitrust policy; Great Britain has been privatizing everything from council-housing to large corporate enterprises; even France has been forced to pull back from its initial great enthusiasm for dirigisme; and New Zealand would appear to have changed direction as well. Certainly the deregulation movement in Canada has already paid off large enough dividends in the form of lower costs and greater efficiency, that it now makes sense to push even further in this direction.

The Fraser Institute has had a long and abiding concern for promoting rational economic policy. It is publishing this volume in the interests of encouraging more informed discussion on the issues raised by the Combines Investigation Act. However, the authors have conducted their research independently, and the views they express may or may not conform singly or collectively with those of the members of the Fraser Institute.

Walter Block
March, 1986

WALTER BLOCK

Walter Block is Senior Economist at The Fraser Institute. Born in Brooklyn, New York, in 1941, Dr. Block received his B.A. from Brooklyn College in 1964 and his Ph.D. from Columbia University in 1972. He has taught Micro-economics, Industrial Organization, Urban Economics, and Political Economy at Stony Brook, State University of New York; the City College of New York, New York University; Baruch College, City University of New York; and Rutgers University, New Jersey; and has worked in various research capacities for the National Bureau of Economic Research, the Tax Foundation, and *Business Week* magazine.

Dr. Block was Editor of *Zoning: Its Costs and Relevance for the 1980s* published by The Fraser Institute. He was also an editor and contributor to *Rent Control: Myths and Realities*, the latest book in the Institute's on-going Housing and Land Economics Series. In addition, he has published numerous articles on economic theory in *Growth & Change*, *Theory and Decision*, *The American Economist*, *The Journal of Libertarian Studies*, *Real Estate Weekly*, *The International Journal for Housing Science*, and *Inquiry*. A former Cato Institute Fellow, Earhart Fellow, and New York State Regents Fellowship winner, he is the author of *Defending the Undefendable*, published by Fleet Press, New York, in 1976.

THE AUTHOR

William Macdonald graduated in 1948 from McGill University with a B.A. in political science and economics. He then attended Osgoode Hall Law School in Toronto and graduated as a barrister-at-law. At the present time he is a partner with McMillan, Binch in Toronto. Mr. Macdonald is editor of the nine-volume Prentice-Hall tax service *Income Taxation in Canada.* He was co-author (with J.W. Popkin) of "Mobilizing the Resources — the Flow of Savings," one of a series of White Paper Tax Reform Studies, published by the Canadian Economic Policy Committee in Montreal. He was co-author of two articles "Bill C-13: An Analysis of Central Issues" (with J.W. Rowley) contained in the volume *Competition Policy in Canada, Stage II, Bill C-13* and "Disclosure of Corporate Information" (with E.K. Weir) contained in the volume *Perspectives on the Royal Commission on Corporate Concentration,* both sponsored by the Institute for Research on Public Policy.

Chapter One

Overview of Competition Law Changes, 1986-Style

William A. Macdonald

I. GOVERNMENT INTERVENTION

During the last two decades, much has changed in Canada and in the world. One of the major changes in Canada and elsewhere is that faith in the efficacy of government intervention in the economy is clearly much less than it was during most of that period. At least in Canada, however, that drop in faith in government has not yet been matched by a corresponding rise in confidence markets or perhaps, more accurately, by a willingness on the part of Canadian politicians to accept the consequences of market reality.

One result is that despite the positive free market rhetoric of the new Conservative government, it has retained powers of intervention that reflect more a lack of faith in unsupervised markets than they do a positive reliance in the benign efficacy of government intervention. This is thus not yet the political environment in which one can achieve the best competition legislation possible. Nonetheless, it is certainly one in which the worst of the overreaching proposals of the past can be avoided. And this is essentially what Bill C-91 achieves.

It is hazardous to predict the future of the economy and resulting public attitudes. Nonetheless, it seems fair to suggest that, while the forces of uncomfortable and even dangerous change are strong in the world economy, the full meaning of these developments has yet to be recognized in Canadian public opinion. The result is that the new Investment Canada legislation dealing with foreign investment and the new competition law proposals contained in Bill C-91 represent at one and the same time both a major improvement over previous approaches — and a failure to reflect fully the realities and necessities of today's world economy.

Powerful economic developments

Three powerful developments characterize the world economy in which Canada must compete successfully to survive and maintain an acceptable standard of living and social policy. The first is that the great expansion of the post-war period, which flowed into the great inflation of the seventies and early eighties, is now ended. The forces of disinflation and the risk of deflation remain strong. Recent oil price weakness is only the latest instance of this phenomenon. Customers everywhere in virtually all markets have the upper hand over suppliers. The second is that technological change has become pervasive in its impact on markets and industrial structures. The third is that newly developed countries are asserting their ambitions more and more strongly; they are thereby reinforcing the already powerful pressures on markets and industrial structure from disinflation and technological change.

There is every reason to expect that these forces will become more, not less, evident in their impact on the Canadian economy and on the everyday lives of Canadians. They mean that this nation must accelerate the pace of adjustment to the new conditions. One of the proposed adjustments relates to new trading arrangements with the United States that assure better access to their markets at the price of more competition in ours. In this world, the worry is not about enough competition to protect American or Canadian consumers but about whether or not American and Canadian producers can meet competition to protect American and Canadian jobs.

Improved process

These realities have had an effect on both substance and process. For most of the period, the approach to competition law reform has been technocratic, substantively all-embracing and confrontational. However, in the past three years, during the last year of the previous Liberal government and under the new Conservative administration, the approach has become largely pragmatic and incremental. One result has been an extensive consultative process which was started by the Grits and continued by the Tories. This resulted in a broadly acceptable but still importantly flawed new Bill C-29 which was introduced but not proceeded with by the previous government prior to the 1984 federal election.

After the federal election, and following a new round of extensive consultations, an improved but still flawed Bill C-91 has now been introduced. It reflects substantial but not complete acceptance by major businesses. This consultative process, on the part of three ministers from two different governments, is not yet fully successful — judged by testing its results against vital national economic policy requirements. Nonetheless, the fact and manner of carrying out the process is extremely important. The serious use of a constructive consultative process is encouraging for the future of economic law-making in Canada at a time when this country must maintain a united front in facing increasingly tough world competition

Government-business alienation

The first version of the Competition Bill was introduced in mid-1971 to a business community that was shell-shocked from the impact of the tax reform process. The Carter Royal Commission Report on Taxation, followed first by the White Paper and then by the massively complex tax reform bill, had signalled a disturbing change in the approach of the federal government to the private sector in Canada. It also started a process of growing alienation between the federal government, both at the political and bureaucratic levels, and the private sector. This went beyond disagreements over substance. It involved a deep chasm in which common objectives and even communication became virtually impossible.

This condition persisted through the seventies and into the eighties. There were only a few but notable exceptions, such as the introduction of the manufacturing tax incentives and personal income tax indexation. As well, there was the blocking of the drive towards the ultimate in social security in terms of costs and coverage, sometimes described as the guaranteed annual income. It only subsided under the combined impact of the highest interest rates and worst recession in Canada since 1945, and when the costs of growing government intervention, of which the National Energy Program and FIRA were only the most notable examples, began to be dimly appreciated.

Business community role

Perhaps one of the most notable features of the long competition policy saga was the fact that the business community, despite the unfavourable environment, was able through persistence and resourcefulness, to prevent the implementation of the worst of the legislative proposals. In retrospect, the turning point involved the coming together of two elements. The first was the growing realization in Ottawa and elsewhere that ever upward and onward automatic economic growth was proving to be an illusion, and that there was a very tough competitive world out there to which only the private sector could respond. The second was a farsighted decision on the part of the Business Council on National Issues. It used a temporary lull in the legislative drive to propose a constructive and fully worked out alternative set of legislative proposals as the basis for new discussions between the government and the business community.

Until these events, the inspiration by the federal government to reform the combines laws of Canada did not come from a concrete assessment of how this Act suited the particular national economic circumstances. Rather, it came from looking into a rear-view mirror which reflected a combination of past United States experience and the most extreme interventionistic academic thinking in that country. This was at a time when the new economic learning and the new economic reality in the U.S. were beginning to initiate the major changes in antitrust policy and legal direction that are now clearly evident.

Canadian versus U.S. developments

The irony of the whole process is that Canada, as a relatively small and economically exposed country, had back in 1971 what one might describe as a minimalist competition law. It prevented price fixing and other such restrictive agreements which had an undue effect on competition; monopoly-making mergers; unfair price discrimination; resale price maintenance; and acts of predation by monopolists or others with unquestioned market power. By contrast, the United States at that time had a maximalist antitrust regime. It was based on a belief in the effectiveness of fine-tuning competition. This belief derived from a simplistic understanding of markets and the competitive process and from the insular perspective of the huge and still largely sequestered United States market.

Since then, the United States has moved steadily closer to the Canadian position of 1971, although they have still some way to go. This about-face reflects two things. The first is that the United States is no longer the huge, relatively untouched secluded economy it seemed to be in the sixties. Now, in a world of technological change that is incredibly costly, rapid and risky, of new economies developing and confronting each other as global rivals, and of pervasive disinflation in many major markets, Americans have directly experienced the vulnerability of their own economy and their own companies and jobs.

Incredible as it may seem, while the Americans were becoming more realistic during the past fifteen years, Canadians, partly insulated by a misguided sense of wealth based on resources, were becoming less so. And all the while, there was a renaissance of vigorous intellectual economic reexamination of antitrust policy in the universities, law schools and courts in the United States. This resulted in a new understanding of market processes at the level of individual firms that was recognizable to the businessmen who operated in those markets. The result in the United States is that perhaps for the first time since antitrust laws were first introduced in the 19th century, there is today an element of uncertainty as to whether antitrust law as generations of lawyers and businessmen have known it will be dead or alive at the centenary of the Sherman Act.

New U.S. initiatives

Indeed, as recently as mid-January, 1986, it was announced that U.S. President Reagan would send Congress a proposal to dramatically overhaul the country's antitrust laws, in an effort to make U.S. industry more competitive in international markets. The President "is convinced that our antitrust laws must reflect that competition is occurring on a global basis, that the U.S. faces stiff competition from many companies abroad," and so will propose what are described as the most sweeping changes in U.S. antitrust laws in 35 years.

No similar intellectual effort to that in the United States took place in Canada during this period. In earlier years, Canadian economic historians such as Harold Innis and William Mackintosh (of the Rowell- Sirois Report) had done realistic and innovative work in this regard. It helped shape the general understanding that prevailed about the nature of the Canadian economy. However, their understanding of the position of Canada in the world economy was increasingly lost in the sixties and seventies. It was replaced with what can only be described as shallow transplants of American views that were already on the way out in their country of origin.

Overview coverage

Presently, the tide continues to run against increased government intervention in market processes in both countries. This extends increasingly to antitrust in the United States, even though it has been until now something of a fundamentalist religion rooted in the economic culture of that country. This raises the question whether in the interests of bringing the long competition reform process to an end, one should accept merger proposals in Bill C-91 that still fall short of what is likely to prove necessary if Canada is to adjust to the new economic situation in which it now finds itself. This is the fundamental substantive question about Bill C-91. Before dealing with that question, however, a number of other broad matters should be commented on: continuing constitutional questions; the choice and nature of the proposed tribunal; the proposed demise of the Restrictive Trade Practices Commission; the proposed changes in the powers of public officials; the alterations in the conspiracy provisions; and the proposed new civil provisions dealing with the abuse of so-called dominant positions.

II. CONSTITUTIONAL ISSUES

There are two constitutional questions raised by the Stage One amendments and the new legislation. They are each discussed at length by S.G.M. Grange, Q.C., (now Mr. Justice Grange of the Ontario Court of Appeal) in the C.D. Howe Research Institute Commentary ''The Constitutionality of Federal Intervention in the Marketplace — The Competition Case.'' The first question relates to the granting of discretionary powers to the Restrictive Trade Practices Commission in the Stage One amendments and to the Competition Tribunal under Bill C-91 to intervene not only in matters affecting international and interprovincial trade, but also in matters affecting local trade within a single province and property and civil rights within a province. The second question concerns the validity of granting a civil cause of action in a manner not clearly ancillary to validly enacted criminal or civil law. The Grange conclusions were essentially negative to constitutionality on both counts. So far, court decisions on each count have gone both ways, and the matter will not be resolved until cases reach and are decided by the Supreme Court of Canada. It will be unfortunate if the continuing failure to address the constitutional concerns, especially those relating to the tribunal powers, should result in a declaration of constitutional invalidity which effectively negates the entire twenty-year reform effort.

Tribunal versus courts

One of the other crucible issues of the long competition reform saga has been the role of a specialized economic tribunal. It had discretionary powers to look at various practices and transactions and to decide whether or not they should be allowed to continue or to proceed. This approach was first proposed in the 1971 bill. It remained a constant throughout the reform process until May 1984 when the then Minister, the Honourable Judy Erola, reversed the position and opted for the Courts. That decision resolved the two major concerns of the business community and others about the earlier tribunal proposals: first, a lack of faith in so-called economic experts to second-guess market processes and outcomes; and second, the absence of a full appeal to the Courts on errors of both fact and law.

The new Minister has reversed the Bill C-29 approach and reverted to a tribunal, but with some differences. To overcome concerns that the tribunal not be able to initiate or undertake investigations, a good many safeguards to ensure due process have been built in. For example, unlike the present Restrictive Trade Practices Commission, the new Competition Tribunal is to be a court of record with no research or investigatory functions; nor will it supervise the use of the Director's powers. Also, while the Competition Tribunal may make its own rules, they are subject to Governor-in-Council (i.e. Cabinet) approval.

Proposed competition tribunal

The Tribunal is to be composed of both federal Court judges and lay members, the latter having expertise in industry, commerce or public affairs (subsection 3(2)-(4), p. 2). Generally, the Tribunal will act in panels of three, but each panel must always be chaired by a judicial member (section 10, p. 4). Moreover, all questions of law will be decided by judicial members exclusively. Lay members will only participate in decision-making on questions of fact and mixed questions of fact and law (section 12, pp. 4-5).

Although proceedings before the Tribunal are to be as informal and expeditious as fairness permits (subsection 9(2), p.4), its decisions must be based on the evidence presented. The latter requirement is important and provides a useful safeguard against decisions being based on the opinions or presumed expertise of panel members. There is concern, however, about the injunction for expeditious dealings. Given that some of the subjects for decision (e.g. mergers) are likely to involve extremely complex factual questions, it might be better to avoid the suggestion that speed of decision-making is an end in and of itself. At the same time, delay in commercial transactions can be fatal.

On the positive side, and for the first time, there will be full appeals from decisions of the Tribunal to the Federal Court of Appeal. This will be on the same basis as appeals from decisions of the Federal Court Trial Division (section 13, p. 5). However, it can only be regarded as regrettable that there is no provision for Cabinet override of Tribunal decisions prohibiting mergers. This is particularly important given the concerns surrounding the substantive merger test and the fundamental importance of the merger process to industrial restructuring.

Regrettable, but not fatal

These represent undoubted improvements over previous approaches to a tribunal for competition matters. Nonetheless, it is in many ways regrettable, albeit not fatal, that the issue of a specialized economic tribunal versus the Courts should have been reopened at this late stage. The scope and nature of decision-making by a tribunal has always been at the heart of the difficulties encountered over the past decade and a half. Whatever the previously perceived merits or demerits of such a tribunal, the reality today is that the very concept of sophisticated economic judgments from appointed experts is broadly discredited in international business circles. It is also increasingly discredited in academic economic circles, which are rediscovering the irresistible power of markets, even in the so-called areas of monopoly and oligopoly.

The overpowering evidence of the traumatic economic events of the past fifteen years, in Canada and elsewhere, is that non-marketplace players, like bureaucrats and government boards, cannot keep pace with the changes encountered every day in the private sector. As a result, to move back to a tribunal and away from the compromise achieved in the previous consultative process may well be seen to be regressive in both Canadian and foreign business and investment communities. A new competition tribunal may thus send the wrong message to these decision-makers. This would be on the basis of a gut feeling that in the light of today's fast changing economic environment, a so-called expert tribunal is the wrong vehicle for overseeing adjustment. A majority is likely to prefer the Courts as best able to respond to those relatively few cases where there may be genuinely insufficient competition in a marketplace for whatever reason.

Courts better choice

All of this indicates that on balance the better approach would have been to employ the Courts to apply clearly established legislative rules. This would involve a twofold approach which combined primary reliance on carefully circumscribed rules applied by the Courts with the potential for Cabinet intervention in special cases. Only practices or transactions which adversely affect competition in a major way should be covered. And the rules determining when this occurs should be established by Parliament in advance. This means primary reliance would be placed on rules established by Parliament in legislation, not on the discretion of appointed so-called experts based on what may be in their minds from time to time.

It is certainly never possible to capture every relevant aspect of evolving economic events in pre-established rules. In today's world, however, this reality is better reflected primarily in rules which are based on confidence in the inherent vitality of competitive forces and which permit all practices without question except those with undoubted major adverse effects on competition. The recourse to the discretionary power of "experts" to decide on the rules as they go along is not likely to create business and investor confidence. There is one hopeful possibility. The rules established in the new legislation which are to be applied by the new Competition Tribunal may prove to be sufficiently clear and precise that there will be little practical difference between the new Competition Tribunal with a full appeal to the Courts and the use of the Courts in the first instance, as well as on appeal.

Cabinet override

In either case, there will still be special cases where pre-established rules applied by the Competition Tribunal or the Courts may nonetheless be perceived as running contrary to broader national economic policy interests. This does not, however, dictate abandoning the use of the Courts, whether in the first instance or only on appeal, to apply rules established by Parliament. This approach will produce the best outcome in the overwhelming majority of cases. What is needed, however, and what would be completely appropriate, is to make a Governor-in-Council (i.e. Cabinet) override available. This would take place in that tiny minority of cases where national economic policy considerations may dictate a different result than that which would arise by applying a set of pre-established rules.

In order to achieve this, a provision not unlike that provided in relation to taxation of all kinds in the Financial Administration Act could be included. This would empower the Cabinet by published order-in-council to permit what might otherwise not be permitted. It could do so either in advance of or after the issue has been dealt with by the Courts. The basis of the exercise of the power by Cabinet would relate to national policy and not legal considerations. Accordingly, the judicial primacy of the Courts in legal matters would be unaffected by an intervention by Cabinet on policy grounds which ran contrary to the effect or potential effect of the legislated rules as applied by the Courts. The precondition to a successful tribunal is credibility in the superior performance of so-called experts. That precondition does not exist in Canada in 1985. The choice of a tribunal is thus not by itself positive. However, the tribunal will be established and circumscribed in ways (including full Court appeals) which is likely to bring it practical operations very close to those of the Courts, albeit with expert member input. This may go a long way to offset most, if not all, of the perceived negatives of the choice of a tribunal over the Courts.

Membership calibre, Cabinet responsibility, are fundamental

One of the unknowns is whether or not high calibre members can be attracted to the Tribunal. A concern is that if there is enough work for the Tribunal to attract the highest quality membership, it will mean the net has been cast too widely and too many situations are being caught up in it. On the other hand, if the net is cast correctly, there may be too little challenging work to attract the most skilled participants. Yet the ablest membership is the only possible justification for the employing of a tribunal rather than the Courts.

Finally, and in any event, economic policy is the ultimate responsibility of the federal government. It should retain, if for only the most major cases, the ability to intervene and allow a merger to go forward. This applies even though the Competition Tribunal and/or the Courts have properly found it should not be based on the facts of the case and the specific rules enacted by Parliament.

One of the effects of the change from criminal to civil law in the areas of mergers and monopolization (abuse of dominance) and of the establishment of the new Tribunal is that the Restrictive Trade Practices Commission (RTPC) will be disbanded. This will produce several positive results. It will no longer be able to initiate inquiries. The Courts, not the new Tribunal, will supervise the exercise of the Director's powers. And no longer will an entity with independent investigatory powers like the RTPC be in a position of passing judgment in individual cases.

Powers reform

There were two basic shortcomings in the previous consultative process, as reflected in Bill C-29. One was the complete failure to come to grips with the issue of appropriate Directors' and RTPC powers. The other related to the threshold test for mergers. This latter shortcoming persists under the present Bill. The former, however, is addressed in the new Bill. This is because since Bill C-29 was introduced, the Department felt a strong need to obtain a revision of its severely curtailed search and seizure powers so that the requirements laid out by the Supreme Court of Canada in the Southam case could be met.

Beyond these reasons, if Canada is to move forward in the face of the present harsh economic environment, the least adversarial and best possible atmosphere between government and business is essential. Traditionally, one of the serious sources of mistrust between business and the federal government in Canada has been in the exercise of the extraordinary combines powers of search and seizure. To respond to these concerns, the existing powers of the Director required significant revisions. The fact that Bill C-91 addresses this requirement in a comprehensive manner is a major step forward for Canadian combines law and for the future character of the relationship between business and the federal government.

III. THREE KEY PRINCIPLES

The Canadian business community and legal profession have long felt that the powers of the Director should be revised to reflect three main principles. First, the powers of search and seizure for those combines matters which remain criminal should reflect the long-standing fundamentals of a citizen's rights to privacy that apply in ordinary criminal cases. This is now required by the Southam decision in any event. That decision vindicated the legitimacy of the business community's long and deeply held convictions about the excessive powers in the hands of combines officials. Second, search and seizure powers, even as revised, should not be available in civil proceedings, nor should the results of their exercise, even in good faith for criminal enforcement purposes, be available directly or indirectly for civil proceedings. Third, the Director has other substantial powers. The exercise of these powers should be subject to the control of an accountable

Minister and to supervision by the Courts, to ensure that due process requirements have been observed.

Vast improvement

The resulting Bill C-91 is a vast improvement over the existing law and over any previous Bill. A complete code governing the extent and use of the Director's investigatory powers is provided. The exercise of all the Director's powers (production of records, oral examination or search warrants) will require judicial approval. Search warrants will be available for both criminal breaches and civilly reviewable matters. The confidentiality obligation of the Director with respect to investigations is strengthened. A procedure for claiming solicitor/client privilege for some communications is provided. The Director no longer has a power to initiate a general inquiry, such as does the present Petroleum Industry Inquiry under Section 47 of the present Act. Parties affected by the exercise of any powers of the Director should now have adequate recourse to the Courts to ensure their exercise is appropriate and not unduly burdensome.

Shortcomings remain

All of this represents substantial and long overdue improvement in the fundamental areas of legitimacy and due process in relation to the large powers granted combines officials. Their sensible administration can do much to reduce the government business gap. But shortcomings and concern still remain which should be addressed. The separation of criminal from civil proceedings under the Act in terms of the officials and powers involved remains to be achieved. The new access to computer records has a potential for major cost and business operation problems if not properly handled. And the right to force a Canadian company to deliver documents from a foreign affiliate has an extra-territorial dimension. This seems inconsistent with the long-standing posture of the Canadian government on extra-territoriality. The timing is also questionable, to say the least. The recent adverse experience of the Bank of Nova Scotia involving the extra-territorial application of U.S. law was strongly objected to by the Canadian government. The issue is also important for the upcoming Canada-U.S. trade negotiations.

Conspiracies essentially unchanged

The most notable aspect of the Bill's treatment of conspiracies is that the essential underpinnings of the present conspiracy section are to remain unchanged. This was also the position under Bill C-29. The basic "undueness" test remains after an earlier effort by combines officials to have it replaced by a "per se" rule. The export agreement exemption to the conspiracy offence is to be broadened and the new tribunal may exempt certain industry specialization agreements from the application of the conspiracy provision. The maximum fine is increased from one million to five million dollars.

For most of the second stage of the competition reform process, the conspiracy provisions were not one of the major issues. They emerged as a potentially important and divisive issue in April 1981 in the document presented by the then Minister entitled "Proposals for Amending the Combines Investigation Act — a Framework for Discussion." What was the primary inspiration for the far-reaching changes in the conspiracy provisions contained in the Framework document? It was the feeling in the Department that the effect of ten unsuccessful cases between 1975 and 1980 had emasculated the long-standing conspiracy provisions of the Combines Act. In addition, Departmental officials at that time sought to go beyond those concerns in an attempt to abandon the long-standing undueness threshold and replace it with the zero threshold of a "per se" offence.

Fortunately, a careful analysis of the cases revealed the Departmental reaction to be a major overreaction. As a result, the only other changes are new evidentiary provisions. Experienced legal counsel in the field believe these do no more than clarify and confirm what they have always believed to be the law in any event.

New civil abuse of dominant positions acceptable

After fifteen years of unsuccessful attempts, Bill C-29, for the first time, dealt with the issue of monopoly in an essentially appropriate and acceptable manner. The underlying theory was that firms which occupy a dominant position owe a special duty not to engage in anti-competitive behaviour. The only concern with the new approach was an overlap between the criminal conspiracy provision and the proposed civil monopoly provisions. This occurs because the new civil clauses apply to essentially the same class of persons as the present criminal law.

The provisos in Bill C-91 are rooted in Bill C-29. Changes have been minor and have led to improvements. While the proposed civil regulation of monopolies (now known as "dominant positions") differs significantly from the criminal law treatment in the present Act, the basic approach continues to be behavioural (that is, based on what you do), rather than structural (that is, based on your share of market position). Despite the lessening of the onus of proof (which comes from the move to a civil from a criminal jurisdiction) and the expanded power of the new proposed Tribunal to effect structural solutions, the new section has a high threshold. This should limit Tribunal intervention only to obvious cases of abuse of market power. The overlap concern, however, remains.

Merger provisions key

The question of mergers is reviewed in depth elsewhere. Nonetheless, mergers are so fundamental to the future restructuring of the Canadian economy that their proposed treatment is a key to any overview of the Bill as a whole. There is one issue which goes to the heart of any merger reform. This is the legal test by which mergers are to be assessed, apart from any question of efficiency (the approach to an efficiency defence contained in both previous Bill C-29 and new Bill C-91 is essentially appropriate).

The choice of legal test depends on one's perspective on how much government intervention is necessary to preserve competition in Canadian markets. A pessimistic view of the vigour of competitive forces produces a concern about any reduction in the number of Canadian-based competitors or in the quality of competition offered. This leads in turn to a test which will allow intervention whenever a merger seems to have anything more than a marginal effect. A more optimistic view of the vigour of competitive forces suggests a test which will only permit intervention if substantial post-merger competition no longer remains. This means that the government, when it makes its policy choice, is also making a statement about two things. The first is about its understanding of the operation of market forces in the Canadian and world economy. The second is about its faith in bureaucratic intervention in the economy.

Consumer in driver's seat

The reality today is that market forces around the world have placed the consumer, not the supplier, in the driver's seat. Even the powerful United States economy has had to come to terms with this reality on an international scale. Technology, product and service substitution and new countries and competitors are dictating business responses everywhere. In no country is there evidence that bureaucratic involvement in this process is economically constructive or necessary to sustain the vigour of these competitive forces.

This is a bold conclusion only to those whose thinking is hamstrung by the past, when quieter times may have suggested possibilities for fruitful bureaucratic intervention. A classic example of the inaccuracy of that pessimistic view, even in quieter times, is the beer case in Canada some three decades ago. The industry was left alone by the Courts, in a decision much criticized by academics. However, the present configuration of competition in the Canadian beer industry bears no relationship to that resulting from the Canadian Breweries merger. This is because substantial competition remained after the merger. A more recent example may be found in the department store mergers of a few years ago. The worry then was that the new union would prove competitively unassailable and would dominate. Today, it would be hard to point to any reduction in competition in retail marketplaces.

Wrong policy choice made

The unavoidable conclusion is that the proper policy choice is a test based on the state of competition after the merger, not on the effect of the merger on competition as it existed prior to the merger. Not only is this test both straightforward and readily understandable. It also tends to keep bureaucratic intervention to a minimum. And of perhaps equal importance, it will provide an unmistakable statement on the part of the government of its belief in market forces and a marketplace system.

By choosing an "effects on pre-merger competition" rather than a "post-merger competition" test, Bill C-91 must be judged to reflect the wrong policy choice. Because of the importance of this area, the business community would be justified, indeed may be said to have a duty, to draw the adverse consequences of this policy choice to the attention of the government and the country. This must be done in a forceful but not adversarial manner. This is more for the benefit of Canada and Canadians, than for business. At the end of the day, if thwarted inside Canada, business can and will redirect and restructure itself outside of our borders. But Canada and Canadians generally have no such choice.

Market forces, sometimes slowly but nonetheless surely, sometimes and increasingly with incredible speed, erode the position of the inefficient. No company, no worker, no industry and no country has escaped from this reality. But this reality is not reflected in the merger provisions of Bill C-91.

It is, however, recognized increasingly in the United States. Moreover, it is not countries or industries that themselves compete, but individual firms. This means that big firms are needed in the big leagues; firms with the financial, organizational and technological strengths to stay the course.

U.S. has got message

White House spokesman Larry Speakes, in announcing proposed new antitrust laws on January 15, 1986, noted that of the fifteen largest industrial corporations in the world, no more than five are based in the United States and that 70 percent of U.S. companies face competition from abroad. Needless to say, none of the top fifteen largest industrial corporations reside in this country and Canadian companies are no less exposed to competition from abroad. Speakes then went on to say

> Many of these firms would like to merge, in order to become more effective, and they are held back because of certain parts of the merger policy. Our goal is to allow them to merge in order to compete on an international basis. In the long run, we believe it would allow them to better serve consumers. The laws now in place are those that have been in place from another era.

Once again, this is not the stance reflected in the merger provisions of Bill C-91, although the case is powerful that if the United States needs to move in this direction, even more so does Canada.

IV. SUMMATION

The following is an overview summation of Bill C-91 as a whole.

1. The reality of market forces and the relative ineffectiveness of government intervention in markets is taking hold in the consciousness of governments and Canadian public opinion, but still has some distance to go.
2. Bill C-91 represents a major gain over previous attempts in terms of the consultative process employed, the accountability and due process of the large powers exercised by combines officials and of economic reality.
3. It would be preferable for all matters to be dealt with by the Courts rather than a new, untried Competition Tribunal. Nonetheless, the ap-

proach taken and the full appeals from its decisions to the Courts may reduce the natural concerns about a tribunal, subject always to the question of the calibre of the Tribunal membership.

4. Industrial restructuring is fundamental to the future of the Canadian economy, and mergers are fundamental to the restructuring process. For this reason, major mergers rejected by the Tribunal or the Courts should nonetheless be able to proceed if the Cabinet believes that they should do so, and is prepared to accept policy responsibility for going beyond the provisions of the law to allow it.

5. Questions of constitutionality remain with respect to the powers of the Tribunal and the civil matters reviewable by it. This is because those powers will extend to issues involving local trade and property and civil rights within a province. This could ultimately invalidate the Tribunal as unconstitutional unless subsequently amended to restrict the scope of civil matters to those involving international and interprovincial trade.

6. There is a major improvement in the subjection of the powers of combines officials to court supervision, but the failure to limit the full powers of officials to criminal cases constitutes a serious defect.

7. The minor changes to conspiracies and the new civil review powers in relation to abuse of dominant positions are acceptable. They involve no major change of substance from the previous law.

8. The approach to mergers is fundamentally flawed by adoption of a threshold test that is far too low for the competitive and market size realities of the Canadian economy. Canada cannot afford the luxury of government interference with mergers so long as substantial competition exists after the merger. The United States is facing this reality and Canada has no choice but to do the same.

9. The business community owes a duty to the country to express its views on the merger provisions forcefully but fairly. The ultimate responsibility rests with the federal government. It should not be allowed to think that the merger provisions will serve the overriding need for much more rapid corporate and industry restructuring in Canada than has yet taken place.

THE AUTHOR

J. William Rowley is a practising barrister and partner in the Toronto law firm of McMillan, Binch. Prior to joining that firm he was one of the legal secretaries to the Supreme Court of Canada, and before that was employed as a special assistant to the Director of the Combines Branch in Ottawa. Educated at the Universities of Carleton and Ottawa he obtained the latter's gold medal on graduation from its LL.B programme. He is a member of the Bars of Ontario and Alberta and has received special calls to the Bars of Quebec and New Brunswick. As well as maintaining an active trial practice in the Ontario and Federal Courts he is a regular instructor in the Ontario Bar Admission Course at Osgoode Hall, and an occasional lecturer in the Ontario Law Society's programme of Continuing Education for the practising Bar. He is also a frequent writer and speaker in the antitrust and trade regulation field both in Canada and abroad. In addition to being a contributor to the Financial Post on the same subject, he has authored a variety of articles in the field and was the co-author with W.T. Stanbury of *Competition Policy in Canada, Stage II*. He was co-author with W.A. Macdonald of a paper "Bill C-13: An Analysis of Central Issues." Mr. Rowley also serves as Vice-Chairman of the Antitrust and Monopolies Committee of the International Bar Association.

Chapter Two

Merger and Pre-Merger Notification

J. William Rowley

Canada's merger laws are 75 years old. Over their history only eight merger cases have been taken through a full trial. Moreover, if one ignores the guilty pleas, there has yet to be a conviction in a contested case which has been sustained on appeal. Against this backdrop complaints from the competition authorities, both about the law and the courts, have been frequent and, at times, shrill. This in turn has contributed to a conventional view that the present merger law is a paper tiger.

This alleged weakness of today's legislation and the asserted adverse public interest effects have stimulated claims that the only remedy is major surgery. This reaction has been widespread and cannot be ignored. However, there are a number of issues which need to be addressed before conclusions as to appropriate merger amendments, if any, can be arrived at:

- is the present law as ineffective as is claimed in some circles?
- even if the present law is more effective than its critics are prepared to acknowledge, are there nonetheless reasons for change?
- do the proposals in C-91 fill the prescription for Canada's needs?

I. THE LAW TODAY

The present Act, under criminal sanction, outlaws mergers which are likely to result in a lessening of competition to the detriment of the public — a two part test. In the early days, despite the public detriment component, it used to be thought that the test was met by market concentration alone. Then, the Supreme Court of Canada, in its *Irving* decision held that this is not automatic and that public detriment cannot invariably be inferred from market concentration alone. Instead, real evidence of public detriment must be shown. This case (and the conclusion that evidence of detriment is required and may not be automatically presumed) is believed by some to have sounded the death knell of enforceability of the current provisions.

Prior to *Irving*, proponents of change and of tougher standards most often cited the celebrated *Canadian Breweries* and *Western Sugar* cases. These decisions, and therefore the law, they argued, were perverse — requiring they said the creation of a monopoly before a conviction could be entered. But these criticisms ignored the fact that two decisions do not make a law — especially trial decisions of the late fifties, neither of which the Crown had bothered to appeal. Certainly, practitioners experienced in the field were not prepared to accept the view that only those mergers which create monopolies were subject to attack.

In addition, it is far from certain that the cases were improperly decided on the facts. For example, in the *Breweries* case (the most often cited example of the ineffectiveness of the law) the complaint had been that Canadian breweries achieved more than 60 percent of the market through a series of mergers. This was said to constitute public detriment. The court did not agree. It held, in effect, that enough competition remained to keep the beer market competitive.

Events since the decision are instructive. They tend to support the view taken by the court. The reality is that enough competition remained to strip away from Canadian breweries during the years following the merger some two-thirds of its merger-achieved market share. These adjustments did not occur overnight, but they did occur over time as the competitive market forces still remaining took hold.

Vigorous markets

The *Breweries* case aside, there is ample evidence that markets are not fragile, as some professional worriers about the marketplace fear, but vital, as the actors in the marketplace well know. The essence of what has become known in the United States as "the New Learning" is that there is an inexorability to market forces. These erode the positions of the inefficient, no matter what the protective devices, private or governmental, where such are aimed at market preservation on any basis other than economic efficiency.

Developments in the United States provide the best examples. Despite the size of its economy and the fact that it constitutes the richest domestic market in the world, the United States has seen entrenched industry after entrenched industry forced into retreat in the face of the power of international market forces. Given that the strength of these forces on Canadian industry can hardly be less, one must consider the present law (or any future law) in conjunction with these market force realities before forming a judgment as to our legislative needs.

How then do the *Irving* requirements, (for both a decrease in competition plus some form of public detriment) stack up in this context? Are they likely to permit, or have they permitted, a succession of mergers which, over time, would or will act to the detriment of the public in Canada? While it is perhaps not possible to answer these questions with absolute certainty, most objective observers would say no. They would point to the fact that mergers are not now going forward (nor have they been) which are obviously damaging to the public interest. Indeed they would be supported in this observation by the recently retired Combines Director, who in his last annual report,* pointed to:

(i)   the recent stabilization of the Canadian post-war trend towards higher industrial concentration;

(ii) the turnover in the relative ranks of leading firms — which shows that positions are not entrenched and that market forces are working; and

(iii) a decrease in horizontal merger activity.

At the end of the day the test of a bad law is whether events are occurring which should not be. The fact is that we cannot readily point to particular mergers which can be said to operate against the public interest. This likely means that the present law is cutting in at the right point to prevent them.

---

*Annual Report of the Director of Investigation and Research for the Year Ending March 31, 1984, p. 8.

Present constraints/reasons for change

The alleged unenforceability of the present law has likely been over-criticized from the standpoint that mergers are now permitted which are against the public interest. But this does not mean that the law is not preventing mergers which should be permitted. As a result of *Irving*, the Crown is now in a position to succeed (if it chose to enforce the law) by proof of lessened competition plus public detriment. There is no requirement that competition be lessened substantially or significantly or to any particular degree — only that it be lessened. As to public detriment, although the Supreme Court has said it may not necessarily be presumed from increased market share, it seems relatively clear that the Crown's options are open. There is nothing to stop an able prosecutor from citing evidence of higher prices or fewer outlets or plant shutdowns in support of an argument of public detriment.

Viewed in this light there is good reason to believe that the present law is not as ineffective as is claimed in some quarters. Indeed, rather than failing to prevent mergers that are contrary to the public interest it is more likely that it prevents or will prevent mergers that are potentially desirable in terms of international competitive market realities and the achievement of beneficial economic efficiencies. This failing, and not the alleged toothlessness of the present wording, is the real reason that change may be desirable.

The fact that the current law is not ineffective, does not mean that those mergers which have taken place without attack will necessarily prove to have been in the public interest — at least in the narrow sense that hoped for economic improvements will be achieved. It does mean, however, that most, if not all, mergers which may subsequently prove not to be economically successful will pay a real economic price that, one way or another, will force adjustment. A market system is not one under which no economic mistakes are made. Rather, it is a self-correcting system in which those who make the mistakes by and large pay for them through the working of the market.

In a properly operating market system, the reality is that mergers and takeover bids, however unwelcome to some shareholders, officers, suppliers or customers of a particular firm, reflect market considerations. The presumption in a market economy is that they should normally proceed. At the same time, such mergers and takeovers may or may not have ultimate economic benefit. This means that the law cannot be premised on either the view that mergers are generally good or that they are generally bad.

Equally, it means that it cannot be premised on the assumption that a third party is likely to have a better view of the merger consequences than the parties themselves.

II. THE MERGER PROPOSALS

Given the conditions of international competition that are likely to prevail, and the importance to Canadian industry of being able to strengthen its organizational, financial and efficiency base, Bill C-91's approach to mergers will, almost certainly, be regarded as the most important component of the new legislation. Its treatment of the subject (and the rules relating to pre-notification) are likely to provoke controversy. If length and complexity were grounds for complaint, concern would certainly be justified.

In principle, however, the substantive rules are comparatively straightforward. The same cannot be said for the pre-notification provisions. Nevertheless there are improvements over Bill C-29 in this area.

There are four themes to the approach to mergers:

(i) a move away from criminal law;
(ii) an attempt to narrow the scope of the section's transactional coverage;
(iii) a substantive test based only on competitive effects; and
(iv) a defence based on resulting efficiencies.

While the significance of dropping the criminal approach is undoubted, the change in the scope of coverage is almost certainly more important.

A new definition — joint ventures exempted

The amended definition is an improvement over both Bill C-29 and the present Act. In each of these former cases too many transactions had the potential to be challenged. The new definition is somewhat narrower but nonetheless still encompasses too many transactions.

Under its terms "... control over or significant interest in the whole or a part of a business ..." must be acquired. Before it was only necessary to establish that the merger resulted in "... *any* control over or interest in ..." the business of another. These changes will tend to limit the application of the section (although not completely) to what might be regarded as mergers of the classic type. The result is that a number of corporate arrangements, including a variety of joint ventures, which come within the present definition will no longer be subject to review.

In addition, there is also to be a further exemption for certain defined joint ventures (new section 67, pp. 51-2). This excludes combinations formed to undertake a specific project or a program of research and development if:

(i) the project or program would not otherwise have taken place or would not reasonably have taken place or be reasonably likely to take place, given the risks involved;

(ii) no change of control over any of the participants in the combination results;

(iii) the parties enter into a written agreement requiring one or more of them to contribute assets, governing a continuing relationship between the parties, restricting the activities of the combination and providing for termination of the agreement on completion of the project or program; and

(iv) the combination does not prevent or lessen or is not likely to lessen competition except to the extent reasonably required to undertake and complete the project or program.

While not all joint ventures are excluded, the exemption will help to relieve anxieties over possible merger review risks in a number of cases. Although not all joint venturers will be satisfied and despite the illogical exclusion of incorporated joint ventures the proposal is a welcome one.

The substantive test

If the merger definition and the joint venture carve-out are improvements, the same may not turn out to be the case for the proposed substantive test. The present Act requires the Crown to prove (under criminal onus) not only that competition has been or is about to be lessened, but also that public detriment will result. Moreover, public detriment may not be implied simply from the fact that a merger under attack has resulted in a high market share. (This is not unreasonable given that firms of considerable size and power are necessary to compete effectively in today's international markets.)

The trouble with the proposed test — which requires only a likelihood of competition being lessened substantially (new section 64(1)) — is the possibility that it sets too low a threshold for merger review and prohibition. Certainly it will be possible for the new Competition Tribunal or the courts (on appeal) to conclude that a merger lessens competition substantially even though it is, on balance, beneficial to the public interest — or at least not contrary to the public interest. This follows from the removal of the need to show public detriment and the fact that a substantial lessening of competition is not in itself the equivalent.

Also, with a test which requires only a substantial lessening of competition what are the Courts to do in Canada's concentrated market universe? What result may we expect, for example, when two of four 25 percent market share competitors merge? One not unreasonable view would be a finding that competition had been lessened substantially — there being only three competitors left in the market, one of which has a 50 percent share. On the other hand, there is a strong argument that the continued existence of two producers with a combined 50 percent market capacity is almost certain to be sufficient to impose the competitive disciplines of the marketplace on the merged enterprise.

Structuralism

To avoid the possibility of the first interpretation, new subsection 64(2) provides that a merger shall not be found to lessen competition substantially "solely on the basis of evidence of concentration or market share." This direction to avoid a structuralist approach will be of some help. However, it will not be definitive. In actual practice, it is far too easy for an adjudicating body to say that its decision was not based on any one aspect of the evidence alone.

In formulating a merger test the question which must always be addressed is whether the proposal sets a sufficiently high threshold for intervention. Too low a threshold permits costly and time-consuming and uncertainty-creating interventions into marketplace dynamics. This is both unnecessary and would be particularly unhealthy in the present Canadian context. Unfortunately the current proposals have the real potential to be interpreted as setting too low a standard. Should this occur it is almost certain to prevent, or at least seriously dampen, the rapid industrial adjustments that are regarded as a necessary step towards making Canadian industries more world competitive.

A final concern about the test is its similarity to that used in the United States. In the U.S., at least at present, the Clayton Act (Section 7) outlaws mergers whose effect "... may be substantially to lessen competition ...." There are two problems. First, given the similar wording, Canadian courts will be tempted to import American jurisprudence. In the past American courts have found that the acquisition of enterprises which have only minor market shares can breach the standard. This could prove disastrous in the Canadian context.

A second and more serious problem arises from recently publicized indictations that U.S. merger laws are about to be changed. Although the precise amendments are not as yet known it is certain that the standard will become more permissive. This is because it is widely recognized that the present law acts as a serious constraint to the sort of industrial rationalization which is required to enable American industries and companies to compete effectively against the more efficient industries and stronger companies of the Pacific basin and a rejuvenated European community. The danger for Canada is that the new test may deny its industries the same ability to reorganize at a time when reorganization will be crucial to survival.

Factors to be considered

Before leaving the substantive test, reference should be made to new subsection 65(1). By its terms, in deciding whether a merger lessens competition substantially, the Tribunal may consider the following factors (or any other factor relevant to competition in the market):

  (i) the extent to which foreign products or competitors provide or are likely to provide effective competition to the businesses of the parties to the merger or proposed merger;
 (ii) whether the business or a part thereof of a party to a merger or proposed merger has failed or is likely to fail;
(iii) the likelihood of availability of acceptable substitutes for products supplied by the parties to the merger or proposed merger;
 (iv) the effect of any tariff barriers or non-tariff barriers or other regulatory controls on the ability to enter the market; and
  (v) whether substantial competition would continue to exist after the merger.

On balance, these factors are an improvement over previous proposed lists. There are fewer of them, and they are more relevant and less prejudicial. Moreover, the first, which points to the relevance of international competition, will ease the worry about the Tribunal taking a primarily domestic market approach. In addition, the last factor may go some way towards directing the court to a sensible interpretation of the ''substantial effects'' test.

An efficiency defence

The third theme of the substantive provisions is a recognition that even those mergers which lessen competition substantially may give rise to efficiency gains which outweigh the competitive impact aspects of the transaction. To this end (as was also the case in Bill C-29) an efficiency defence which overrides the Tribunal's right to prohibit or dissolve a merger is provided (new section 68, p. 52).

By its terms no order may be made if resulting efficiencies are likely to be ''... greater than, and will offset, the effects ...'' of the merger on competition. The section also requires the Tribunal to determine efficiency gains by looking at whether exports will increase or imports will fall.

The new defence is a better and more simplified version of the comparable provision in Bill C-29. Its importance should not be underestimated, given the need of the Canadian business community to be in a position to rationalize production facilities in the face of international competition. Moreover, it appears superior in most respects to previous proposals, chiefly because it is based on ''likelihoods'' rather than certainties that efficiencies will result.

III. POWERS OF THE TRIBUNAL

Finally, although the Tribunal is to be given reasonably broad powers to correct negative competitive effects, these powers are generally not pro-active. Thus, in the case of a merger which has not been completed (subsection 64(1)(f), pp. 49-50) the merging firms will never risk more than an order not to complete. At the same time, however, the Tribunal is given the power to make consent orders or what are, in effect, conditional orders permitting completion of the transaction on terms.

In the case of completed mergers the powers of dissolution are somewhat more broadly described than at present (see subsection 64(1)(e), p. 49). Instead of a simple power to dissolve, the Tribunal may also order asset or share disposal. However, despite the greater clarity of this provision it is doubtful that the court's powers (except with respect to consent orders) are much greater than those under the present Act. In addition, their use is further restricted by a new 3-year limitation period (section 69, p. 53). Moreover, as in Bill C-29, the ability to intervene is considerably more circumscribed than that found in earlier Bills and published discussion papers.

Turning briefly to procedures, mention should be made both of advance ruling or pre-clearance certificates and of the Tribunal's power to make interim orders. With respect to the former, section 74, p. 56 sets out a desirable procedure whereby a party to a proposed merger may protect itself from subsequent attack. The procedure, involving advance and confidential disclosure of the details of the transaction, is straightforward and a useful addition to the Act.

Interim orders — two regimes

As to the Tribunal's new interim order powers, the position is not so straightforward. This is because there are really two regimes. One is for cases where the Director has not yet made a formal application against a merger (new section 72, p. 54). The other is for cases where the Director seeks interim relief following the institution of a formal application (new section 76, p. 56).

In the first case, which might be expected to be reserved for situations where the Director must move quickly, two requirements must generally be met. First, the court must be satisfied that the merger is reasonably likely to lessen competition substantially (i.e., the Director must make a *prima facie* case). Second, the Director will have to show that in the absence of an interim order action is likely to be taken that would impair substantially the Tribunal's ability ultimately to remedy the merger's effect on competition.

Although it is clear that this two-part test sets a reasonably tough standard, it is evidently less onerous for the government than dealing with interim injunctions in the present Act. In the circumstances perhaps the most important aspect of the new section is that any order made will have a maximum duration of 21 days (except in cases of failure to pre-notify), which term is not subject to extension.

The interim order power also applies to cases where there is an obligation to pre-notify, which has been ignored. In such a case the test is straightforward — was there an obligation and has it been ignored? In these cases the intent is to prohibit the completion of the merger until after pre-notification has occurred and the requisite waiting periods (dealt with below) have been complied with. Whether or not the language used achieves the objective is doubtful and it may be that a minor amendment to subsection 72(5) will be required.

As to the second type of interim order, the provisions of new section 76 apply generally to any application the Director might be disposed to bring under new Part VII (ie. the new part which now contains all civilly reviewable matters). Put another way, they are not merger specific. However, in so far as they relate to mergers it might be expected that an application would be brought only after a formal application against the merger had been commenced. In such cases it is intended that the Tribunal's power to intervene be the same as the court's in an ordinary commercial case, i.e., the assessment as to whether an order should be made would be on a "balance of convenience" basis.

Merger pre-notification

Certain mergers, but not all, will have to be pre-notified to the Combines Director. Those subject to these requirements are the so-called notifiable transactions (note the merger definition is not used). Similar provisions were found in Bill C-29. Even though the drafting has improved in the present Bill the provisions (contained in 17 new sections covering 16 pages) remain detailed and complex. However, the concepts are simple. There are three objectives:

(i) The requirement to pre-notify should apply only to a limited number of transactions. To this end, a series of dollar value exemptions is provided. Where transactions or the size of the parties involved do not exceed the dollar value limits there is no requirement to pre-notify.

(ii) Provision is made for two forms of pre-notification (short and long) either of which may be chosen initially. The short form should be comparatively easy to comply with and has been designed to avoid excessive costs. The long form involves considerable detail. The information sought has been designed to enable the Director to make a preliminary assessment of the competitive impact of a proposed transaction so as to permit him to determine quickly whether to oppose or not.

(iii) In cases where pre-notification is required the parties to the transaction are prohibited from completing it until the conclusion of a waiting period. This period begins to run upon the filing of a pre-notification form with the Director. Where a short form is used the waiting period is a brief 7 days (although the Director has the right to require the filing of a long form — and thus extend the waiting period — at his discretion). Where the long form is used (or required) the waiting period is 21 days — except in the case of a share acquisition. For share acquisitions to be effected through a stock exchange in Canada the parties are free to complete the transaction if the Director fails to take action within 10 days, or such longer period, not exceeding 21 days, as may be allowed by the rules of the stock exchange before shares must be taken up.

Before turning to the details of the pre-notification procedure, the absence of the term "merger" requires explanation. Put simply, the definition of merger contained in section 63 is quite broad. Had it been used in the pre-notification provisions, it would have required this preliminary step in many more instances than would have been acceptable. The use of a more narrowly defined "notifiable transaction" is sensible. However, the better approach might have been (and may still be) to modify further the definition of merger to exclude transactions which are not really mergers.

Pre-notification provisions

The interim solution has been to seek to limit the application of the pre-notification provisions by restricting their coverage to share and asset "acquisitions," "amalgamations," and unincorporated "combinations." As a consequence, and subject to the exemptions described below, pre-notification is required for four types of notifiable transactions:

   (i) Share Acquisitions:
        Where a person (with affiliates) acquiring shares would own shares that carry more than 20 percent or 50 percent of the voting rights of publicly traded companies, or 35 percent or 50 percent of privately held companies (new subsection 82(3), pp. 60-61).
  (ii) Asset Acquisitions:
        Where the aggregate value of the assets to be acquired or the gross revenues from sales generated from those assets exceed $35 million (new subsection 82(1), pp.59-60).
 (iii) Amalgamations:
        Where the aggregate value of the assets in Canada owned by the continuing corporation or the gross revenues from sales in or from Canada generated from its assets exceed $70 million (new subsection 82(4), pp. 61-62).
  (iv) Unincorporated Combinations:
        Where the aggregate value of the assets in Canada owned by such a combination or the gross revenues from sales in or from Canada

generated from those assets exceed $35 million (new subsection 82(5), p. 62).

Exemptions

If a transaction is of a type described above, pre-notification is required unless it also fits within one of the exemptions. The basic exemptions are as follows:

(i) If the transaction does not involve an operating business (a defined term meaning a business undertaking in Canada to which employees employed in connection with the undertaking ordinarily report (new subsection 80(1), p. 58)), then pre-notification is not required.

(ii) A similar exemption exists where the parties (together with their affiliates) have assets in Canada or gross revenues from sales in, from or into Canada of less than $500 million in aggregate value (new subsection 81(1), p. 59).

(iii) Pre-notification is not required where:

    (a) the transaction is exclusively amongst affiliates;

    (b) the Director has issued an Advance Ruling Certificate;

    (c) the transaction was entered into prior to the enactment of the Bill and is substantially completed within one year of its proclamation;

    (d) the transaction is a share acquisition where the aggregate assets or gross revenues from sales generated from those assets of the company in which shares are being acquired are less than $35 million;

    (e) the transaction constitutes a joint venture (as defined in section 84);

    (f) the transaction involves the acquisition of real property or goods in the ordinary course of business. This exemption does not apply to transactions involving the acquisition of all of the assets of the business;

    (g) the transaction involves shares which are being acquired solely for purposes of underwriting;

    (h) the transaction is one by way of gift or transfer on death;

    (i) certain transactions by way of asset or share acquisition by a creditor triggered by a debtor's default are exempt. Financial institutions should note that there is no exemption for transactions whereby the same creditor seeks to dispose of assets so acquired;

    (j) the transaction involves the acquisition of a Canadian resource property (as defined in the Income Tax Act) pursuant to an agreement providing for transfer of the property only if exploration and development expenses are incurred;

(k) the transaction involves the acquisition of voting shares of a corporation pursuant to an agreement providing for the issuance of the shares only if exploration and development expenses are incurred in connection with a Canadian resource property; and

(l) other classes of transactions described by regulation by the Governor-in-Council.

Where an asset value test is provided, assets are expected to be valued on net book basis. Valuation methods are later to be prescribed by regulation.

Some controversy may be expected in connection with these provisions if only because they will be costly to comply with, especially for smaller companies. Having said this, the legislative draftsman has made a considerable effort to exempt unimportant transactions. And although the approach is similar to that in the Hart/Scott/Rodino legislation in the United States, the current draft would appear to be less onerous and compliance with the provisions should be less costly.

The operation of the pre-notification provisions are described diagramatically at the end of the chapter.

IV. CONCLUSIONS

Neither the merger nor the pre-notification proposals in Bill C-91 are perfect. It is apparent, however, that each has benefited considerably from the consultative process conducted by both the present and the previous governments. Gone, for example, are earlier proposals for market share thresholds. Gone too are suggested reverse onus provisions. These departures from past thinking, when coupled with a more realistic merger definition, a major move to a civil jurisdiction, the introduction of a more workable efficiency defence and a directive to avoid placing undue weight on concentration indicate that significant progress has been made.

However, when one comes to the heart of the proposals — the substantive test — a harsher evaluation is required. Put simply the proposed threshold fails the test of economic reality. If this is not apparent in purely Canadian terms, events in the United States (and the current trade negotiations) indicate the need for improvement. Merger policy in our closest and biggest competitor is undergoing nothing short of a radical transformation. This is best illustrated by some dramatic figures on merger activity and antitrust challenges to it. In the case of mergers requiring pre-notification under the Hart/Scott/Rodino legislation, in 1980, there were some 825 reported mergers and 24 challenges. In 1984, there were some 1400 reported mergers and only 12 challenges (or less than 1 percent). There is no doubt that merger activity, for reasons of financial strength and business rationalization, is fundamental to restructuring the Canadian-owned part of the private sector. It is also essential that government stay out of the way of a process bound to have painful elements, unless the result will be an absence of substantial competition in the marketplace. As a consequence, it is the merger provisions in the new Bill which will need the most attention and effort. This must be undertaken to ensure that they are right in terms of the massive financial and industrial adjustment requirements facing the Canadian economy.

NOTIFIABLE TRANSACTIONS

PROPOSED TRANSACTIONS
Sections 80 to 96 inclusive

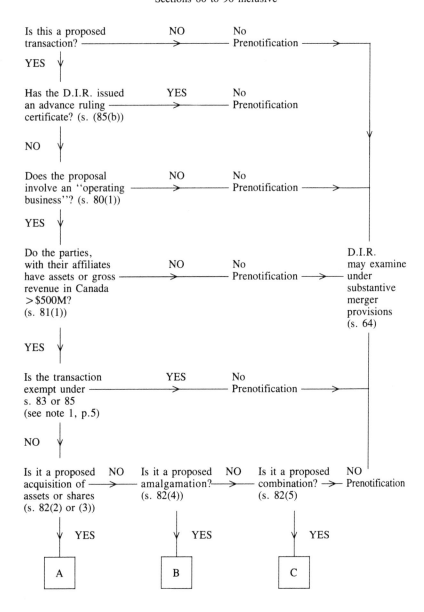

Is this a proposed transaction?   **NO →**   No Prenotification →

YES ↓

Has the D.I.R. issued an advance ruling certificate? (s. (85(b))   **YES →**   No Prenotification

NO ↓

Does the proposal involve an "operating business"? (s. 80(1))   **NO →**   No Prenotification →

YES ↓

Do the parties, with their affiliates have assets or gross revenue in Canada >$500M? (s. 81(1))   **NO →**   No Prenotification →   D.I.R. may examine under substantive merger provisions (s. 64)

YES ↓

Is the transaction exempt under s. 83 or 85 (see note 1, p.5)   **YES →**   No Prenotification →

NO ↓

Is it a proposed acquisition of assets or shares (s. 82(2) or (3))   **NO →**   Is it a proposed amalgamation? (s. 82(4))   **NO →**   Is it a proposed combination? (s. 82(5))   **NO →**   Prenotification

↓ YES   ↓ YES   ↓ YES

[A]   [B]   [C]

PROPOSED AQUISITIONS
Is it a Proposed Acquisition?

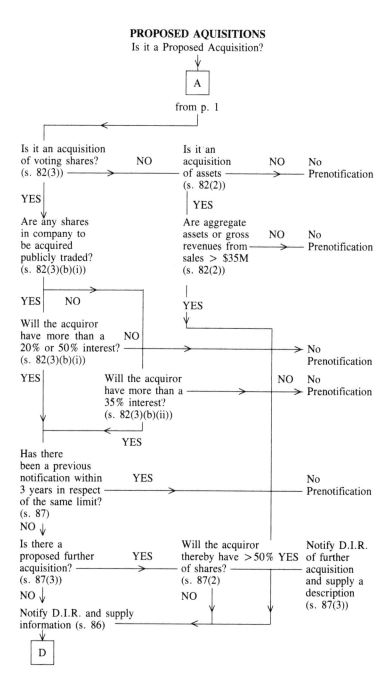

PROPOSED AMALGAMATION

```
                    ┌───┐
                    │ B │
                    └─┬─┘
                      │
          Is it a Proposed Amalgamation?
                   (s. 82(4))
                      │
                     YES
                      ↓
   Will continuing corporation have assets    NO   No
   or gross revenues from sales of > $70M?   ──→──  Prenotification
                (s. 82(4)(a)(b))
                      │
                     YES
                      ↓
        Notify D.I.R. and supply information
                    (s. 86)
                      ↓
                    ┌───┐
                    │ D │
                    └───┘
```

PROPOSED COMBINATION

```
                    ┌───┐
                    │ C │
                    └─┬─┘
                      │
          Is it a proposed combination?
                   (s. 82(5))
                      │
                     YES
                      ↓
        Does it involve assets or       NO      No
        gross revenues > $35M?         ──→──    Prenotification
              (s. 82(5)(a)(b))
                      │
                     YES
                      ↓
   Does the joint venture exemption apply    YES  No
                   (s. 84)                   ──→── Prenotification
                      │
                      NO
                      ↓
        Notify D.I.R. and supply information
                    (s. 86)
                      ↓
                    ┌───┐
                    │ D │
                    └───┘
```

INFORMATION REQUIREMENTS

$\boxed{\text{D}}$

Notify D.I.R. and supply information
(s. 86 and 92-94)

↓

Is more than one person required to
notify and supply information

NO ↓ YES

Will there be
joint filing
(s. 86(2))?

NO ← YES

Person elects NO
short forms filing? →
(s. 92(a))

↓

YES

↓

Short form filing   Long form
(individual or joint)   filing elected?
(s. 93)   (s. 92(b))

↓   YES

Does D.I.R. require   YES   Long form filing
long form filing   →   (individual or joint)
(s. 92)   (s. 94)

↓   Is transaction a
NO   voting share
                                     acquisition using a
                                     stock exchange

                          YES ← → NO

Transaction is not to	Transaction is not to be	Transaction is not to
be completed within 7	completed within 10 trading	be completed within
days of the giving of	days of notice, up to	21 days of the giving
notice.*	maximum of 21 days of	of notice.*
(s. 95(a))	exchange rules.*	(s. 95(b))
	(s. 95(c))	

* Unless D.I.R. before expiration of that time gives notice that he does not intend
to make an application under s. 95 in respect of the proposed transaction.

Note: Classes of transactions exempt from the application of the sections 82 and 86 (prenotifications provisions):

- s. 83 no prenotification for acquisition where,

  (a) acquisitions of real property or goods in the ordinary course of business (not all the assets of a business)
  (b) acquisitions for underwriting purposes
  (c) gifts or transfers on death
  (d) certain acquisitions by a creditor due to a debtor's default
  (e) acquisitions of Canadian resource property where exploration or development expenses incurred
  (f) acquisitions of shares issued where exploration or development expenses incurred for a Canadian resource property

- s. 85 no prenotification where,

  (a) transaction among affiliates
  (b) D.I.R. gives advance ruling certificate
  (c) transactions entered into prior to the passage of this law and completed within one year thereafter
  (d) other classes of transactions prescribed

AUTHOR

C.J. Michael Flavell was born in Quebec, and earned the bachelor's degree from Bishop's University, a law school degree from McGill University, and the Master of Laws from Harvard University Law School. A partner in Courtois, Clarkson, Parsons and Tetrault, Mr. Flavell is the author of *Canadian Competition Law: A Business Guide* and has pubished on the topics of anti-dumping, corporate structure, and finance. He is a member of the Montreal, Quebec and Canadian Bar Associations, and has won numerous honours, prizes and scholarships in civil law, criminal law, and history.

Chapter Three

The Monopoly Provision: Abuse of Dominant Position

C.J. Michael Flavell

I. INTRODUCTION

The substantive provisions proposed by Bill C-91 to deal with monopoly are found in Sections 50 and 51. It has been observed that this is a new concept in Canadian competition legislation and that, though popularly it may be referred to as the "monopoly" provision, the word "monopoly" is never used. This indicates a clear break with the previous law.[1]

Before analyzing the rules set out in Bill C-91, it behooves us to take a look at the law as it presently stands under the Combines Investigation Act. This will enable us to see how radically different the new proposals are, especially to the extent that they set out recourses for the situation euphemistically described as "Joint Monopoly."

The present law

Under the present law, monopoly is outlawed as a criminal offence by the combined effect of the definition of monopoly, found in Section 2, and the statement of the offence in Section 33, as follows:

> "monopoly" means a situation where one or more persons either substantially or completely control throughout Canada or any area

thereof the class or species of business in which they are engaged and have operated such business or are likely to operate it to the detriment or against the interest of the public, whether consumers, producers or others, but a situation shall not be deemed a monopoly within the meaning of this definition by reason only of the exercise of any right or enjoyment or any interest derived under the Patent Act, or any other Act of the Parliament of Canada.

33.   Every person who is a party or privy to or knowingly assists in, or in the formation of a merger or monopoly is guilty of an indictable offence and is liable to imprisonment for two years.

A few introductory observations are in order as to the wording of present Sections 2 and 33:

(a) The law requires that one or more persons ''substantially or complete-ly control'' a class or species of business in a market; thus, a high percentage of market share is a prerequisite to any charge;
(b) The detriment required to be proved is to the public, defined as being ''consumers, producers or others''; this avoids the argument that the injury must be to the public at large or to the ''general public.''

Some useful general remarks as to the present provision can be found in a speech of a former Director of Investigation and Research:

There are several general points that should be made about this provi-sion. In the first place, this provision has scarcely been tested in the courts and the limits of its application have therefore not yet been defined.

In the second place, it is clear that to be in a monopoly position is not a *per se* offence; it is only an offence if the monopoly is operated to the detriment or against the interest of the public. As in the case of mergers, what constitutes detriment to the public will ultimately have to be determined by the courts or by Parliament.

It is considered by the Director and his staff that the provision is in-tended to protect the public against monopolization, that is, the ac-quisition of market power and the use of that power, firstly, to ex-clude competitors and dominate the market, and secondly, to main-tain that monopoly position. In discussions with businessmen and lawyers under the program of compliance, the director generally in-forms them that he would be likely to investigate not monopoly *per* se but "abuse of monopoly" which constitutes conduct designed to extend, entrench or maintain the monopoly position, including the inhibiting of competition at lower levels of distribution as, for example, by setting up exclusive dealing and tying arrangements and refusing to sell to a reasonable number of outlets so as to permit competition to develop in the chain of distribution.

Further, it should be noted that monopoly, as defined, embraces more than single firm monopoly by reason of the express reference to "one or more persons." It is our current view that this provision is capable of being extended to oligopoly situations, where a small number of firms tend to act as a monopoly and this is an aspect that will ultimately have to be tested in the courts.[2]

A double test

Thus, under the old law, bigness was not necessarily badness and to justify a conviction, bigness plus badness had to be shown, both beyond a reasonable doubt. For this reason, the offence was not often invoked and was even less often successfully prosecuted. It was felt by commentators that, without legislative change, such a history would have continued.

The first major Canadian monopoly case was *Eddy Match*,[3] a not very helpful precedent, since the accused was clearly in a monopoly position and was found to have used such flagrantly anti-competitive measures as almost to guarantee conviction. Numerous mergers, industrial spying, and the use of fighting brands and secret discounts made the illegality so clear that the case is of little use for most other situations.

Thus, under the old law, for there to be a monopoly violation of the Section 33 criminal provision, two requirements had to be demonstrated beyond a reasonable doubt:

(a) substantial or complete control by one or more persons throughout Canada or any area thereof of a class or species of business; and,
(b) operation or likely operation of the business to the detriment or against the interest of the public.

The requirement of substantial or complete control required a very major market share, likely in the vicinity of 75 percent and up, market power tantamount to being able to operate virtually free of competition.

Motivation

The second criterion was that the monopoly be, or be likely to be, operated ''to the detriment or against the interest of the public, whether consumers, producers or others.'' The net effect of the case law under Section 33 was that the required degree of detriment is shown by demonstrating anti-competitive or predatory behaviour characterized by the motive of preserving or entrenching or increasing the monopoly power. A few examples of such behaviour were:

(a) The type of practices by a monopolist demonstrated in the *Eddy Match* case.

(b) Acquisition of competitors by merger in order to reduce competition in the market, or acquisition of potential or would-be competitors to forestall their entry to the market.[4]

(c) The act of forestalling potential competition from fellow suppliers by signing one's customers to long-term contracts.[5]

(d) The act of forestalling sources of supply to would-be competitors by long-term contracts with the suppliers.[6]

(e) Use of a patent to extend the market power or monopoly lawfully conferred by the patent into other areas or products.[7]

(f) Use by a monopolist of a policy of predatory pricing with the aim of removing or forestalling competition.[8]

(g) Attempts at foreclosure of would-be competitors by other ''roadblock'' activities; for example, in the *Anthes* situation, there was evidence that it made representations to Canadian Pacific Railway to discourage the sale by CPR of a real estate site to a party wishing to set up shop as a competitor of Anthes in the area in question.

Allied Chemical

As mentioned above, bigness is not necessarily badness under existing Canadian competition law. The requirement of proof beyond a reasonable doubt of detriment to the public was underlined in the *Allied Chemical* case,[9] where the accused, Allied Chemical, enjoying a monopoly in the manufacture and sale of sulphuric acid in certain areas of British Columbia, entered into an agreement with another company whereby Allied obtained all its requirements for sulphuric acid from this company, and subsequently closed its own manufacturing facility. This action, though found to be that of a monopolist, was also found to have resulted solely from the fact that the accused, Allied, was able to obtain the best economic result by purchasing acid rather than continuing to make it. The case was dismissed as to the monopoly charge for simple failure to demonstrate the required degree of detriment.

The question arose as to whether proof of complete monopoly in itself logically implied, or at least created a presumption, of detriment to the public. In the *Eddy Match* case, it was found that the accused had achieved a very major degree of control and it was suggested that this created a presumption of detriment to the public.

> Such a condition creates a presumption that the public is being deprived of all the benefits of free competition and this deprivation, being a negation of the public right, is necessarily to the detriment or against the interest of the public.[10]

Thus, it was felt by some observers (including, no doubt, the Combines Branch) that, once there was proof of complete control, a presumption arose of detriment to the public, meaning that the burden of proof was then on the accused to rebut that presumption.

Irving

This notion was bluntly put to rest by the *K.C. Irving Ltd.* case.[11] In *Irving*, the Trial court had convicted the accused, finding detriment to the public. The New Brunswick Court of Appeal differed on the basis that detriment to the public had not been proved and the Supreme Court of Canada confirmed the Court of Appeal. The Crown had argued, on the basis of the *Eddy Match* case, that there was a presumption of detriment once complete control had been demonstrated. Mr. Chief Justice Laskin flatly stated the proposition that there could be no such presumption and that both bigness and badness had to be demonstrated beyond a reasonable doubt:[12]

> I do not think that it is open to a court in a criminal case to raise a presumption such as is contended for by the Crown in this case in the absence of legislative direction.

Thus, it seemed clear that, under the existing law, a monopoly prosecution would not be successful unless there can be demonstrated beyond a reasonable doubt both the fact of the monopoly power *and* practices of the type demonstrated in *Eddy Match, ERCO,* and *Canada Safeway.*[13]

As to the concept of ''joint monopoly'' under the old law, it must be recalled that the definition of ''monopoly'' included the phrase ''one or more persons'' having the required degree of market power. The case of *R. v. Canadian General Electric Company*[14] was an attempt by the Combines Branch to show that Section 33 envisaged what might be called the ''several firm'' monopoly. The case contained evidence that the companies were parties to traditional Section 32 conspiracy, resale price maintenance and uniform consignment practices; however, the criminal complaint was not restricted to these specific offences in the normal manner of procedure but rather alleged them in their own right and as part of a ''several firm'' monopoly under Section 33. As to the Section 32 charge, the court found sufficient evidence of mutually co-ordinated parallel behaviour as to justify a finding of an illegal conspiracy under this heading. The monopoly charge raised the interesting issue as to whether or not several arms-length firms could, together, be found to have committed a monopoly offence. This marked the first attempt by the Crown to establish the proposition of the ''shared monopoly'' or ''multi-firm monopoly'' as a violation of Section 33, where the firms involved were not related or affiliated.

The finding

The trial judge found that a monopoly case can be made against more than one independent company where they work together as a unit. However, the evidence upon which he based the conclusion that the companies were working together as a unit was the same as that upon which he had relied in finding that the companies had illegally conspired under Section 32 of the Act. This was the provision traditionally reserved for a conspiracy charge against independent (non-affiliated) companies. Not wishing to use the same evidence to find two completely different offences, he concluded that, having found the multi-firm monopoly, there must be independent proof of ''detriment to the public'' other than the acts found to be the basis of the Section 32 conviction. He then proceeded to make a finding of fact that the Crown had not satisfied its burden of proving beyond a reasonable doubt that such independent acts of detriment to the public had occurred. Thus, under the old law, the concept of ''shared monopoly'' has been accepted by at least one court at the trial level.

Under the old law, the penalty for illegal monopolization was ''liability to imprisonment for two years.'' Usually, and necessarily, in the case of charges against corporations, this was replaced by a fine, the amount of which was without limit and in the discretion of the court. There was also available, as a weapon of enforcement, the prohibition order, generally forbidding the continuation or repetition of the offence but also, in some instances, forestalling new or additional activity of like manner.

Any party provably injured by criminal monopolization was empowered by Section 31.1 of the Statute to seek civil damages, a recourse which has been suspect constitutionally and not often used.

In conclusion, it is safe to say that the double requirement of proof beyond a reasonable doubt of monopoly power *and* of detriment to the public by abusive or predatory practices, left Canadian anti-trust law pretty short of successful monopoly prosecutions. The Combines Branch has characterized this as a failure of effective enforcement while others have argued that Parliament forbade only clear abuses of monopoly power and that instances of this have simply not been proved. Whichever view is correct, there can be no doubt that there has been strong pressure from various sources to remove the monopoly provision from the criminal jurisdiction and recharacterize it as a reviewable practice under the aegis of a civil authority such as the Competition Tribunal proposed by Bill C-91.

II. THE NEW PROPOSALS: BILL C-91

The essential changes proposed by Bill C-91 are as follows:

(a) re-characterization of monopoly as abuse of dominant position;
(b) removal of the "offence" from the criminal jurisdiction into the civil ambit of the new Competition Tribunal where it is classified as a "reviewable practice," along with such other existing reviewable practices as "exclusive dealing," "tied selling," and the like;
(c) replacement of the test of "detriment to the public" by the concept of "preventing or lessening competition substantially in a market";
(d) statutory definition (by way of examples) of the "anti- competitive acts" which constitute reviewable abuse of dominant position.

Proposed Section 51(1) of Bill C-91 reads as follows:

> 51(1) Where, on application by the Director, the Tribunal finds that
>
> (a) one or more persons substantially or completely control, throughout Canada or any area thereof, a class or species of business,
>
> (b) that person or those persons have engaged in or are engaging in

a practice of anti-competitive acts, and the object of the practice is to lessen competition, and

(c) the practice has had, is having or is likely to have the effect of preventing or lessening competition substantially in a market,

the Tribunal may make an order prohibiting all or any of those persons from engaging in that practice.

The concepts of substantial or complete control will require a definition by the Tribunal as will the terms "Canada or any area thereof" and "class or species of business."

The concept of "control"

Though the concept of substantial or complete control survives from the old Act, there was very little judicial comment on the subject and so resort must be had to the normal dictionary meanings of the word "control." Complete control is an easier concept than substantial control and the latter will have to be defined, presumably at least in part by some threshold of market share percentage. This, then, raises the question (in seeking the relevant "class or species of business") as to what is the appropriate product (goods or services). This necessitates the definition of the applicable market. Put another way, we may ask, Should a "class or species of business" be narrowly interpreted to cover only a very specific product? Should not competitive and substitute products be included in seeking to define both the "class or species of business" mentioned in paragraph 51(1)(a) and the "market" in paragraph 51(1)(c)? In the *Eddy Match* case,[15] the question arose as to whether wooden matches constituted a "class or species of business" or whether the definition should be broader and include other competitive lighting devices such as other types of matches and mechanical lighter devices. The court held that wooden matches could be distinguished from other lighting devices and, therefore, formed a "class or species of business." It is doubtful whether such a narrow definition would be accepted by the new Competition Tribunal which will undoubtedly enjoy the input of economists and other experts in market definition both by reference to product and geography. (Also, of course, times have changed in the lighting device market since 1952.)

The term "Canada or any area thereof" would, at first glance, indicate that the "area" could be very small indeed; perhaps even a single village or municipality. However, it is suggested that the "area" must be large enough to form a distinguishable market; thus, the corner druggist in Alfred, Ontario, will not be found to be a monopolist if three miles down the road there is a drugstore available to consumers as a source of competition.

A "practice"

The next requirement of Section 51 is that there must have been a practice of anti-competitive acts with the object of lessening competition.

According to the wording of the legislation, this "practice has had, is having or is likely to have the effect of preventing or lessening competition substantially in a market." The requirement that there be a "practice" indicates, on the basis of case law under other sections of the present enactment, that the behaviour complained of has continued over some period of time and is not of the nature of a one-shot or one-time activity.[16] The concept of "lessening competition substantially" is one found elsewhere in the Bill and in the present law. There is not much interpretive help in the case law to date. One wonders how the Tribunal will measure for substantiality of effect and what will be the relevance of the respective market shares of the monopolist and the party or parties against which his market power is being exercised.

Necessarily, the monopolist will be a substantial player in the market in order to meet the test of paragraph 51(1)(a) but one must wonder, if the target of the monopoly power is relatively small or insignificant, whether the predatory activity can have a substantial anti-competitive effect in the market.

Malevolent intent

Section 51 requires that the monopolist(s) "have engaged in or are engaging in a practice of anti-competitive acts" with the object of lessening competition. (It is noteworthy that there is always the requirement of malevolent intent.) Section 50 gives a non-exhaustive list of "anti-competitive acts" and a quick look at these show the wide diversity of activity which the authorities feel to be unacceptable when practiced by a monopolist. The listed anti-competitive acts, and commentary on several of them, follow;

> (a) squeezing, by a vertically integrated supplier, of the margin available to an unintegrated customer who competes with the supplier, for the purpose of impeding or preventing the customer's entry into, or expansion in a market;

This covers the type of situation where a manufacturer who is also a retailer sells to other retailers who compete with his own outlet; the rivals can be squeezed either by the manufacturer raising its prices to them or by causing his own outlet to reduce its prices to end users or both. This impacts on the rivals either by raising their costs or by forcing them to realize less revenue and is felt to be an unjustified use of monopoly power.

(b) acquisition by a supplier of a customer who would otherwise be available to a competitor of the supplier, or acquisition by a customer of a supplier who would otherwise be available to a competitor of the customer, for the purpose of impeding or preventing the competitor's entry into, or eliminating him from, a market;

The buying up of a customer who would otherwise, perhaps, do business with a competitor or the acquisition by a customer of a supplier who might otherwise supply to a competitor of the customer both forestall competition which would otherwise take place. It is conceivable that the new merger provisions would have applicability here as well.

(c) freight equalization on the plant of a competitor for the purpose of impeding or preventing his entry into, or eliminating him from, a market;

(d) use of fighting brands introduced selectively on a temporary basis to discipline or eliminate a competitor;

We saw above that this type of activity was indulged in by *Eddy Match* and was one of the main bases of the conviction in that case.

(e) pre-emption of scarce facilities or resources required by a competitor for the operation of a business, with the object of withholding the facilities or resources from a market;

(f) buying up of products to prevent the erosion of existing price levels;

The provisions of (e) and (f) are self-explanatory and are clearly meant to cover the situation where the activity is undertaken not for the purpose of maximizing profit but for the purpose of disciplining or destroying a competitor.

(g) adoption of product specifications that are incompatible with products produced by any other person and are designed to prevent his entry into, or to eliminate him from, a market;

This can be a very effective anti-competitive manoevre where products are relatively complex and product specification can be used as an anticompetitive tool against a competitor.

(h) requiring or inducing a supplier to sell only or primarily to certain customers, or to refrain from selling to a competitor, with the object of preventing a competitor's entry into, or expansion in, a market.

Where the buyer has sufficient market power to influence a supplier in his decisions to sell to other competing customers, the use of that power to disadvantage competitors is clearly anti-competitive and an unjustified extension of market power.

Predation

The phraseology of the examples of "anti-competitive acts" makes it clear that what distinguishes these activities from acceptable good tough competition is predatory intent. This is usually couched in terms of purposefully impeding or preventing entry into a market or of disciplining or eliminating a competitor. This would mean, at the very least, that in most situations where the dominant competitor was engaging in one or more of the anti-competitive acts described in Section 50 as a reaction to aggressive competitive moves by rivals, the Tribunal, presumably, would find that the requisite anti-competitive or predatory intent was not shown. However, in subsections 50(a) and (h), the monopolist is restrained from seeking to prevent a competitor's "expansion" in a market. This would seem to curtail even defensive moves. Generally, there is no doubt that any business entity which could be classified as a monopolist has to be very careful in fighting the competitive battle since constraints are placed on him which do not attach to his rivals.

Where the Tribunal finds abuse of dominant position pursuant to Sections 50 and 51, it can prohibit such person(s) from engaging in the suspect practice. According to subsection 51(2), the Tribunal can go further if it finds that a simple prohibition order would not be likely to restore competition in the market. It can also "make an order directing any or all persons against whom an order is sought to take such actions, including the divestiture of assets or shares, as are reasonable and as are necessary to overcome the effects of the practice in that market.'' Given the radical nature of the divestiture power, subsection 51(3) goes on to state that ''the Tribunal shall make the order in such terms as will in its opinion interfere with the rights of any person to whom the order is directed...only to the extent necessary to achieve the purpose of the order.'' The decision to utilize the divestiture power is one which, in the present author's view, should be exercised only on such occasions where the activity of the monopolist has so destroyed competition as to make divestiture the only reasonable alternative.

Exceptions

Section 51 goes on to set out a series of exceptions, exemptions or defences available to the ''accused'' where proceedings for abuse of dominant position are brought to the Tribunal by the Director. It is notable that *only* the Director can commence the proceedings; this has drawn criticism from some quarters. However, to allow private complainants to initiate the proceedings raises constitutional issues which the authorities presumably wish to avoid.

Under subsection 51(4), it is stated that no order is to be made where the substantial lessening of competition is a result of the superior competitive performance of the person against whom the order is sought. This will be a very difficult juggling act indeed; it will require the Tribunal to decide whether the lessening of competition resulted from market power or from superior competitive performance. One can hardly envy the Tribunal members in this task.

The difficulties inherent in the application of this so-called ''efficiency defence'' were recognized in the *Consultation Paper* issued by the Minister of Consumer and Corporate Affairs, the Honourable Michel Cote, in March, 1985:

> There is strong support for an efficiency defence when reduced competition in a market dominated by one or more firms results from superior economic efficiency and not anti-competitive practices. The primary concern with an efficiency defence is that it could become a gateway for anti-competitive practices since, in certain circumstances, it may be difficult to determine whether reduced competition stems from superior economic efficiency or anti-competitive conduct. Moreover, critics have argued that it is difficult to measure superior economic

efficiency. This is of concern to some because it could result in lengthy proceedings and create uncertainty in the law.

Bill C-91 makes no attempt to resolve this dilemma.

Intellectual property

Another defence is expressed in subsection 51(5) of the Bill:

> (5) For the purpose of this section, an act engaged in pursuant only to the exercise of any right or enjoyment of any interest derived under the *Copyright Act, Industrial Design Act, Patent Act, Trade Marks Act* or any other Act of Parliament is not an anti-competitive act.

This provision recognizes that the lawful exercise of rights conferred by intellectual property statutes cannot be considered an anti-competitive act such as to constitute a reviewable abuse of dominant position. This would not permit, however, the extension of such monopoly rights beyond the terms of the statutes conferring them or the use of intellectual property rights to extend economic power into other or related fields. Concern has been expressed "that the provisions of subsection (5) as now proposed are not broad enough to cover intellectual or industrial property rights arising at common law, such as trade secrets, know-how and rights between franchisors and franchisees."[17]

Remembering that only the Director can make an application to the Tribunal in respect of abuse of dominant position, the application must be made not more than three years after the practice has ceased [subsection 51(6)]. This is a somewhat unusual method of setting a limitation of action provision. It means, of course, that a practice can be attacked ten, twenty or thirty years after inception as long as it is not later than three years after cessation.

Recognizing the overlap that obviously can occur under the new law as between the abuse of dominant position (monopoly), and conspiracy and merger subsection, 51(7) provides that no application can be made under the monopoly provision where proceedings have been commenced under Section 32 (conspiracy) or where an order has been sought under Section 64 (merger). This applies to the extent that the application would be based on the same or substantially the same facts as would be alleged in the proceedings under Sections 32 or 64.

Conscious parallelism

In the present writer's view, the most controversial aspect of the dominant position provisions is the concept of joint monopoly and the related issue of the status of conscious parallelism in Canadian competition law. Subsection 51(1) makes it clear that the reviewable practice of monopolization can be carried on by "one or more persons." The list of anti-competitive acts in Section 50 can clearly, according to subsection 51(1), be undertaken by one or more persons. There is no requirement that the several persons (found to be substantially or completely controlling the class or species of business) be acting in concert or pursuant to overt or tacit agreement. It is arguable that several persons found to be in a dominant position could be held to be in violation of the provision for purely independent but similar behaviour. Likewise, it seems possible that a party less than dominant could be grouped with others to find a dominant collectivity and then be subject to these provisions for independent acts which, if committed by that party alone, would not constitute abuse because of lack of dominant position. This raises again the whole issue as to whether, in this and other amendments (specifically in Section 32), the Combines Branch is not seeking to obtain the ability to attack close oligopolies and conscious parallelism. If this is their intent, it is not only bad law but bad economics.

The United States anti-trust authority long ago gave up any crusade against conscious parallelism on the simple basis that no agreement or conspiracy was behind such behaviour. Canadian courts have held likewise under Section 32 prosecutions. Ours is a small economy in the international context. It is necessarily characterized by numerous oligopolistic industries which achieve in that manner the required efficiencies of scale to compete abroad and at home against foreign competition. There is no sense in rendering oligopoly and conscious parallelism suspect by a provision as broad as the joint monopoly features of Sections 50 and 51 of Bill C-91. The Bill should be amended to make it clear that joint monopolization requires concerted action or action pursuant to tacit or overt agreement.

III. CONCLUSION

In this writer's view, the dominant position provisions are an improvement over predecessor bills and proposals but suffer two weaknesses:

(a) the considerable difficulty of "apportioning" the cause of a substantial lessening of competition as between apparently anti-competitive acts and the superior competitive performance mentioned in subsection 51(4); and,

(b) where more than one person is engaging in anti-competitive acts and only together do they reach the ''dominant position'' threshold, they should not be actionable as a collectivity unless it is shown that they have acted in concert or pursuant to agreement, overt or tacit.

Notes

1. See the notes of an address by John H.C. Clarry at the Conference on Amendments to the Combines Investigation Act, sponsored by The Canadian Institute for Professional Development, at Toronto, January 24, 1986.

2. D.H.W. Henry, Q.C., now Mr. Justice Henry of the Ontario Supreme Court, in W.C.J. Meredith Memorial Lectures—1971 Series, pages 71 and 72.

3. *R. v. Eddy Match Company Limited et al.* (1952), 13 C.R. 217, (1954), 18 C.R. 357, (1953), 109 C.C.C. 1.

4. See the *ERCO* case; *R. v. Electric Reduction Company of Canada Ltd.* (1970), 61 C.P.R. 235. See also the *Anthes* Report (Restrictive Trade Practices Commission) as commented on in W.C.J. Meredith Memorial Lectures—1971 Series, D.H.W. Henry, *op. cit.*, pages 80 and following. These cases deal with mergers by persons with monopoly power; the offence was a monopolization offence more than a merger offence.

5. See the *ERCO* case cited above.

6. Ibid.

7. See the *Union Carbide Canada Limited* proceedings under the provision in the Statute enabling limitation of patent rights. A summary of the case and of the resulting order is found in W.C.J. Meredith Memorial Lectures—1971 Series, D.H.W. Henry, *op. cit.*, page 77.

8. See *Regina v. Canada Safeway Ltd.* 41 DLR (3d) 264.

9. *Regina v. Allied Chemical Canada Ltd. and Cominco Ltd.*, 24 C.P.R. (2d) 221.

10. *Op. cit., Eddy Match,* (1953), 109 C.C.C. 1.

11. *Regina v. K.C. Irving Ltd. et al.,* 45 D.L.R. (3d) 45; 11 N.B.R. (2d) 181 (Appeal); 72 D.L.R. (3d) 82 (Supreme Court of Canada).

12. *Ibid.*

13. *Canada Safeway* (reported at 41 D.L.R. (3d) 264) was shown to have a monopoly in the grocery retailing industry in Calgary and in Edmonton, and to have consistently discouraged competition and thè growth of small competitors by selectively lowering its prices to meet any new or expanded competition. Further information as to *Canada Safeway* can be found in the 1974 publication of the *Annual Report* of the Director of Investigation and Research—Combines Investigation Act.

14. *R. v. Canadian General Electric Company,* (1976) 15 O.R. (2d) 360.

15. *Op. cit.* the *Eddy Match* case, footnote 3.

16. See *Canadian Competition Law—A Business Guide;* McGraw-Hill Ryerson Limited; 1979; pages 216 and 217, dealing with the term "practice" as found in Section 34 of the Combines Investigation Act.

17. *Op. cit.,* John H.C. Clarry, note 1.

THE AUTHOR

Louis-Philippe de Grandpré was born and educated in Quebec. He received his B.A. from the University of Montreal, the B.C.L. from McGill University, and holds the LL.D. (Hon.) from both McGill and Ottawa Universities. A partner in the firm of Lafluer, Brown, de Grandpré, he is a member of the bars of Montreal, Quebec, the Canadian Bar Association, the Law Societies of both Upper Canada and Saskatchewan, and is a fellow of the American College of Trial Lawyers. Mr. de Grandpré holds directorships to numerous Canadian corporations, and was decorated with the Companion of the Order of Canada.

Chapter Four

Legal Powers

L. Philippe de Grandpré

I. INTRODUCTION

Within the past two decades, much has been written about the jurisdiction of the Canadian Parliament to legislate over matters of competition. Canada's philosophy concerning its business community has been twofold:

— On the one hand, freer rein should be given to the corporate community, thus establishing Canada's place in the world markets;
— On the other hand, the protection of the consumer should be embodied in stricter statutory guidelines.

Bill C-91, *An Act to establish the Competition Tribunal and to amend the Combines Investigation Act*, which received first reading on December 17, 1985, is a result of this apparent contradiction.

Has Parliament jurisdiction to enter the civil law field by invoking one or the other of its jurisdictions under section 91 of the *Constitution Act, 1867?*

Could the Peace, Order and Good Government power be the basis of such a statute?

Is Parliament justified in relying on its Trade and Commerce power?

Before attempting to answer these questions, a few words are in order about the Criminal Law power which, up to now, has been used by Parliament as the basis of its jurisdiction.

This examination of the federal powers must, of course, be related to the jurisdiction of the Provinces over property and civil rights in the Provinces.

Two questions must also be answered:

(1) Does the Bill establish procedural safeguards to conform with the Charter of Human Rights and Freedoms?

(2) Has Parliament the power to create a non-court tribunal to exercise jurisdiction over the matters listed in Part VII of the Bill?

The Criminal Law power

It is the Criminal Law power which is the present constitutional base for the federal competition legislation. In *A.-G. Ontario* v. *Hamilton Street Ry* (1903) A.C. 524, the Privy Council stated that "it is ... the criminal law in its widest sense that is reserved" for the exclusive authority under section 91(27) of the *Constitution Act, 1867.*

In *Re Board of Commerce Act* (1922) 1 A.C. 191 (hereinafter referred to as *"Board of Commerce"*), Viscount Haldane's introduced a limited view of the section 91(27) power by referring to it "as enabling the Dominion Parliament to exercise exclusive legislative power where the subject matter is one which by its very nature belongs to the domain of criminal jurisprudence." This view cast doubt upon whether anti-combines legislation could be supported under the Criminal power.

However, in *Proprietary Articles Trade Association* v. *Attorney General Canada* (1931) A.C. 310 (hereinafter referred to as the *"P.A.T.A. case"*), Lord Atkin refused to follow Viscount Haldane's restrictive view and instead upheld the 1923 combines law. He stated at p. 324:

> Criminal law means the criminal law in its widest sense. ... The criminal quality of an act cannot be discerned by intuition; nor can it be discerned by reference to any standard but one: Is the act prohibited with penal consequences.

To quote other cases would only burden this short paper. It is sufficient to recall that Laskin in *Canadian Constitutional Law*, 4th ed. (1973) at p. 824, wrote that resorting to "the criminal law power to proscribe undesirable commercial practices is today as characteristic of its exercise as has been resorted thereto to curb violence or immoral conduct.''

Peace, Order and Good Government (POGG)

Most proponents of this federal head of power claim that anti-combines law can be supported under the ''national dimensions'' doctrine introduced in the *A.-G. Ontario* v. *A.-G. Canada* (1896) A.C. 348 (hereinafter referred to as the *"Local Prohibition* case''). Their contention can be validly challenged by Viscount Haldane's judgment in *Board of Commerce* which narrowed the application of the POGG power to ''emergency'' functions. Later, in *A.-G. of Ontario* v. *Canada Temperance Federation* (1946) A.C. 193, at p. 205, the Court attempted to broaden this power to include any legislation which ''goes beyond local or provincial concern or interests and must from its inherent nature be the concern of the Dominion as a whole.''

The latter interpretation represented the ''national dimensions'' doctrine prior to the *Anti-Inflation Act Reference* (1976) 2 S.C.R. 373. This case, for the present, seems to have settled the debate. The Court stated that the POGG power had only two aspects: (1) a residual aspect for constitutional matters which did not fall within the enumerated heads in section 91 and section 92, and (2) an emergency aspect ''a la'' Board of Commerce.

Assuming there is no competition or anti-combines state of emergency in Canada, we would be stretching the imagination by stating that the area of competition falls within the residual aspect of POGG. Therefore, the federal Legislature cannot, by the force of the POGG power alone, uphold its claim that Bill C-91 falls within its sphere.

The regulation of Trade and Commerce

It is obvious that Parliament is being asked to sustain the proposed legislation with the Trade and Commerce power. Clause 18 of the Bill proposes that the long title of the Combines Investigation Act be repealed and that the following be substituted therefore:

> An Act to provide for the *general regulation of* trade and commerce in respect of conspiracies, trade practices and mergers affecting competition.

Despite the breadth of the expression ''Trade and Commerce,'' the Privy Council in *Citizens Insurance Co.* v. *Parsons* (1881) 7 A.C. 96 hereinafter referred to as *"Parsons''*), narrowed it down considerably. Trade and Commerce was confined to (1) interprovincial trade, (2) international trade, and (3) general regulation of trade affecting the whole Dominion.

In an attempt to challenge the Criminal Law power as the constitutional base of anti-combines legislation, "Trade and Commerce" was further reduced to a second class power. In *Board of Commerce,* Viscount Haldane struck down the *Combines and Fair Prices Act* and this power was rejected with one blow: Section 91(2) "did not, by itself, enable interference with particular trades in which Canadians would ... be free to engage in the Provinces."

However, this power was resurrected in an *obiter* by Lord Atkin in the *P.A.T.A.* case. He stated, at page 326, that the words Trade and Commerce "must receive their proper construction where they stand as giving independent authority to Parliament over the particular subject matter." The importance of this judgment was that the Court left open the question whether the *Combines Investigation Act* could be sustained under the Trade and Commerce power.

Later, in another constitutional challenge to an anti-combines law, Chief Justice Duff in *Re Dominion Trade and Industry Commission Act* (1936) S.C.R. 379, held the Act *ultra vires* the federal government and referred to the Trade and Commerce power in this manner:

> If confined to external trade and interprovincial trade, the section might well be competent under head number 2 of Section 91; and if the legislation were in substance concerned with such trade, incidental legislation in relation to local trade necessary in order to prevent the defeat of the competent provisions might also be competent, but as it stands, we think this section is invalid (at p. 382).

Consequently, the two attempts, namely *Board of Commerce* and *Re Dominion Trade and Industry Commission Act, supra,* to justify a non-criminal federal board to monitor combines cases were unsuccessful.

II. CONSTITUTIONAL BASE

It seems obvious that the Legislature in drafting Bill C-91 considered the above case law. One would simply have to read clauses 18 and 19 to discern Parliament's intention to conform with the various guidelines established by the judges in order to make the Trade and Commerce power the valid constitutional base for this Bill.

For instance, as was previously mentioned, clause 18 of Bill C-91 refers to the long title of the Act as being "An Act to provide for the *general regulation* of trade and commerce ...."

This complies with Sir Montague Smith's third category in the *Parsons* case, whereby Trade and Commerce could comprehend "the *general regulation of trade* affecting the whole Dominion." It also takes heed of the judgment in the *Local Prohibition* case which affirmed that through the use of the general Trade and Commerce power, Parliament could enact uniform laws with respect to combines matters even if it may incidentally affect provincial heads of power.

The latter case complied with Chief Justice Duff's judgment in *Re Dominion Trade and Industry Commission Act, supra,* and it appears to be the harbinger for the manner in which clause 19, which defines the purpose of the Act, was drafted. Clause 19 of Bill C-91 reads as follows:

PURPOSE

1.1   The purpose of this Act is to maintain and encourage competition in Canada in order to promote the efficiency and adaptability of the Canadian economy, in order to expand opportunities for Canadian participation in world markets while at the same time recognizing the role of foreign competition in Canada, in order to ensure that small and medium-sized enterprises have an equitable opportunity to participate in the Canadian economy and in order to provide consumers with competitive prices and product choices.

There is an emphasis upon international trade and the ensuing necessity of an efficient Canadian economy. As such, a valid argument can be raised in the event that the Act is constitutionally challenged on the basis that it infringes upon the Provinces' jurisdiction, specifically sections 92(13) and (16) powers.

According to this view, which I share, Bill C-91 would be, in pith and substance, an Act to promote the economic efficiency of Canada faced with an increasingly competitive world market. The fact that it may infringe upon property and civil rights in the Provinces would only be incidental to its main objective.

The Bill and the Charter

Bill C-91 has completely recodified the investigatory powers needed to deal effectively with competition matters in Canada.

In *Hunter, Director of Investigation and Research of the Combines In-*

vestigation Branch v. *Southam Inc.* (1984) 2 S.C.R. 145 (hereinafter referred to as the *"Southam* case"), the Supreme Court of Canada examined the constitutionality of search powers in the *Combines Investigation Act.* It did so in light of section 8 of the *Charter* which states that "everyone has the right to be secure against unreasonable search or seizure." The Court, in a judgment rendered by Dickson J. (as he then was), held that the three-step procedure set out in section 10 providing for a prior authorization of searches by a member of the "Restrictive Trade Practices Commission" was unconstitutional in two respects, namely that it failed to specify an appropriate standard for the issuance of warrants and that it designated an improper arbiter to issue them. The Court found that the guarantee of security from unreasonable search and seizure required that there be a valid procedure for prior authorization of searches:

> For such an authorization procedure to be meaningful, it is necessary for the person authorizing the search to be able to assess the evidence as to whether the standard has been met, in an entirely neutral and impartial manner .... The person performing this function need not be a judge, but he must at a minimum be capable of acting judicially.

Under the present Act, the Court held that the dual role of the Commission to investigate and to adjudicate violated "the ability of a member of the Commission to act in a judicial capacity when authorizing a search or seizure." In order to correct these constitutional defects, the proposed Competition Bill has been restructured. For one thing, the Commission itself has been abolished so that the Director of investigation no longer has any adjudicating powers. For another, all orders for oral examination, production of record and written return and warrants for entry to premises will emanate from a judge of a Superior, County or Federal Court upon application of the Director or of an authorized representative (ss. 9 and 13). These changes were clearly devised to ensure the impartiality required by the *Southam* case.

In conformity with the "minimum standard" set out by Dickson J. (as he then was) in *Southam,* the proposed Bill also sets out explicit criteria by which warrants to enter premises may be authorized. While the present Act merely states that the Director "may grant an authorization" upon a certificate from a member of the Commission, Bill C-91 now requires the authorizing party, a judge, to satisfy himself "by information on oath" that there are reasonable grounds to believe that an offence has been committed under the Act (s. 13). The wording would appear to fulfill the *Southam* standard which requires that there be "reasonable and probable grounds, established upon oath, to believe that an offence has been committed and that there is evidence to be found at the place of search."

True nature of Tribunal

Bill C-91 would abolish the "Restrictive Trade Practices Commission" and establish in its place a "Competition Tribunal" (clause 3). This Tribunal will consist of twelve members, four selected from the Federal Court and eight lay members (clause 3(2)). Only the judicial members of the Tribunal will determine questions of law.

The jurisdiction of this Tribunal will be to hear and determine all applications under a much enlarged Part VII of the Act (clause 8).

The Tribunal will have the power to make prohibition orders against persons engaging in the practice of abusing dominant positions, of consignment selling, of exclusive dealing or tied selling and of engaging in delivered pricing. It will also be able to order a supplier to accept a person as a customer, order the reduction or removal of customs duties, order the divestiture of assets or shares, order that no measure be taken in Canada to implement foreign judgments, laws or directives, order one to sell a product or not deal in a product when a foreign supplier has refused to supply such a product, approve a "specialization agreement" whereby parties agree to discontinue producing one or more products in order to rationalize and restructure certain industries.

In respect of completed mergers, the Tribunal will have the power to dissolve them or order the disposition of assets or shares. In the cases of proposed mergers, it will have the power to order that such "merger not proceed." The Tribunal may make orders under the provision that they may be rescinded or varied if certain conditions have occurred whereby it would no longer be preventing or lessening competition substantially.

The substance of the jurisdiction is therefore to do and to undo contracts, to refuse to recognize contractual relationships or to impose such relationships.

The power of the federal Parliament to establish federal courts under certain conditions is, of course, conferred by section 101 of the *Constitution Act, 1867.* There is also no doubt that Parliament may establish administrative tribunals to administer federal matters. The question here is whether, under the guise of establishing such an administrative tribunal, Parliament would not in fact create a Court, the characteristics of which would not conform to the minimum ones without which there cannot be a true Court.

Tribunal or Court?

The powers that would be exercised by the Competition Tribunal are of such importance, going to the roots of our economic life, that it is wise to remember the words of P.H. Russell in *The Effect of a Charter of Rights on the Policy-making Role of Canadian Courts* (1982), at p. 18:

> Perhaps the most difficult and important decisions a democratic society must make are precisely those involving the competing claims of diversity and order, equality and liberty, welfare and economy.

Given the nature and the extent of the adjudicative role that would be exercised by the Competition Tribunal, it may well be argued that this role should be exercised only by a true Court. Otherwise, a large segment of the nation's life would be left in the hands of the Executive power of the State to the exclusion of the Judicial power.

Assuming the conclusion that only a true Court should pass upon the subject matters entrusted by the Bill to the Competition Tribunal, it is obvious that the latter does not pass the test, as expressed by Lord Hailsham on September 27, 1984 in an address to the Judicial Studies Board Seminar Dinner:

> In Britain, and in all free constitutions based on Cabinet Government and derived from it, the importance of a judiciary secure in its tenure, impartial, applying objectively identifiable rules of law, which are binding until altered remains fundamental to a free constitution.

Eight lay members with a tenure limited to seven years cannot be considered true judges. The recent judgment of the Supreme Court of Canada in *Walter Valente* v. *The Queen* (judgment rendered December 19, 1985, unreported to date) sheds light on the problems involved.

The fact that all the decisions of the Tribunal, whether final, interlocutory or interim, are subject to appeal to the Federal Court of Appeal (section 13), would not validate the exercise of Judicial power by an administrative tribunal.

A true Court of Appeal presupposes a true Court of first instance.

III. CONCLUSION

It is my submission

(1) that Bill C-91 is a valid exercise of the federal power under section 91(2) of the *Constitution Act, 1867,* namely Trade and Commerce;

(2) that the powers entrusted by the Bill to the Competition Tribunal should be exercised by a true Court.

THE AUTHOR

Donald E. Armstrong obtained Arts and Commerce degrees *cum laude* at the University of Alberta and a Ph.D in Economics at McGill University, with one year of post-graduate study at the University of Manchester. He set up a new Graduate School of Business (now the Faculty of Management) at McGill University where he served for four years as its first Director.

On the public side of his consulting and research activities, Dr. Armstrong has prepared studies or has acted as advisor or expert witness for the Gordon Commission, the Borden Commission, the Royal Commission on the Revision of the Financial Terms of Union Between Newfoundland and Canada, the Royal Commission on Transportation and the Royal Commission on Bilingualism and Biculturalism. It is, however, as a consultant for industry that he has done most of his work. He has served as a Project Director at the Stanford Research Institute in California, and has acted as the Manager of a Canadian firm of economic consultants. Currently Dr. Armstrong is a principal in Manecon — A Meco Company offering economic consulting services to industry. He recently acted as an expert witness for the Aluminium and Sugar cases both of which were won by his clients.

Dr. Armstrong wrote *Competition versus Monopoly* which was published by the Fraser Institute in 1982.

Chapter Five

The Sugar Case as a Reason for "Strengthening" the Combines Act

An Economic Perspective

Donald E. Armstrong

I. INTRODUCTION

The case of *Regina v. Atlantic Sugar Refiners Co. Ltd., Redpath Industries Limited, St. Lawrence Sugar Limited, and S.L.S.R. Holdings Limited* (hereinafter referred to as the Sugar Case) has been cited by Consumer and Corporate Affairs[1] as evidence that there is a "Need to Reform" the Combines Investigation Act. The eventual acquittal of the accused produced a number of criticisms of either the weakness of the Act or the softness and ineffectiveness of the courts.[2][3][4] It is the contention of this paper that if one looked at all the evidence and the testimony — as well as the judgments — and if one assessed this information on the basis of a more realistic model of the firm and of competition than that provided by main-line price theory, one would come to the very opposite conclusion.

What the sugar case demonstrates is that under the existing Combines Investigation Act companies can be punished with long and expensive trials. It shows that they can come perilously close to being fined and to having their executives imprisoned for up to five years — for behaviour that is innocent of any criminal or economic wrong doing.

The sugar case offers many examples of the power of the existing law and of the difficulties that can be encountered by defendants. The sugar companies were charged with eight different offenses (only one of which had to be won by the Crown in order to obtain a conviction). To do justice to all of the issues raised by these trials within a trial would require a lengthy book, not a short article. Attention will therefore be limited to only one of the issues. The one that has been chosen is the alleged tacit agreement among the sugar companies to share the market.

Not guilty, guilty, not guilty

After a lengthy and very expensive trial in the Criminal Division of the Superior Court of Quebec, the sugar companies were acquitted on all eight charges. But the Crown took the case to appeal and the finding of the trial judge was reversed on the charge of market sharing. The companies were found guilty and fined a total of $2,250,000. The conviction was appealed and the companies won before the Supreme Court of Canada, but not without a dissenting opinion.

The key element in the reversal of the trial judge's decision by the Court of Appeal is the one that has been chosen as the focus of this paper.

The submission of the Crown on this issue as recited by the trial judge reads as follows:

> ... all three accused adopted a policy of maintaining their traditional established share of the market for refined sugar, refusing to compete for a larger share although conditions in the industry existed which ought to have encouraged such an effort and that even after Cartier [a new relatively small entrant in the market] became established and acquired a portion of the market, the respective shares of the accused remained proportionally, the same as before.[5]

The trial judge summarized the theory of the Crown in these words:

> There existed a market sharing agreement which was maintained by the accused for many years despite changing circumstances and the fact that any one of the accused could readily have obtained a greater share of the market by inter alia:
>
> (a) giving greater discounts to customers,
> (b) more vigourous advertising,
> (c) better packaging,

(d) abolishing the basing point pricing and freight absorption system of marketing,

(e) using maximum plant capacity and the agreement had the effect of lessening competition.[6]

The defense

The theory of the defense was summarized in a short paragraph:

> The only way to increase sales of an homogeneous product in an oligopoly is to reduce prices, the result of which is either a depletion of supplies and depressed earnings by the firm lowering its prices or a price war. Since the results in either case are disastrous, the only alternative is for each member of the oligopoly to seek to maintain its traditional market share.[7]

An attempt to increase market share

After setting out the market shares (roughly 43 percent, 35 percent, and 22 percent) the judge went on to describe what happened when Redpath tried to increase its market share after the opening of its Toronto refinery.

> During the next decade, the market shares varied slightly. But in 1958, Redpath having just opened its Toronto refinery and being anxious to increase sales and recoup some of the heavy expenses involved, surreptitiously began to cut prices in the Toronto area. Atlantic felt the loss of sales in that area and so began to cut its prices there, although this represented a serious expense, due to the absorption by Atlantic of the unsubsidized portion of the freight from the refinery in St. John to the nearest basing point which was now Toronto instead of Montreal as it had been before the new refinery was constructed. The price was spread to include St. Lawrence. There were two results -
>
> First: Redpath increased its market share at the expense of the others from 42.8 percent in 1957 to 46.6 percent in 1958.
>
> Second: it lost the price war against its two-well funded opponents, and having sustained serious financial losses it was ripe for a take over by Tate and Lyle.[8]

II. THE FATEFUL TERM: "TACIT AGREEMENT"

Then followed the conclusion and the labelling of the result as a "tacit agreement."

> Thereafter, each of the accused settled down to a policy of maintaining their traditional market shares. Although each stressed that this was the result of an independent decision, one would be ingenuous not to be aware that there was and continues to be a *tacit agreement* to this effect.[9] (Underlining added)

Even if one's knowledge of the case is limited to a reading of the judgment, the appearance of the term "tacit agreement" with regard to market share must come as a surprise in the light of (i) the analysis that the trial judge undertook with regard to pricing, (ii) the fact that he dismissed the Crown's contention that the accused had conspired to set prices and (iii) the almost complete absence of any discussion of the problem of market shares except the observation that attempts to change them turned out to be rather disastrous.

In view of the rather cursory treatment of market shares by the trial judge it is doubly important to describe the reality of competition and the alternatives open to the sugar companies in the kind of market in which they carried on their business.

Market characteristics

1. Industrial refined sugar is a relatively homogeneous product (or set of products).
2. Economies of scale and transportation costs decree that, especially in the limited Canadian markets, there cannot be more than a few suppliers of most sugar products.
3. Industrial sugar is sold in an "expert" market; the refiners do not sell directly to the public. Buyers and sellers are usually experienced, have and use many sources of information, and are generally very knowledgeable.
4. Firms in such a market will be mutually interdependent and must recognize this fact. That is to say, intelligent managers will know that whatever they do will be known to their competitors, will affect their competitors, and will cause their competitors to react.
5. All buyers and sellers in this type of market know that product prices

must be very similar. Posted, list, advertised or pro forma prices have to be virtually identical for any one product at any one location and at any one time. Actual prices must be almost the same. This equality of prices will hold whether prices are relatively stable or whether they are changing rapidly over time.

6. According to the Crown, the sugar companies had excess capacity. This condition is quite normal in this type of industry; indeed, in markets with fluctuating demand, excess capacity is almost inevitable most of the time.[10]

7. In many if not most large-firm industries and in all industries with excess capacity, the additional or marginal cost per unit of producing some significant amount of additional output will be below the average cost, and will also normally be well below price. From this it follows that atomistic price cutting will be a constant threat to the industry.

8. The atomistically competitive behaviour of a firm would require that it ignore mutually interdependency and that it look at each possible sale without any thought of what effect its terms would have on all the other sales made by itself or its competitors. A firm that was competing in this manner might try to increase its market share and profits by keeping,or trying to keep, its existing prices on existing business constant; at the same time it might shave prices for new customers and thereby bribe them away from competitors. While this strategy might work in markets with differentiated products, it will not work in the case of a product like industrial sugar. "New" business gained by one firm is "old" business lost for a competitor. The firm that has lost a customer and therefore some market share will under most circumstances be obliged to cut prices to maintain or regain customers.

When the Crown argued before the trial judge that "any one of the accused could readily have obtained a greater share of the market by ... giving greater discounts..." [11] etc. it was simply in error. The evidence cited by the trial judge proved this error beyond reasonable doubt.

While the sugar companies were constantly skirmishing, shading prices, obtaining and losing customers, they could not have believed (and after Redpath's experience it would have been foolish of them to believe) that they could *easily* increase their market share. If they could do so at all it would only be after a long and costly fight.

9. Engaging a long and costly fight could hardly have been a sensible policy for any sugar company unless it had the capacity, the low costs and the financial reserves to eliminate a rival and therefore to remove some ex-

cess capacity from the industry.[12] It seems very doubtful that during the period of the alleged offense any of the companies were in a position to benefit from a fight to the finish; nor is it self-evident that in the long run even the customers would benefit from such a war. The irony in all of this is that even if one of the sugar companies did happen to be able to eliminate a competitor and thus reduce excess capacity in the industry, it could easily have found itself in trouble with a charge of predatory competition under Section 34 of the Combines Investigation Act. Damned if you don't, and damned if you do! Yet this elimination of excess capacity is implicit in the charge by the Crown that the firms were not reacting as they should have to the existence of excess capacity, i.e. the strong were not cutting price and expanding sales in order to eliminate the weak.

Competitive options facing the sugar companies

Given the reality of a homogeneous, expert, oligopolistic market, a sugar company would have three possible options that it might follow with respect to price and market share.

1. At one extreme it could wage a price war in the hope of eliminating a competitor and in the further hope of being able to recoup the lost income once a larger market share had been obtained.
2. At the other extreme it could try to enter into an explicit price and market-sharing agreement with its competitors.[13]
3. Finally it could try to operate in "the middle," avoiding destructive and possible illegal predatory competition on the one side and collusive and illegal non-competition on the other. The evidence clearly showed that the sugar companies were competing in this middle ground.

Competition in between collusion and predation

Companies that operate in expert, homogeneous markets and that must at the same time steer a course between collusion and predatory behaviour must face the realities of the kind of market they are in. The competitive solution they adopt must recognize that:

– they are mutually interdependent,
– their marginal costs are usually below their average costs, i.e. they cannot afford to sell at marginal cost,

- pro forma prices must be virtually identical and actual prices must be nearly so,
- pro forma and actual prices must be held above the atomistically competitive floor of marginal costs,
- price and marketing skirmishing must not degenerate into either total war or total peace.

Now it *will* be obvious to anyone who has ever operated in such a market, and it *should* be obvious to any one who has thought about the matter, that in order to satisfy the above conditions there must be

> conscious parallelism, (c.p.) or a
> way of doing business, or a
> procedure, or an
> arrangement, or an
> understanding, or a
> convention, or a
> shared wisdom, or a
> decision rule, or a
> predictability of behavior, or a
> practice, or
> something (hereafter referred to as [c.p.etc.])

that makes market prices and market shares behave the way we know they must.

The law and "tacit agreement"

The law having declared the Scylla of predation and the Charybdis of collusion to be illegal, *it must not now declare to be illegal that narrow band of water in between*. If it does, it will deny to us the made-in-Canada products that must be produced by homogeneous oligopolies. If [c.p.etc.] is also to carry the optional label of "tacit agreement," that does no harm just so long as this practice does not also constitute an illegal conspiracy. If "tacit agreement" is to be a criminal offence then it must on no account be used to describe the [c.p.etc.] processes by which the competitive activities of homogeneous oligopolies are described.

The trial judge on prices

The evidence put before the trail judge clearly indicated that Redpath was the price leader and that the pro forma prices of the accused were almost always the same.

The two smaller sugar producers stated quite categorically in court that they knew the formula (based on the London Daily Price) by which Redpath established the posted price from day to day and that their posted prices followed.

In view of the trial judge's subsequent labelling of the sugar companies' market-sharing performance as a tacit agreement, one cannot help but wonder, along with the Supreme Court Judges,[14] why this follow-the-leader on prices was not also labelled a tacit agreement. After all, with respect to posted prices the trial judge had solid, unrefuted evidence of shared knowledge and an easy-to-follow and easy-to-understand formula. This was much more than he had in the case of market shares.

Economic sense

That the judge did not use tacit agreement to apply to pricing can perhaps be explained by the fact that there is a considerable amount of applied economic and managerial good sense that has found its way into the court rooms on the matter of pricing in homogeneous markets. In his written judgment the trial judge quotes various economists and concludes:

> In an oligopolistic situation where the product is homogeneous — as is sugar — the price of the product must inevitably be the same, for if one member priced his product higher than the others he would have no sales. If he posted a lower price he would soon be inundated with buyers, would realize his price was too low, perhaps unprofitable, and raise it. Thus by natural osmosis the price of an homogeneous product tends to reach the same level. But this process might be costly and is certainly inefficient. There are two ways to avoid it. Firstly, by the members of the industry conspiring to fix prices, which is illegal, or by the members of the industry making a conscious effort to parallel the prices of the leader.[15]

He includes a long quotation from the Director of Investigation and Research — which is worth quoting again.

Frequently these price changes concern staple commodities entering into the cost of living of consumers. Markets for these commodities are usually such that price changes are effected by all competitors on or about the same day and an impression of simultaneous decision invariably arises. Often this is interpreted by the public as evidence of collusion on the part of the sellers and questions are raised to the possible application of the remedies provided under the Combines Investigation Act.

.....

A searching inquiry into the facts will often show that the speed with which a price change becomes general is not inconsistent with independent action on the part of each seller and does not give rise to a valid inference that there has been collusive action. *Except during brief periods of change, the price of any homogeneous commodity will tend to be the same for all sellers and buyers in a given market area. At the first suggestion of any permanent differential, buyers will switch their custom to the company offering the lowest price and sellers therefore will have to bring their prices to meet that of the lowest competitors. Consequently, in those commodity markets where sellers are few and many sales are made daily to wholesalers, retailers and consumers, a price change instituted by any one seller will usually be communicated within the hour to his competitors and the necessary adjustments made almost instantly.*[16] (Underlining in original)

Follow the leader

The trial judge was assured by all of the sugar company executives that they knew precisely how pro forma prices were set, and it must have been evident to him that each company knew that competitors had followed the leader in the past and would probably do so in the future. He was also assured that this arrangement came about by each company deciding independently that this course of action, [c.p.etc.] was undertaken independently as the logical and, we might add, inevitable thing to do.

If the judge was tempted to call the pricing method a tacit agreement he was perhaps deterred from doing so by the evidence that there was still considerable rivalry concerning price. When buyers set out to negotiate contracts they received *different* quotes from different sellers, and were thus able to chose from among different competing offers. While it was never suggested (nor could it be expected) that the differences in competing offers at any one time were large, they were apparently large enough to convince the judge that there was a reasonable degree of rivalry in the industry. Anyone else reviewing the evidence would be very likely to come to the same conclusion.

III. MARKET SHARES

While the trial judge presented a careful review of expert opinion and of the evidence with respect to pricing there is only a brief analysis of, and very little by way of review of the evidence with respect to, market shares. There is not a hint of how the situation with regard to the adoption of parallel policies on market shares differed from the obviously parallel policies on pricing. Nor did there seem to be any awareness that price rivalry and market-share rivalry were so inextricably intertwined that when companies were fighting over price they were at the same time fighting over sales and market shares. Logic would suggest that if the trial judge was satisfied with the amount of competition on price, which he seemed to be, he should have been equally satisfied with the amount of competition on sales.

In what little analysis there was, the judge did quite wisely dismiss the Crown's suggestion that a greater market share could be readily obtained by advertising, packaging, or greater use of plant capacity (!) And he dismissed as undesirable the abolition of the basing point and freight absorption which would have reconstituted the industry into a series of local monopolies.

Price cutting

The judge was left with the conclusion that "the only method of increasing them [market shares] [was] by price cutting through extensive discounts."[17]

But on the evidence it is clear that not even price cutting could produce a lasting increase in market shares (unless, of course, a competitor was eliminated). As the judge pointed out, Redpath had indeed tried price cutting. While it did succeed in increasing shares for a time the battle did not end until its competitors regained their market shares. As added punishment, the then management of Redpath subsequently lost control of the company. It is doubtful whether any sugar company had at its disposal any rational policy that would have produced a significant increase in its market share save the elimination of a competitor. It is unlikely that such a plan would have maximized profits or minimized court costs.

The judgment reads:

On the evidence, I find that the maintenance of traditional market shares—which were adjusted but in the same proportion when Cartier came on stream—was the result of a tacit agreement between the accused. But in my opinion, it has not been shown that this agreement was arrived at with the intention of unduly preventing or lessening competition. The reason for maintaining traditional market shares was to avoid a price war which would have resulted had the accused taken the only method of increasing them by price cutting through extensive discounts. Nor am I able to infer from the totality of the evidence on this point, including overt acts, that market shares were maintained for the purpose of stifling competition. On the contrary, Cartier was launched in 1964 and none of its initial difficulties were due to the maintenance of market shares. Westcane was launched successfully in 1969. Austin attempted to launch Austin Sugar Refineries Limited in the Cornwall area with Government support in 1971.... That this project was never realized was in no way due to the maintenance of market shares by the accused.[18]

The fundamental question is whether this "tacit agreement," this [c.p.etc.], was anything more than the knowledge shared by the sugar companies that list prices were determined in a certain way. Was it any more than the knowledge that in this industry there was leadership and followership? Was it any more than the shared knowledge that if price erosion got out of hand there would probably be a repeat of past disasters? Was it any more than the knowledge that when one company introduced liquid sugar, the others had to follow in order to protect their market share or that when one company introduced plastic bags for brown sugar the others had to defend their market position by introducing their own plastic bags just as quickly as possible?

The facts on market shares

Two topics that have been almost completely missing from discussions of the Sugar Case are the *facts* on the fluctuations of market shares and what *"bench marks"* there might be against which actual fluctuations can be compared so that an illegal conspiracy can be proven or at least inferred.

Mr. Justice Estey wrote the dissenting opinion in the Supreme Court which would have retained the guilty verdict against the sugar companies. It is instructive that he referred to "the maintenance of *fixed* proportions of the eastern Canada sugar market."[19] Later, he spoke of "the *strange sight* of the three accused sharing virtually all the eastern Canada sugar market *in constant proportions* for eleven years and thereafter sharing ninety percent of the market in the *same proportions* for another fourteen years.''[20] (underlining added)

Just how ''constant'' or ''fixed'' were these shares? In this regard a picture is worth a thousand words, and what follows (see Chart A) is a picture of the market share of domestic sales by Redpath on a monthly basis (only a ten-year interval is shown so that the graph can be compared directly with a ten year simulation on Chart B).

It would hardly seem appropriate, in view of the reality of the market performance, to use the term ''fixed'' or ''constant'' to apply to the actual fluctuations in market shares. They in fact involved large and inconvenient swings in sales.

The Crown had no right to claim that market shares were fixed; they obviously were not. Nor is it at all self-evident that the observed fluctuations prove or infer an illegal conspiracy. If the Crown believed that fluctuations should have been greater and, in the absence of an illegal conspiracy, would have been greater, such a contention should have been backed by analysis or data or evidence of conspiracy. But by themselves the actual fluctuations prove nothing more than that market shares were *not* constant.

Appropriate expectations on market shares

The Crown did not offer any guidance on what fluctuations in market shares one should expect in a non-conspiring, but mutually interdependent, expert, homogeneous, oligopolistic, mature, relatively unchanging and gently growing, stable product market. On *a priori* grounds there are several reasons for expecting relative stability of market shares in such a market. In the light of the particular circumstance of the sugar market it is difficult to think of *any* convincing reason to expect fluctuations to be greater than they actually were.

Some of the factors promoting relative stability of market shares are as follows:

1. Equal growth and therefore equal shares are to be expected so long as the industries being served by the sugar companies are themselves growing at a reasonably stable rate. Sugar refining is a stable, mature industry serving a number of stable, mature industries.
2. Stable market shares are suggested by the nearly equal balance of financial power among the refiners — there were no ''weak sisters'' to be squeezed out.

CHART A   **Simulated Market Share
on a Monthly Basis**

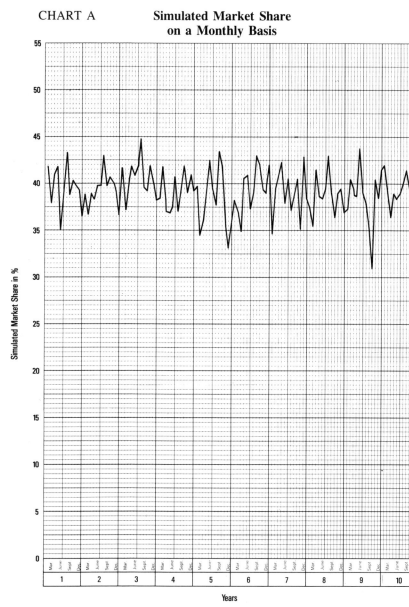

Capacity of Plant A =   55 Units
Capacity of Plant B =   45 Units
Capacity of Plant C =   35 Units

Total capacity   135 Units

Total market   90 Units

CHART B

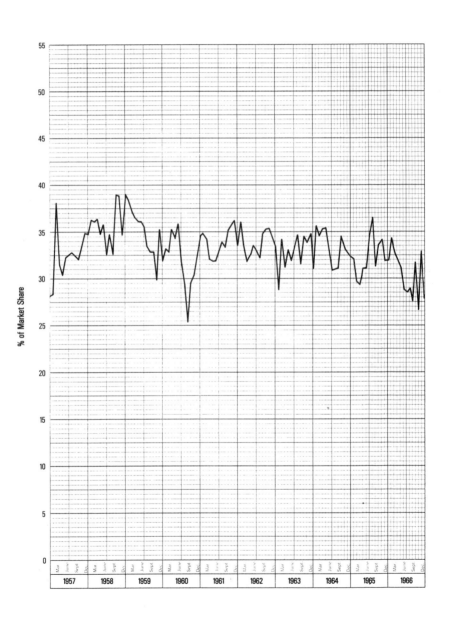

3. The pace and nature of production and product innovation in the period promoted stability. Technological innovations in production tended to occur outside the industry and were available to all, while the product and service innovations that occurred within the industry were generally non-patentable and easily copied.

4. Some aspects of growth are related to company size and therefore tend to perpetuate the results of the past. For example, a company that has enjoyed 35 percent of the market could be expected to have 35 percent of the sales force and to put forth about 35 percent of the sales effort. It would therefore be in a good position to pick up about 35 percent of the business in the future.

5. This inertia is usually reinforced by the inevitable planning-forecasting function of a firm. In a mature, steadily growing industry, decisions about the future will be based to a considerable extent on extrapolation of the past. Historical stability encourages planning activities that will promote future stability. For example, the sugar companies must purchase raw sugar many months ahead of refined sugar sales. How much raw sugar should a company buy? It would obviously be tempting to purchase on the assumption that final sales in, say, January 1972 will be about the same as they were in January, 1971 plus average market growth over the previous few years. Once such a decision is made it tends to become a self-fulfilling prophecy. For when the sugar is refined, the production volume becomes the sales target. Sales that are too high will mean shortages and unfilled contracts. Sales that are too low will mean excess inventory.

6. Past stability produces future stability and in this case it must be remembered that historical stability was reinforced in this industry by many years of government controls when market shares *were* fixed by government regulation.

7. Finally the determination of competitors, and their *proclaimed* determination, to maintain "their" market shares, is an efficient way of keeping the peace. Neither political scientists familiar with rivalry between nation states nor naturalists familiar with the territorial imperative should have any trouble believing that territory can be defended by threats, warlike preparations and border skirmishes that show a determination to hold on to one's territory or, presumably, to one's market share.

Market-share bench marks

The Crown did not provide the Court with a bench mark against which the actual fluctuations of market shares could be judged. But for amusement, if not enlightenment, the reader might compare the market share in the following diagram with the actual market share of Redpath shown on Chart A.

The reader can be assured that the market fluctuations are *not* the result of collusion because they were generated by a computer that picked sales for each company at random from all of the possible permutations and combinations of sales by three companies serving a total market demand of 90 units per month but with individual plant capacities enabling maximum deliveries of 50, 40 and 30 for plants A, B, and C, giving a total possible supply of 120 units.

The computer simulation demonstrates that by taking a simple set of constraints, even a random (atomistic) picking of market shares produces a pattern of market sharing over time remarkably similar to the market shares that proved to the Crown that there had been a criminal conspiracy.

Market shares after entry of new firm

The Supreme Court Justice who held the companies guilty of an illegal collusion found it very "strange" that the three sugar companies should end up with the same—we should say *about* the same—market share after the entry of a new competitor as they had before. It is quite likely that this "strangeness" had a good deal to do with the choice of the term "tacit agreement" by the trial judge and with the writing of a dissenting opinion in the Supreme Court decision. But let us put the question the other way around. Why would the market shares of the "old" refiners *not* be about the same relative to each other after a new firm has entered the market?

Chart C presents the question as a formal statistical exercise in probability. Assume that there are 1000 customers, all represented by balls in an urn, and that 45 percent "belong" to company A, 35 percent to company B and 20 percent to company C. If the new firm "steals" 10 percent of the balls out of the urn it is going to leave the 3 firms with 90 percent of their former customers.

But Company A is still going to have about 45 percent, B 35 percent and C 20 percent of the 90 percent of the market that is left to the three companies.

What would have been "strange" and what would have needed explaining is a *post-entry distribution of market shares among the three companies that was significantly different than it was before.*

IV. EVIDENCE OF NON-COLLUSION

Prosecuting attorneys are fond of saying that collusive acts are done in secret and only by inference and luck can the Crown be successful in prosecuting conspiracies. In this case, however, the evidence clearly establishes that non-collusive competition was the weapon used to obtain market shares.

The Redpath marketing memo quoted at some length in the Supreme Court judgment (but not by the trial judge) clearly indicated that this firm was speculating about the action of its competitors. Yes, Redpath believed that other sugar companies would behave in a certain way, but the language of the memo is simply not consistent with the existence of a collusive agreement.

While most of the evidence seemed to spotlight the price side of the price-sales function, there were clear indications of the existence of rivalry where the emphasis did rest on the volume side of the function.

The testimony of Thomas Moorse, a former sugar buyer for Neilsons and Lowneys, contained a number of references to the importance placed by the sugar companies on volume and to the concessions that they were willing to make to obtain expanded sales.[21]

Price competition IS competition for market share

The main body of evidence concerning market shares was simply overlooked because the Court did not seem to appreciate the logical connection between price and volume. The trial judge was satisfied with the degree of price competition, and flatly rejected the Crown's contention that they were determined by a criminal conspiracy. But price is just one-half of the "demand curve": it is just one half of the price-sales relationship. The sugar companies engaged in price competition for only one reason — to obtain sales and therefore market share. Each and every example that the Court heard concerning price rivalry could just as easily, and indeed more accurately, have been relabelled as sales or market-share rivalry.

It is logically unacceptable to find that there is sufficient rivalry on price but insufficient rivalry — indeed a criminal conspiracy — with respect to volume! If the sugar companies had really agreed to divide the market in fixed percentages, then surely they would not have had to resort to the prac-

CHART C

In the urn there are 1000
"customers"

450 **◐**   =   45 percent
350 **●** and =   35 percent
200 ○   =   20 percent
being the
customers = 100 percent

of firm A **◐**
        B **●**
   and C ○

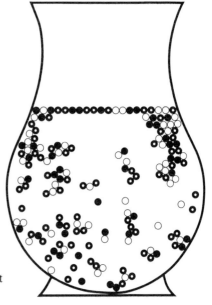

If a new firm D draws 10 percent
of the customers out of the urn
at random then it is most likely that
the new firm will require about

10 percent of the A (**◐**) customers or 45   **◐**'s
10 percent of the B (**●**) customers or 35   **●**'s and
10 percent of the C (○) customers or 20   ○'s

The old firms will be left with
(450-45) 405   **◐**'s which is 45 percent of 900
(350-35) 315   **●**'s which is 35 percent of 900
(200-20) 180   ○'s which is 20 percent of 900
          and 900 total is   100 percent of 900

tices of stealing each other's customers, and of making price and other concessions to obtain the market share that was allocated to them by "collusion."

What's in a name?

Unfortunately for the sugar companies, the judgment, as we have seen, reads "On the evidence, I find ... a tacit agreement."[22]

These words will continue to pose a problem for lawyers and economists (not to mention the managers who must work in this type of market). These words also created difficulties for the Supreme Court. If "tacit agreement" is just another synonym to be added to the list in [c.p.etc.] as descriptive of how a mutually interdependent expert, homogeneous, oligopolistic industry must operate, in order to avoid the illegality of too much or too little competition, then the problem vanishes. But if "tacit agreement" is to refer to an illegal conspiracy punishable by fines and imprisonment, then the decision of the trial judge simply had to be challenged on either his interpretation of the facts or on his use of the term. The Supreme Court chose the latter course.

V. "TACIT AGREEMENT" EQUALS CONSCIOUS PARALLELISM

That the Supreme Court saw the tacit agreement as akin to conscious parallelism can be seen in the following quote — even if it does end with a question.

> Counsel for St.Lawrence Sugar Ltd. has contended that such a 'tacit agreement,' being merely the conscious adoption of a uniform course of action without any communication, assent or promise, did not amount to a conspiracy. He pointed out that there was no illegality in the independent adoption of such a policy of limited competition. A conspiracy requires agreement. Is a finding of a 'tacit agreement' sufficient?

It must be accepted that a conspiracy may be effected in any way and may be established by inference.

In dealing with the refiners' uniform prices, the trial judge felt that they raised an inference of collusion. However he accepted (at p. 98) that this was a result of independent decisions called "conscious parallelism" which is not illegal. The evidence was clear, however, that not only were its competitors immediately aware of Redpath's list price the moment a new price was posted in its lobby, they also in time were able to discover Redpath's pricing formula by a process of deduction from available data. Yet the trial judge held, correctly I think, that this did not constitute a conspiracy to maintain uniform prices according to Redpath's formula but merely ''conscious parallelism.'' Could this not be just as accurately called ''parallelism by tacit agreement?''[23]

Of course once ''tacit agreement'' was linked to legal conscious parallelism for *proforma* prices it was self-evident that the competitive interactions of market shares and real prices were even ''less parallel'' and, therefore, that much further away from being an illegal conspiracy.

''Tacit agreement'' and competition

If the matter could be left with a simple decision by the Supreme Court that tacit agreement is just another word to describe legal conscious parallelism etc. the net effect of the Sugar Case on the need to strengthen or weaken the Combines Act would be quite straightforward. It would simply demonstrate how easy it is for the Crown to prosecute homogeneous oligopolies, and it would also show how serious are the risks of being found guilty for inevitable business practices that follow from mutual interdependency. If revision of the Act's conspiracy provisions is warranted at all, then it might consist of adding a preamble that would point out some of the facts of competitive life in homogeneous oligopolistic markets.

Unfortunately the Supreme Court decision did not merely equate tacit agreement with [c.p.etc.]; it seemed also to accept the proposition that ''tacit agreements'' and therefore presumably conscious parallelism — and all of the other ''things'' that we included in [c.p.etc.] — limit competition. This finding of the Supreme Court crystallized the position of the Crown in the statement

> ... the Crown's contention implies ... that ... each of the refiners was obliged to endeavour to increase its market share at the expense of the others, otherwise it was agreeing to lessen competition unduly.[24]

Good sense prevailed in both the trial court and the Supreme Court and the judgment continued,

> In my view, the trial judge was correct in rejecting this submission.[25]

So far so good. The companies were not conspiring: they were pursuing policies that were necessary to avoid bankruptcy and, very likely, to avoid prosecution for predatory behaviour.

Innocence

What the Supreme Court justices should have said at this point, is that the sugar companies' actions involved only conscious parallelism, there was absolutely no hint of a criminal conspiracy, and the companies were therefore innocent of any wrong doing. This is approximately what the Supreme Court decision said, but unfortunately in saying it, the judge used the following words:

> As I have already indicated, I cannot agree with the submission that this "tacit agreement" to maintain market shares involved the elimination of competition. On the contrary, as we have just seen, *the evidence is clear that it involved only a lessening of competition.* [26] (underlining added)

What the Supreme Court decision seems to have done is to equate "tacit agreement" with [c.p.etc.] that are the normal and necessary attributes of competitive behaviour in this special type of market. It has always been the understanding of most executives in this type of industry that so long as they avoided conspiracies, the courts would recognize that necessary patterns of conscious parallelism were legal and, indeed, unavoidable.

Risk and uncertainty

Given the decision of the Supreme Court there must be considerable uncertainty and more risk in doing business in a homogeneous oligopoly. We seem to have a verdict from the highest court in the land, based on the existing Combines Investigations Act, to the effect that whatever companies do in a homogeneous, expert, oligopolistic market to avoid an atomistic price war is by definition a limiting of competition.

The effect of this decision will be that every company in this type of industry brought to trial will automatically be found guilty by the Court and by the newspapers of what is presumably an *economic* misdemeanour of limiting competition. The only matter to be settled will be whether the executives have gone far enough in their "antisocial" behaviour to warrant five million dollar fines and five year jail sentences. The room left to navigate between the sea monster and the whirlpool has been peerlessly narrowed. The Sugar Case has already enhanced the power of the Combine Investigation Branch. "Strengthening" the Act to make it even easier for the Crown to win future cases against oligopolies producing homogeneous products is unwarranted. The Crown did not have a legitimate conspiracy case against the sugar refiners, and adjusting the law to enhance the prosecution side is certainly unwarranted.

Notes

1. Consumers and Corporate Affairs, *Competition Law Amendments: A Guide*, Minister of Supply and Services, Canada, 1985, pp. 26-7.

2. Green, Christopher, *Canadian Industrial Organization and Policy*, McGraw-Hill Ryerson, 1980, pp. 178-79.

3. Stanbury W.T., Reschenthaler G.B., "Oligololy and Conscious Parallelism: Theory, Policy and the Canadian Cases," *Osgoode Hall Law Journal* vol. 15, No. 3 especially pp. 644-52.

4. McFetridge, Donald G., Wong, Stanley, "Agreements to Lessen Competition After Atlantic Sugar," *Canadian Business Law Journal*, Vol. 5, p. 329.

5. Regina v. Atlantic Sugar Refineries Co. Ltd.,*et al. Judgment*-Combines Investigation act, Mackay J. 19 December 1975. (hereafter R. v. Atlantic Sugar *et al.*) p. 48.

6. Ibid., pp. 94-5.

7. Ibid., p. 95.

8. Ibid., p. 95.

9. Ibid., p. 95.

10. Excess capacity is a much abused concept in the economic literature, and it generally receives a very bad press. From the point of view of conventional wisdom it is not surprising that those in charge of the Sugar Case appeared to believe that there should have been a price war to stamp out the evil of resource-wasting excess capacity. Of course, the construction of *new* excess capacity would almost by definition be a waste of resources. But what if that some capacity was labelled "a safety factor," "reserve capacity," or "stand-by capicity," "capacity to handle peak loads," etc.?

    If the prevention of *new* excess capacity is open to question, the case for the elimination of *existing* excess capacity is even weaker.

11. Ibid., p. 94.

12. The elimination of excess capacity is more difficult than the elimination of a particular competitor. A price war that bankrupts a company does not destroy its physical plant. What is likely to happen is that the financial assets of the bankrupt firm will get written down/perhaps to zero — and a reconstituted firm will rise from the ashes to operate at the old physical capacity at reduced or zero financial cost.

    A price war is very likely therefore to accomplish nothing more than the replacement of a high-cost competitor with a low-lost competitor — at least for the life of the plant.

13. According to most economists who write in this field it is presumed to be easy for firms to conspire. If price theory really did describe the real world one might agree, but the real world has too many variables to make an effective agreement easy or even possible. For a further discussion of this point see Armstrong D.E. *Competition versus Monopoly*, 1982 especially pages 75-84, 148-158.

14. Supreme Court of Canada, Atlantic Sugar Refineries C. Ltd. *et al.* and The Attorney General of Canada. Judgment July 18, 1980.

    "The basis for an inference of "tacit agreement" was in a way stronger for the uniform price list than for the maintenance of market shares," p. 10.

15. R. v. Atlantic Sugar *et al.*, p. 88.

16. Ibid., p. 89.

17. Ibid., p. 96.

18. Ibid., p. 96.

19. Supreme Court, op.cit., Minority Report, p.6.

20. Ibid., p. 6.

21. See *Transcript of trial in Montreal,* especially Vol. 5.

22. R. v. Atlantic Sugar, *et al.*, p. 96.

23. Supreme Court, Op.Cit., pp. 9-10.

24. Ibid., p. 11.

25. Ibid., p. 11.

26. Ibid., p. 11..

THE AUTHOR

Colin K. Irving was born in Montreal, and received his B.A. and B.C.L. degrees from McGill University. Counsel for the firm of Phillips and Vineberg, he is a member of the bars of Quebec, Ontario, and of the Canadian Bar Association. Mr. Irving's main areas of interest include repatriation, natural resource ownership, Indian land ownership, bilingualism, taxation, and of course, combines policy. He is a Fellow of the American College of Trial Lawyers, and a member of the International Business Council of Canada's arbitrators.

Chapter Six

The "Errors" in Atlantic Sugar et al. V.R

Colin Irving

I. INTRODUCTION

With a view to correcting perceived errors in the decision of the Supreme Court of Canada in *Atlantic Sugar* and to a lesser extent *Aetna*, Bill C-91 adds two new subsections to section 32 of the Act, which deal with criminal conspiracies. The first of these states as follows:

> (1.2) In a prosecution under subsection (1), the court may infer the existence of a conspiracy, combination, agreement or arrangement from circumstantial evidence, with or without direct evidence of communication between or among the alleged parties thereto, but, for greater certainty, the conspiracy, combination, agreement or arrangement must be proved beyond a reasonable doubt.

Insofar as the new subsection 1.2 provides that a conspiracy may be inferred from circumstantial evidence it adds nothing to the law as it had been understood since the last century. Indeed in the *Atlantic Sugar* case the trial judge's conclusion that there was a "tacit agreement" to maintain market share was based entirely on circumstantial evidence. In the Supreme Court the majority judgment noted:

> It must be accepted that a conspiracy may be effected in any way and may be established by inference.[1]

Nor has there ever been any doubt that communication between the parties to a conspiracy may be proved by circumstantial evidence. In this, as in all other matters, circumstantial evidence, provided it is sufficiently cogent, is perfectly acceptable and has been the basis of many convictions.

Perceived error

What then is this amendment intended to achieve? It is aimed, we are told, at a perceived error in the judgment of the Supreme Court in *Atlantic Sugar*. To understand the supposed error it is intended to correct, it is necessary to return briefly to the facts of the Sugar Case.

In the two years following the opening of a new refinery by Redpath in Toronto, there was a fierce price war amongst the eastern refiners. This had been triggered by Redpath which was determined to increase its market share to fill up its new capacity. In the early going Redpath's market share did increase. But as the competitive response of Atlantic and St. Lawrence made itself felt, the early gains were eventually eliminated. In the process Redpath suffered substantial losses, the market value of its common shares, almost all of which were in Canadian hands, fell by almost 50 percent and it was taken over by Tate & Lyle. The new management decided immediately to end the price war. In a series of internal meetings, it elaborated a new long-term marketing plan. The essence of the new plan was that Redpath would seek to maintain its historical share of market and that its price cutting activities would be limited to this aim. In minutes of the Redpath management committee which were introduced in evidence at the trial, the executive responsible for preparing the marketing plan noted that in all likelihood the competing companies would sooner or later discern Redpath's aim. It was his hope (perhaps unfortunately set out in the minutes) that when this inevitable discovery was made, the other companies would react by adopting a similar goal. There was no suggestion by the Crown that this decision was made in concert with the competition or that it was ever communicated to any other company.

Criminality

It is somewhat difficult to conceive of such a corporate decision constituting a criminal act, but that was precisely the contention of the Crown. The Crown submission was that the making of such a decision, believing that it would become known to competitors, was a form of indirect communication with them and that when, as indeed happened, they responded with

parallel conduct, there was an offence against section 32.
In the Supreme Court of Canada this contention received short shrift.
Mr. Justice Pigeon for six of the seven judges had this to say:

> But there was no such communication of the marketing policy. In those circumstances did the 'tacit agreement' resulting from the expected adoption of a similar policy by the competitors amount to a conspiracy? I have great difficulty in agreeing that it did because the author of Redpath's marketing policy was conscious that its competitors would inevitably after some time become aware of it in a general way and also expected them to adopt a similar policy which would also become apparent.
>
> It appears to me that the Crown's contention implies (and this is apparent from what the trial judge says at page 101) that in the situation of the sugar industry in Eastern Canada each of the refiners was obliged to endeavour to increase its market share at the expense of the others, otherwise it was agreeing to lessen competition unduly. In my view the trial judge was correct in rejecting this submission. None of the refiners was obliged to compete more strongly than it felt desirable in its own interest.[2]

If this passage is considered to constitute an error and if the amendment is intended to ensure that a different result would be arrived at if conduct of the same kind was repeated, then a major change in the notion of criminality is being proposed.

The evidence in the *Sugar* case indicated that virtually all decisions by the refiners which affected marketing became known to the competitors in short order. They were, after all, dealing with the same customers and one of their salesmen's functions was to obtain useful intelligence on the activities of competitors. It is hardly possible to imagine any marketing decision which would not become known to competitors in this way. Nor is this a situation unique to sugar refiners. Yet if the finding of the Supreme Court is wrong, and if it is corrected by legislation, the consequence will be that virtually any such decision may be found to constitute a criminal act if it finally evokes a parallel response by one or more competitors.

II. INTENT

A criminal conspiracy, as the name suggests, involves criminal intent. An action taken by an individual company on its own, and without collusion, ought not to be potentially criminal depending upon whether or not others correctly discern its purpose and act in the same way. When in such circumstances would criminality arise and where is the criminal intent?

If the amendment is successful in overturning the conclusion of the Supreme Court on this issue it will have produced a profound and disturbing change in Canadian concepts of criminal conspiracy. It seems unlikely that the amendment will achieve any such result since it appears to do nothing but restate the fact that the Department of Consumer and Corporate Affairs seems to feel that such a change is desirable. Yet it is still cause enough for concern.

The second proposed amendment to section 32 reads as follows:

> (1.3) For greater certainty, in establishing that a conspiracy, combination, agreement, or arrangement is in contravention of subsection (1), it is necessary to prove that the parties thereto intended to and did enter into the conspiracy, combination, agreement or arrangement, but it is not necessary to prove that the parties intended that the conspiracy, combination, agreement or arrangement have an effect set out in subsection (1).

This subsection is intended to eliminate the so-called double-intent requirement which the Supreme Court is apparently thought to have imposed in *Aetna Insurance* and in *Atlantic Sugar*. It is said that as a consequence of those decisions there may be an onus on the Crown to prove beyond reasonable doubt not only that the accused intended to make an agreement to lessen competition, but that they intended also that the lessening of competition should be "undue."

Double-onus

There are passages in both judgments in which reference is made to the onus on the Crown to prove that the parties "intented to lessen competition unduly." However, it is made perfectly clear in the *Atlantic Sugar* case that the supposed double-onus does not apply. The statements regarding intention to lessen competition unduly are nothing more than a statement of the requirement which exists in all criminal cases that the Crown prove that the parties intended to commit the offence in question, in this case to lessen competition unduly.

Mr. Justice Pigeon left no doubt on this issue in *Atlantic Sugar* when after quoting the following passage from the judgment of Mr. Justice Ritchie in *Aetna*:

What is criminal is an agreement that is intended to lessen competition improperly, inordinately, excessively, oppressively or when intended to have the effect of virtually relieving the conspirators from the free influence of free competition.

He went on to say:

While the offence charged is truly criminal in nature and therefore requires mens rea this does not mean that assuming that the tacit agreement was illegal the accused or rather their officials who are their directing minds had to be conscious of its illegality. If it had been intended to lessen competition 'unduly' it would have been no defence that the accused mistakenly thought that the intended lessening of competition would not be undue. It is always for the Court to decide on the facts whether an agreement to lessen competition means that competition is to be lessened 'unduly' and the views of the accused on that are irrelevant.[3]

Non-existent

It is difficult to imagine a clearer statement. The test is that the parties must intend to enter into an agreement to lessen competition to an extent which the Court finds to be "undue" but it is no part of the onus on the Crown to prove that the parties realized and therefore intended that it should be "undue." There is thus no need for an amendment to remove the double-intent onus. Such an onus has never existed.

In legislating to eliminate a non-existent double-intent, however, the draftsman may well have eliminated the onus of proving any criminal intent. If this amendment becomes law it will not be "necessary to prove that the parties intended that the conspiracy ... have an effect set out in subsection (1)." The Crown may thus be free of the onus of showing that the parties intended to lessen competition at all, much less that they intended to decrease it unduly.

While this may ease the path for prosecutors, it is hardly consistent with accepted principles of criminal law. If the intention is to change the nature of the offence from one which is "truly criminal and therefore requires mens rea" to quote Mr. Justice Pigeon there is, here again, serious cause for concern and a serious question of constitutional validity as well.

Notes

1. [1980] 2 S.C.R. 644 at p. 656.
2. id at p. 657.
3. id at p. 660.

THE AUTHOR

Steven Globerman received his Ph.D. in economics from New York University and has taught in the business faculty at York University, the University of British Columbia and is presently at Simon Fraser University in Burnaby. His area of specialization is industrial organization and he has published monographs and journal articles on regulation and competition policy in a number of industries including telecommunications, petroleum products and the cultural industries. Professor Globerman has been on the research staff for the Royal Commission on Corporate Concentration and was advisor to the industrial organization research group for the Macdonald Royal Commission. He acted as consultant on combines matters for Imperial Oil, Bell Canada and other companies and has consulted on regulatory issues for Bell Canada and B.C. Tel.

He has published a book on *Cultural Regulation in Canada*. Another extensive area of research has been international business and investment and this includes a textbook entitled *Fundamentals of International Business Management* to be published by Prentice-Hall in the spring of 1986.

Chapter Seven

The Merger Provisions of Bill C-91: An Evaluation

Steven Globerman

I. INTRODUCTION

A long-standing concern on the part of many academic economists concerning the Combines Investigation Act is the difficulty associated with treating mergers and monopoly in the context of criminal law. Indeed, the failure of the Crown to overturn a single domestic merger under the Act has been pointed to by critics, over the years, as evidence that the Act effectively cannot prevent mergers that have serious anti-competitive consequences.

Bill C-91 represents the government's effort to redress what it saw as the major weakness of the Act. [1] Under the amendments to the Act, mergers and monopolies will be adjudicated under a civil law framework by a specialized competition tribunal. It is argued that this major change will permit more sophisticated judgment of the social consequences of large mergers and a more flexible and effective approach toward dealing with them. [2]

Revision of the Act has been a long and tortuous process. The latest proposed amendments involved extensive negotiations with different constituencies, including corporate leaders. As a consequence, it has aroused much less indignation from the private sector than did earlier bills of amendment. According to one observer, the preferences of the business community were rejected in only one area of true importance — the test for judging mergers. The purpose of this paper is to review and evaluate amendments to the

merger provisions of the Act against the background of evidence surrounding the causes and consequences of mergers.

Background to the merger amendments

In reviewing and evaluating the merger amendments* of Bill C-91, it is
important to note that any large mergers involving a foreign-owned company remain subject to a similar review procedure under the Investment
Canada Act. Specifically, acquisitions of Canadian businesses by non-
Canadians are reviewable if the business acquired has assets with a value
of $5 million or more. The purchase of a foreign parent corporation with
a Canadian subsidiary, if the Canadian assets involved are less than half
of the overall assets of such international business, is reviewable only if
the Canadian division has assets with a value of $50 million or more.

Takeovers of Canadian businesses by non-Canadians may require only
notification of Investment Canada, or may require review and the Minister's
approval. A set of rules are prescribed for determining whether an organization is Canadian. The purchase of more than 50 percent of the voting shares
of a corporation is deemed to be an acquisition of control of that firm. The
procurement of less than one-third of the voting shares is deemed not to
be an acquisition of control.

When merger requires review and Ministerial approval, the criterion is
whether the investment offers a ''net benefit'' to Canada. This must take
into account criteria such as the effect on the level and nature of economic
activity in Canada; participation by Canadians in the business; the effect
on productivity, industrial efficiency and technological development; the
effect on competition; compatibility of the acquisition with national industrial
and economic policies and the effect on Canada's ability to compete in world
markets. These criteria are largely the same as those applied under the old
Foreign Investment Review Act.

After Investment Canada receives an application, the Minister has 45 days
to review the transaction and decide whether or not to approve it. If no
notice is sent to the applicant within this 45-day period, the investment is
deemed to be accepted. After an investment has been approved, the applicant is required to submit information from time to time as requested by

---

*See chapter two of the present volume — ed.

Investment Canada. This permits monitoring of the investment and any undertakings given.[4]

Similarity

This brief overview of the merger provisions of the Investment Canada Act, which parallel those of the old Foreign Investment Review Act, suggest a strong similarity to the Amendments of Bill C-91. In both cases, a group of government-appointed representatives are charged with the responsibility of establishing whether the social benefits of a particular transaction outweigh the social costs. In the case of foreign acquisitions, however, bureaucrats rather than tribunal members, "adjudicate" the merits of specific mergers. The ostensible tradeoff in both cases is improved efficiency and growth prospects against reductions in competition, albeit the criteria in the Investment Canada Act are somewhat more extensive.

These similarities suggest that an insight into the effects of the proposed C-91 amendments might be gained by reviewing the merger review experience under the Foreign Investment Review Act. We undertake this review in a later section. Before doing so, however, it is useful to consider in more detail the rationale behind a merger review procedure. In particular, it seems relevant to consider whether a *per se* rule regarding the legality or illegality of mergers might be preferable to the discretionary approach suggested.

Alternative approaches to merger policy

At one extreme, all mergers would be considered legal and beyond review by the government. This *per se* approach would be appropriate in an environment where mergers had no significant anti-competitive consequences.

At the other extreme, all mergers would be prohibited. This alternative *per se* approach would be appropriate in an environment where mergers, as a rule, significantly reduced competition but offered no offsetting efficiency advantages. No participant in the debate has taken this extreme stance. In light of evidence that most mergers involve the acquisition of relatively small firms, a *per se* illegal policy would not seem to merit further consideration. In the absence of sufficient evidence to justify a *per se* policy, the merits of alternative approaches, including a screening procedure, must be considered. What would count as support for instituting tighter merger review procedures? This would be provided by evidence that the net social benefits of mergers are increased beyond the additional costs associated with the most efficient merger surveillance procedure. This would apply to all mergers covered by the relevant legislation. The potential costs of tighter merger surveillance include the direct expenses of staffing and maintaining the review apparatus. As well, there are the indirect costs associated with a reduction in the number of socially beneficial mergers undertaken. Potentially beneficial mergers may be discouraged. This may come about as a result of added administrative costs and uncertainties imposed upon potential acquirers and (or) acquirees. Alternatively, it may take place as a result of merger board rejections which reflect mistakes in judgment on the part of review personnel. [5]

In summary, a *per se* approach presumes that the social consequences of mergers are so substantially negative if illegal (or positive or neutral, if legal). Alternatively, they could be so easily addressed by other means as to outweigh (on net balance) the costs of trying to screen mergers. And what of an evaluative approach towards mergers and acquisitions? Whether on a guideline or case-by-case basis, this presumes that the net social benefits of overall merger activity can be increased, beyond the costs of the review process, by evaluating the potential consequences of mergers in greater or lesser detail.

In the following section, we consider the theoretical costs and benefits of mergers in more detail and review available evidence.

II. THE BENEFITS AND COSTS OF MERGERS

As noted in the preceding section, the major public policy objection to adopting a *per se* legal stance is that some mergers may have significant anti-competitive effects. For this to be so, a merger must either create new or increased market power in some section of the economy, or else facilitate the exercise of power that previously existed but was not utilized.In one simple version of the "market power" motivation for mergers, power is created or enhanced by a reduction in the number of independent economic units. In a more indirect version, potential competitors are eliminated from the market through mergers. The view here is that if a newcomer did not enter a market by acquiring an extant firm, it would have entered *de novo*, and more competitors would exist as a result.

As the Amendments to the merger provisions acknowledge, the exercise of market power depends critically on conditions of entry and exit. Indeed, modern industrial organization theory focuses on entry and exit conditions as the critical factors determining how efficiently and competitively firms will perform. [6] A reduction in the number of firms in a market may provide a temporary "window" for those remaining, which will enable them to extract wealth from their customers or their suppliers. But the long-run competitive consequences of a merger (according to modern theory) will depend upon whether the merger increases the costs of entry and exit into the relevant market. If it does not, there is no reason to believe that the remaining firms will act any less efficiently or charge higher prices than before the merger took place.

The critical issue is thus whether mergers can affect entry and exit conditions. However, it is difficult to put forth a plausible rationale for why mergers should make entry and exit more difficult. One might argue that entry into a more highly concentrated market increases the likelihood that a new entrant will be "squashed" by the "elephants" which inhabit the industry. Investors will therefore be more reluctant to lend money to would-be entrants than would be the case if the industry's market structure was more fragmented; that is, if it had more firms of lower average size. But this argument rests on a view that capital markets are inefficient or, at least, that investors are extremely reluctant to take risks. For if existing firms are earning "unfairly excessive" profits, and if new ones could provide the same level and quality of service at lower prices, investors could expect to continue to capture market share from extant firms. They could do this while sharing in the lucrative returns being earned by other investors in the industry. Furthermore, if the entrants are as or more efficient than extant firms, efforts by the latter to drive the former out of existence are doomed to failure.

Monopsony power

Another argument might maintain that the market power created by mergers creates — or enhances — barriers to entry, since it enables resulting firms to extract lower prices from suppliers of all sorts of inputs, thereby leaving potential entrants at a competitive disadvantage. Existing firms might also "encourage" their suppliers not to deal with new firms. In fact, already established businesses might acquire their suppliers, i.e., merge vertically, in order to deprive entrants of low cost input factors. The latter possibility has long been a concern of critics of large vertical mergers. It represents the most extreme potential case of entry foreclosure operating through input markets. However, this possibility rests upon the notion that integrated entry is either difficult or impossible. Otherwise, the newcomer could itself enter the market both as a supplier and user of critical inputs. Alternatively, entrants in the "downstream" portion of the industry could agree to long-term contracts with independent newcomers "upstream." The point is that vertical integration itself is unlikely to create barriers to entry where none before existed. It is also unlikely to even significantly enhance already existing barriers.[7]

At the other extreme, it seems more plausible to argue that mergers represent a particularly effective vehicle for quick entry into a market, and that they also reduce potential exit costs. It obviously takes more time to build a new plant than to buy an already existing one. And it takes more time to establish a new distribution network than to take over one that already exists. Hence, a potential entrant who saw the possibility of operating more efficiently than extant firms might favour the merger route to entry. However, it should be noted that the seller of the assets might capture all of the advantages of the speeded-up entry in the form of higher prices for the assets sold.

Ease of exit

A more plausible argument for the pro-competitive effects of mergers is that an unrestricted merger environment facilitates exit from an industry. This is because the salvage value of specialized assets is likely to be higher in an environment where they can be sold, intact, to a potential user. The more fungible the assets in a business, the lower the sunk costs, all other things constant. And it is the magnitude of sunk costs that economists have come to recognize as the major barrier to exit. Furthermore, the lower the barriers to exit, the lower the risks of new entry, and (presumably) the greater the willingness of new firms to enter an industry, all else the same.[8]

It has been well recognized in the economics literature that mergers can facilitate entry and thereby promote competition. However, the new studies on contestability heighten the importance of this potential relationship. One hopes that if the current amendments are passed into law, the Tribunal will be as ready to entertain pro-competitive as anti-competitive arguments regarding specific mergers.

Perversity

Proponents of merger review might still maintain that this procedure will have net benefits, in that internal competition will be preserved in markets characterized by durable barriers to entry. But the broader issue for competition policy is how to address barriers to entry and exit. In this regard, government policy has too often played a perverse role. Specifically, governments at both the federal and provincial levels have imposed both tariff and non-tariff barriers to trade. They have erected barriers to investment that seriously erode the salutary benefits of potential market entry. Examples of government restrictions on competition abound. In most cases, they are imposed on foreign firms. Some of the more notorious examples, such as the quotas on Japanese automobiles, are in the manufacturing sector. But the service sector, which is the largest sector of the economy, is especially rife with government sanctioned barriers to competition. In the financial, communications and transportation fields, participation by foreign firms is extremely inhibited. Foreign consultants are barred from working in Canada by immigration laws. Entry into many of the professions is limited by government sanctioned licensing requirements. This is only the tip of the iceberg. It seems ludicrous, not to say schizophrenic, for government to erect an anti-merger apparatus to treat a lack of competitiveness in the Canadian economy when this is the consequence of ill-conceived economic policies of its own devising. Far better to change the policies that reduce market competition in the first place. Then, concerns about mergers need never arise.

In an open economy such as Canada's, international trade and investment offers a powerful and fairly rapid source of entry into domestic industries. With the elimination of important tariff and non-tariff barriers, along with the panoply of licensing restrictions and marketing boards that litter Canada's economic landscape, the potential for significant long-run anti-competitive consequences from even large mergers would be largely eliminated.[9]

Concentration

Several other issues related to the benefits and costs of mergers must be raised. One is the view that the concentration of economic wealth in a small number of hands is a potential social evil. This is held by some to be true even if the direct economic consequences of a high aggregate concentration of wealth are benign. Consider in this regard the proposed merger between the Power and Argus Corporations, which led to the formation of the Royal Commission on Corporate Concentration. This generated concerns about the accumulation of corporate wealth, and social and political influence, by a small number of decision-makers. Without passing judgment on these concerns, it is worth noting that the research undertaken by the Royal Commission on Corporate Concentration failed to identify any clear social impacts of "big business."[10]

It might still be argued that for those cases where entry is restricted by "natural" market forces, the competitive benefits of a merger review procedure will substantially outweigh any direct or indirect costs.[11] This is certainly the "conventional" view of the economics' profession.[12] Before accepting this view for Canada, however, it is worth taking a closer look at the potential costs of a domestic merger review.

The potential costs of a merger review process

One potential cost of such a process is that mergers which would promote a more efficient utilization of resources will be discouraged or prevented. This concern raises an empirical question: how substantial are the efficiency gains from mergers? The relevant literature here is extremely large and diffuse. Furthermore, it permits no easy summarization.

For example, some conglomerate mergers appear to provide shareholders with an efficient diversification of risk.[13] Others appear to offer no unique diversification benefits. Some studies find that diversifying firms have outperformed the stock market, while others find that they provided below-average returns to investors.[14] With respect to mergers between companies in related businesses, some studies find that such mergers have facilitated the capture of economies of scale at either the plant or firm level. Others find no compelling evidence of efficiency gains resulting from horizontal mergers.[15]

These mixed results are not entirely surprising. In a world of imperfect information and changing economic circumstances, many investments may not pan out as planned. The available evidence does suggest that, on average, mergers enhance efficiency. But these gains are difficult to identify even *ex post*. Against this background, it is hard to be optimistic about the ability of a Tribunal to estimate the efficiency gains that will result from a merger. Certainly, the merger candidates will ordinarily have no trouble demonstrating the existence of *ex ante* efficiency gains. One suspects that the Tribunal will come to emphasize more easily quantifiable criteria, such as the planned exports of the merged unit, or the extent of import displacement. Yet these latter criteria may have nothing at all to do with efficiency.

III. F.I.R.A.

The experience under the Foreign Investment Review Act is instructive in this regard. Unfortunately, the reasons for the acceptance or rejection of reviewable acquisitions under the Act did not have to be made public. Hence, it is impossible to determine how many socially beneficial acquisitions were directly or indirectly discouraged through the review process. However, several observations can be made. One is that the overwhelming majority of proposed foreign acquisitions have been approved by the government over time. However, the attitude of the bureaucrats toward these acquisitions was apparently sensitive to the priorities of the government. In particular, a more lenient attitude was adopted during periods of severe recession. In periods of relatively strong economic growth, a more restrictive attitude toward foreign acquisitions was adopted. Pressure from nationalist influences in Parliament have also apparently influenced the treatment of foreign acquisitions[16]

The treatment of several individual acquisitions was also apparently influenced by lobbying efforts within government. The attempted purchase of Westinghouse Canada Limited's appliance division by White Consolidated Industries Ltd., a U.S. firm, offers a case in point. A review of this case suggests that FIRA bureaucrats felt that the acquisition could be supported on efficiency grounds. However, a rival bid by GSW Ltd., a Canadian firm, drew important support from government officials who believed that the appliance industry should be "Canadianized."

Political influence

While public information about the case is limited, there is some indication that securing general economic benefits for Canada was not the overriding concern in the government's favouring the GSW Ltd. bid. Certainly, economic considerations alone favoured WCI Ltd. Indeed, it has been suggested that FIRA and Donald Jamieson (then Minister of Industry, Trade and Commerce) recommended WCI be given approval to take over Westinghouse's appliance division. Jamieson's department was split on the question, with some department officials arguing against WCI on grounds that a GSW takeover would help to Canadianize the appliance industry. Jamieson took FIRA's view to Cabinet and was overruled. Insiders in Ottawa cite the case as evidence that government decisions about foreign investment in Canada are political as much as technical. In the WCI case the technical decision seemed to favour the American company, while the political decision did not.[17]

It is obviously dangerous to generalize from a limited data base; however, the experience of the Foreign Investment Review Act suggests how difficult it is to separate economic decision-making in the public sector from political imperatives. The potential for (economically) arbitrary reversals of decisions taken in the marketplace represents a significant potential cost of a merger review process. We ignore this only at our peril. Indeed, the likelihood that government policies and regulations will be subverted to serve narrowly defined interest groups is a powerful reason for limiting the economic power that government can exercise in the marketplace.

IV. CONCLUSIONS

If the experience under the Foreign Investment Review Act is any guide, a relatively small number of contested mergers will be rejected by the Tribunal. Some (unknown) percentage will fail to be initiated because of the existence of the review procedure. Some subset of these rejected or discouraged mergers may have conveyed efficiency gains on the economy. In addition, as we have seen, the important barriers to competition in the Canadian economy remain, by and large, government imposed.

The recent Amendments to the Combines Act do not, therefore, represent a substantial step forward toward promoting free and fair competition. Rather, they continue a tradition of substituting the judgment of government appointed "experts" for the judgment of the marketplace. Whether Canadians would be better off without the merger amendments or, indeed, without the entire Combines Act, is at least a debatable question. However, it seems absurd to make the elimination of specific barriers to entry contingent on specific mergers taking place. Shouldn't the central focus of competition policy be the elimination of these barriers? It is of course politically difficult to rescind protection that has been long afforded to specific interest groups. But the largest payoff to the typical Canadian will come from the efforts of the Director and his staff to have these barriers to competition dismantled and to prevent new ones from being imposed. Making this effort subsidiary to speculating about the wide-ranging effects of specific mergers seems (at best) a substantial misdirection of public policy.

Notes

1. The House of Commons of Canada, Bill C-91, First Session, 33rd Parliament, 33-34 Elizabeth II, 1984-85.

2. Consumer and Corporate Affairs Canada, *Competition Law Amendments: A Guide,* Ottawa: Minister of Supply and Services Canada, December 1985.

3. Ronald Anderson, "Competition Bill Felt Step Forward," *The Globe and Mail*, January 14, 1986, B2.

4. This description is taken from McDonald and Hayden, Investment Canada Act Summary, Toronto, mimeo, June 30, 1985.

5. A more comprehensive discussion of the criteria underlying a merger review procedure can be found in Steven Globerman, *Mergers and Acquisitions in Canada*, Royal Commission on Corporate Concentration, Study Number 34, Ottawa: Minister of Supply and Services Canada, 1977.

6. Contemporary industrial organization models have come to focus on the "contestability" of markets, where this is largely determined by ease of entry and exit into and out of a market. For a readable introduction to this literature, see William J. Baumol, "Contestable Markets: An Uprising in the Theory of Industry Structure," *American Economic Review*, March 1982, Vol. 72, pp. 1-15.

7. An extended analysis of this argument can be found in Sam Peltzman, "Issues in Vertical Integration Policy," in J.F. Weston and S. Peltzman, eds., *Public Policy Toward Merger*, Pacific Palisades: Goodyear Publishing Company, 1969.

8. A fairly recent study provides evidence that the risk arising from sunk costs constitutes a strong barrier to entry. See Ioannes Kessides, "Toward a Testable Model of Entry: A Study of U.S. Manufacturing Industries," Princeton University, mimeo, 1982.

9. One might also include in this category entry restrictions associated with conventional regulation. For example, entry into the market for long-distance telephone service is restricted by CRTC policy.

10. A brief review of this research can be found in Steven Globerman, "The Report of the Royal Commission on Corporate Concentration and Its Implications for Competition Policy," in J.R.S. Prichard, W.T. Stanbury and T.A. Wilson, *Canadian Competition Policy: Essays in Law and Economics*, Toronto: Butterworths, 1979.

11. The benefits, in turn, could largely encompass a socially undesirable transfer of wealth from consumers to producers. The allocative effects are more complicated to analyze. In particular, if merging facilitates more effective price discrimination, total output after a merger may go up rather than down.

12. This view is represented quite well in Richard E. Caves, "Industrial Concentration, Corporate Size and Market Power: Economic Evidence and Strategic Choice for Canadian Competition Policy," in J.R.S. Prichard, W.T. Stanbury and T.A. Wilson, eds., op. cit.

13. See, for example, D.H. Ciscel and R.D. Evans, "Returns to Corporate Diversification in the 1970," *Managerial Decision Economics*, Col. 5, June 1984, pp. 67-71.

14. See Donald J. Lecraw and Donald N. Thompson, *Conglomerate Mergers in Canada,* Ottawa: Supply and Services Canada, 1977.

15. See Steven Globerman, *Mergers and Acquisitions in Canada,* Ottawa, Supply and Services Canada, 1977.

16. For relevant evidence supporting these observations, see Steven Globerman, "The Consistency of the Foreign Investment Review Act: A Temporal Analysis," *Journal of International Business Studies,* Summer 1984.

17. These details are taken from Steven Globerman, *U.S. Ownership of Firms in Canada,* Montreal: C.D. Howe Research Institute, 1979, pp. 86-94.

THE AUTHORS

Gabrielle A. Brenner received her Ph.D. at the University of Chicago, and is now an assistant professor at Ecole des Hautes Etudes Commerciales, Université de Montréal. She has been a consultant for private organizations, and has published articles in the *Journal of Business*, *International Journal of Law and Economics*, *Journal of Gambling Behavior*, *l'Analyste*, *Gestion*.

Reuven Brenner is an associate professor in the Department of Economics, Université de Montréal and member of the research staff at the Centre de recherche et développement en économique, Université de Montréal. He taught at the University of Chicago and New York University, and has published studies for Shell Canada Ltd., the C.D. Howe Institute, and the Economic Council of Canada. He is the author of numerous articles and three books: *History—The Human Gamble* (1983), *Betting on Ideas: Wars, Invention, Inflation* (1986), both published by the University of Chicago Press, and a third, on competition, anti-combines legislation, and state-owned enterprises, is due in 1987.

Chapter Eight

Innovations and the Competition Act

Gabrielle A. Brenner and Reuven Brenner

The Competition Act defines its purpose in words that, if left unaltered, will provide occupation for an army of economists and lawyers — and that certainly should not be its objective.

The Act's goals are: a) "to encourage competition in Canada in order to promote the efficiency and adaptability of the Canadian economy" — which is just fine, provided the words "competition," "efficiency," "adaptability" were properly defined in the Act — but they are not; and b) to "ensure that small and medium-sized enterprises have an equitable opportunity to participate in the Canadian economy" — but this goal is questionable and may be inconsistent with the first. This erroneous beginning of the Act is not accidental. The faulty reasoning behind it is reflected elsewhere as well; it stems, unfortunately, from a misunderstanding of the competitive process itself.

I. "COMPETITION" — WHAT DOES IT MEAN?

The notion of "competition" implicitly used when stating the second goal of the Act seems to be borrowed from its traditional meaning in economic analysis. This meaning is significantly different from its everyday use, and it has been misused in the analyses of antitrust cases.[1] The source of the error is that "competition" is defined in orthodox economic analysis with reference to a long-run equilibrium (similarly defined are the words "profits," "costs," "market"; they may look familiar, but they mean something radically different for economists than they do for businessmen). But this analysis totally neglects the process of innovations, and inventions in particular by which such a fixed state, frozen in time, is reached. Forgetting the limitations of this model, some economists have looked at the world through its lenses and misused the vocabulary defined within it. The erroneous results can be seen in Mr. Côté's recently suggested Competition Act.

Only by remembering that within the aforementioned "classic" model "competition" is linked to the existence of numerous *small* sellers (of a single homogeneous product) can one understand why the Act makes reference to the size of enterprises. Also, it is only by keeping in mind this long-run equilibrium model that one can understand the reference to "equitable opportunity" and the suspicion of relatively large enterprises. For, assuming away innovations, inventions, entrepreneurial and managerial talent, on what grounds but collusive, exploitive behaviour, could one explain concentration within such a model?!

Non-sequitur

Thus, imbedded in the statement of the goals is a fatal equivocation: when stating that the purpose of the law is to encourage "competition," the Act implicitly refers to the competitive *process*. Here, it recognizes that what matters is the special role played by innovations of any kind, technological or managerial. But where the Act mentions "equitable opportunity" and makes reference to the size of enterprises, it implicitly relies on the definition of competition within a model where all innovations have long been made, all demands have long been anticipated, where differences in entrepreneurial and managerial talents play no role, and the various industries have settled down to the quiet, comfortable life that economists call the "steady state."[2]

The first revision that one can recommend for the new bill is therefore to define the word "competition" with precision. This can be done in the following way:

> 'Competition' means a situation where businessmen pursue strategies
> to discover a combination of customers and services in order to obtain
> an advantage over those whom they perceive as competitors.

The definition is not exactly novel: this seems to be the way businessmen

view competition, and Adam Smith understood the concept in this way too.
For him, competition meant a conscious driving against other business firms
for patronage of buyers with price or non-price strategies, specifically including inventions. This simple process is called "rivalry," but economists
who advocate and support combines legislation largely ignore it. In contrast, "competition" came to mean something radically different. Thus,
the Smithian and modern definition of competition is incompatible: while
in the *Wealth of Nations* competition and growth are two aspects of the same
process, within the now widespread economic approach, competition and
lack of growth are two sides of the same coin.[3] Since Canada's goal is
economic growth, there should be no doubt about which definition of "competition" the Act should rely on.

Definition

Once it is recognized that this is indeed the definition of competition, the
"Purpose of the Act" can be stated in this brief sentence:

> The purpose of this Act is to maintain and encourage competition in
> Canada.

All the rest of the proposed "Purpose" is unnecessary, and worse,
misleading. The phase "in order to promote the efficiency and adaptability
of the Canadian economy" not only does not add anything, but it may be
confusing. "Efficiency" has a precise meaning within the static economic
analysis. It implies a relationship between price and marginal costs. But
this is devoid of any interest or practical application in the real, uncertain
world. When one talks about "promoting efficiency" in everyday conver-
sation, one refers to a variety of strategies (increasing productivity, changing managerial and advertising strategies, innovating, etc.) through which
firms can discover either how to lower costs, reach more customers, or
both. It is this latter context that is the Act's true interest. But since it is
already incorporated in the definition of "competition," one can simply
discard this without losing anything. As for the term "adaptability" — it
is simply redundant, since it is exactly through the competitive process,
by trial and error, that people try to adapt.

II. COMPETITION AND THE SIZE OF ENTERPRISES

Now consider economic analyses which incorporate entrepreneurial and managerial skill, innovations, uncertainty and chance. In these models, the size distribution of firms within an industry has no necessary correlation with conditions of competition. One cannot infer non-competitive from high industrial concentration. The reason is simple: dominant position can also be obtained because of chance, and the greater entrepreneurial skill of some individuals. This result should not surprise economists for two reasons: first, their particular "industry" is characterized by this feature too; there are a tiny number of economists whose ideas have long dominated the field (Smith, Marx, Keynes) and they, their ideas, provide employment for all the others who seem to adopt them and adapt to them. Why should the distribution of talent and ability be different in any industry than in this particular field of the social sciences?

Second, the evidence regarding the size distribution of firms within an industry is consistent with the prediction of models that accord these factors (entrepreneurial talent and chance) a central role. Scherer (1980) presents the following numerical example: suppose an industry comes into being with 50 firms, each with 2 percent share of sales and $100,000 of sales. Each firm may have the same average growth every year, but with a variation around the trend. In any year some may be luckier, growing more rapidly than the average, while others are unlucky, increasing by less. Let the probability distribution of growth rates confronting each firm be normal, with a mean of 6 percent and a standard deviation of 16 percent. (Scherer chose these parameters to reflect the average year-to-year growth actually experienced between 1954-1960 by 369 companies on Fortune's list of the 500 largest industrial corporations for 1955.) If every firm's growth in each period is determined through a random sampling from the aforementioned distribution of growth rates, one of the results obtained is that after 100 periods, the four-firm concentration ratios range between 33.5 percent to 64.4 percent, with a mean of 46.7 percent. This is a distribution that often fits real-world industries. Scherer's view is that stochastic factors — due to one form or other of entrepreneurial, innovative skill and chance — seem to determine the size distribution of enterprises. This is not a novel perspective. He admits that his numerical example conforms to Gibrat's "law of proportionate growth," since the number of firms was fixed, the distribution of growth rates confronting each firm was the same, independent of both firm size and past growth history. Such growth processes generate a log normal size distribution of firms, and statistical studies reveal that such distributions often fit the data.

An objection

But one may object that if entrepreneurial talent is interpreted as the central force in the process, then there is a contradiction with the assumption of growth as independent of firm size and past history. Thus, it may be useful to note that in other simulation studies, Ijiri and Simon (1964) have shown that size distributions similar to those generated by Gibrat's models can also be obtained when there is serial correlation in a firm's year-to-year growth rates. Simon and Bonini (1958), reasoning backward from observation to hypothesis, concluded that some form of stochastic process must thus explain size distributions since they show such a "regular and docile conformity" (p. 608).[4]

The conclusion is obvious: if indeed the goal of the Act is to encourage competition, no reference should be made to the size of enterprises and to ensuring "equitable opportunities." Businesses may be small or medium-sized because that scope fits the talents of their decision-makers. As to chance — it should not be the purpose of the Competition Act to compensate for errors and misfortune. In order to encourage competition, one must look at the *behaviour* of enterprises rather than at their size.[5]

III. MONOPOLISTIC AND COMPETITIVE BEHAVIOUR, AND THE NOTION OF INTENT

Since according to our definition competition implies innovations, a secured monopolistic position implies their absence.

The existing Competition Act defines "monopoly" as a "situation where one or more persons either substantially or completely control throughout Canada or any area thereof the class or species of business in which they are engaged." If one interpreted the term literally, everybody would be a monopolist since people are not the same: there are no two grocers, no two singers, and not even two MacDonalds who are exactly alike (the location, at least, is different). Of course, this is not what Cournot, Marshall, and before them, Adam Smith had in their minds when writing about and condemning "monopolies." Rather, they referred to situations where the entry of would-be-producers of close substitutes was severely limited (in Smith's case by regulations inherited from the Middle Ages). This enabled the incumbent firm to profit from a "quiet life" (as Hicks once put it).

But barriers to entry only exist when the incumbent firm can refrain from competing, without thereby inducing entry. This applies, of course, only when the word "competition" is used as defined above. In other words, the firm may successfully abstain from pursuing innovative strategies. Notice, however, that this negative impact — of lack of innovations — occurs only if the one seller knows that entry is blocked. If the dominant position was obtained because of superior skills, this conclusion is incorrect. For, the managers may notice that there might be others too, who, perceiving their success, may try their luck. Fearing entry, the dominant firm worries about potential competition, and may continue to innovate. This is a further reason why one should not pay attention to the size distribution of firms within an industry (even in the case of "one-seller"), but only to the behaviour of this firm (or firms). While the Competition Act does indeed refer to the issue of superior skills, it still makes reference to the size of enterprises — and thus misses the point.

Monopoly power?

How, then, can outsiders infer (in the absence of obvious legal restrictions on entry) the possession of secured monopoly power? The answer is simple: a necessary, but not sufficient, condition is to observe lack of innovation. Neither information on firm size, on concentration ratios, on profits nor, as it will be pointed out below, on pricing and other strategies, can shed light on this question. Any size distribution, and thus any concentration ratio, can be generated by a distribution of entrepreneurial and managerial skills and chance. Persisting relatively high rates of profit can be attributed to these factors too.

It must be admitted that the criterion of "lack of innovations" for inferring non-competitive behaviour will not always be easy to use. Yet, it is applicable to, and may provide useful insights into some well-known antitrust cases. Data on the fraction of revenues of a firm derived from products not in existence, for example five years before, is available. It can provide one with rough information on whether or not decision-makers within these companies were sitting on their laurels.

Innovation

What is this fraction for various firms and industries?

The fact that 80 percent of the revenues of I.B.M.'s data processing divisions came from products manufactured since 1979 implies that this company is quite innovative. With this evidence in hand, we can safely discard the interpretation that I.B.M.'s decision-makers have used various pricing strategies (accused by its competitors to be "predatory") in order to just maintain its dominant position. On the contrary, the changes in pricing strategies occurred simultaneously with innovations. Choffray and Lilien (1980, pp. 4-5) present this evidence in the scientific instruments area. The Office of Economic and Cultural Development reported that in many American firms, 60 to 80 percent of sales are from products that were not in existence five years earlier. In the same industry, according to Utterback (1969, p. 30), 17 percent of 1960 sales were of products not in existence in 1956, and even this relatively low fraction ranked the industry (based on this measure) second to aircraft. For 223 manufacturers, the percentage of 1966 sales attributable to the sale of products first marketed by the company within the past five years was 20 percent. According to Pearson (1982, p. 22), 3M Corporation has a record of introducing new products at such a rate that between 20 and 25 percent of any year's sales are from products introduced within the immediate past five years. At Hewlett-Packard in 1985, 75 percent of the sales were in products that have been introduced during the preceding five year period (Hammond, 1982, p. 124). A look at Du Pont's 1972 sales reveals that 25 percent of sales was in dyes introduced in the previous five years, 40 percent in the previous 10, and 75 percent in the previous 20 years. In 1973, the company produced three times as many pounds of nylon with only 20 percent more people as in 1963, selling them profitably at prices 35 percent lower (and there was no deflation in these ten years). For the company as a whole, Gee and Tyler (1976, p. 36) found that 25 of 1973 sales were generated by products introduced in the previous 15 years, and the price index for Du Pont's entire output was 73 percent of that of 15 years earlier. Relative to all these numbers, I.B.M.'s performance seems outstanding. It is thus difficult to justify the widespread accusations of its enjoying a secured monopoly power (i.e. that entry is blocked and I.B.M. can raise prices of existing products without fear of consequences).

Taking into account this measure, one can suggest a definite criterion for the much debated point on the relevance of evidence regarding "intent" to pursue non-competitive strategies. While according to structural and pricing criteria (derived from static models) competitive and predatory intents are confused, the criterion of whether or not innovations have been pursued within an enterprise indicates something clear about its perception of entry and intention to compete.[6]

The Competition Act should be interested in this behaviour and not, as section 32 (1.2) now indicates, in inferring "the existence of conspiracy, combination, agreement or arrangement from circumstantial evidence." This proposed addition is unnecessary. Alternatively, clear cut information in the public domain indicating whether or not the accused company was engaged in innovative strategies enables one to learn something about the existence of conspiracy.

Dominant firms

The definition of "monopoly," as a single seller which fears no intrusion suggests that such cases must be extremely rare. It raises the question, Why does the law refer to monopolies so often? Closer inspection of cases in which companies have been accused of being "monopolies" reveals that, indeed, language was abused. The word was used as a synonym for *any* large-scale business, whether it competed and innovated or not. Once again "form" (i.e. language defining a particular form of structure) seemed to be interpreted as "substance" (i.e., implying a particular type of behaviour).

Indeed, many studies have pointed out that monopolies are rare, but then argued that the same theory applies to situations where one "dominant" firm coexists with numerous small ones. This inference is flawed, for the existence of small firms suggests that entry is *not* blocked. Thus, one must explain both why the smaller firms do not expand or others intrude (if indeed the dominant firm employs non-competitive strategies), and why the dominant firm's decision-makers do not take into account the threat of expansion and entry.[7]

However, no convincing evidence suggests that this type of structure does indeed imply non-competitive behaviour. Scherer (1980) summarizing an extremely wide range of evidence concludes:

> Prices often hover closer to cost than one would predict from an analysis that takes into account only the fewness of sellers, ignoring coordination obstacles and long-run constraints. These more subtle structural and behavioural variables (threats of entry) help explain why pricing performance in modern industrial markets has on the whole been fairly satisfactory despite significant departures from the structural ideal of pure economic theory. (p. 266)

The unavoidable question is therefore, Why should anyone pay any attention — the Competition Act in particular — to the "ideals" of "pure economic theory" (by which Scherer refers to models where entrepreneurial, managerial skills and uncertainty are not taken into account), since they do not shed light on the facts?

The explanation for single seller status or dominant position may be quite simple. They are due to entrepreneurial, managerial skills and chance. There are only a few financial or industrial Napoleons just as there are a severely limited number of Adam Smiths, Darwins, Walt Disneys or Picassos. Some firm's dominant position may have been obtained not only by securing a patented innovation, but also because they happened to have the "right" men, at the "right" time and at the "right" place at their helm. Because of this combination of entrepreneurship and good fortune, they were able to sell a good of a higher quality, or at a lower price, to eliminate or discourage their competitors. Indeed, by definition, they possess some power due either to having such skills, or the smile of Fortune.[8]

The presently suggested Act indicates that "the offence relating to monopoly would be replaced by provisions relating to abuse of dominant position" (Clause 20, p. 7a). As the arguments and evidence presented above suggest, no reference should be made to "dominant" position, or any size: the Act's concern should be to condemn *anti-competitive behaviour* rather than any form of structure.

Oligopolies

Theories of oligopoly attempt to predict the behaviour in markets where rivals are "few." As Judge Bork (1978) has correctly noted, "The lack of rigor in that theory may be suggested by the observation that there appear to be about as many oligopoly theories as there are economists who have written on the subject" (p. 102). This disorder should have been expected since the departure point — looking at number and size of firms to infer behaviour — is mistaken.[9]

There is simply no way to determine on *a priori* grounds where oligopoly turns into a competitive structure. The key to the distinction is subjective—it depends on whether or not the decision-makers at the helm of the few firms consider themselves rivals and/or perceive threats of entry. It is useful to note that while this reservation has been made (Scherer, 1980, p. 11), it has not always been drawn to its logical conclusion.

The conclusion had to be that on *a priori* grounds one cannot give a negative connotation to the existence of one or few sellers, since the crucial question is whether or not these firms face threats of entry. If they do, the outcome is competitive and the number of firms cannot shed light on behaviour. In order to infer whether or not decision-makers need take competition into account, one may look at the fraction of revenues generated by relatively recent innovations, as compared with other industries (or with the same industry in other countries). Only if this fraction compares unfavourably, should suspicions rise and further investigations be pursued. Instead, the law focuses on pricing and other strategies. This has led to perverse uses of the antitrust legislation in the U.S. Instead of promoting competition, the law was used by declining companies to constrain those who were more vigorous. In a recent study Baumol and Ordover (1985) note that

> Chrysler and Ford, the horizontal competitors of the joint ventures...,
> have pressed the Federal Trade Commission to reject the (GM-Toyota)
> venture on the grounds that it will restrain competition... Recently,
> the FTC approved the joint venture. Undeterred, Chrysler has been
> pressing a private antitrust action in an attempt to accomplish what
> if failed to do at the FTC. (p. 256)

According to these writers the accusations must be false, for if the enterprise were in fact likely to acquire monopoly power and charge excessive prices, that should have benefited Chrysler and Ford, since they could have competed more easily. Their interest was to inhibit a formidable competitor. Baumol and Ordover also examine MCI's case against AT & T and conclude that "the staunchest advocates of full-cost pricing have been firms anxious to hobble their disquietingly effective rivals" (p. 258). A large number of such perverse uses of the FTC and antitrust laws are documented in Plouffe (1985), and Brenner (1986).

In its present form, Canadians too can expect such perverse use of the law.

IV. ON INFERRING NON-COMPETITIVE BEHAVIOUR

Both in Canada and the U.S. combines and antitrust prosecutions frequently revolve around whether or not the observed pricing behaviour of the firms was evidence of a conspiracy.

Why was so much attention paid to pricing behaviour in isolation from the rest of the accused firm's strategies? Once again, the answer stems from the erroneous reliance on the textbook model of "competition" and its accompanying vocabulary. Since, as emphasized, this model assumes stationary conditions (thus all innovative behaviour is automatically disregarded), the viewpoint is that if firms do not compete on pricing, they cannot compete at all, since price competition is the only possible option. Of course, one can argue that the idea of cutting prices is an innovation too. But the textbook approach disposes of this possibility by assuming that prices are given to all firms in a "perfectly competitive" market, to which they passively adjust.

Once one realizes that this definition of "competition" is not practical, and accepts the view that firms compete by using a great variety of strategies (inventions, marketing, service, advertising, etc.), no justification can be given for limiting one's attention to pricing behaviour. This strategy reflects just one aspect of the deeper entrepreneurial decision-making process that takes place.

Observed prices

The focus on observed prices is most peculiar since not only are they not the only variables by which firms compete, but they are not even always the ones that concern customers most. The "price" one pays for a commodity involve characteristics such as search, time, quality and location, among others.[11] Consumers do not just purchase "gasoline," they prefer buying it at convenient locations (saving time and thus lowering the "full price" they pay for it), and want to be relatively sure of the quality of the product sold. Some may wish their oil checked at the pump, their windows cleaned and their cars washed, and may prefer credit transactions rather than paying cash, etc. All these characteristics determine "the full price" that consumers actually pay when filling their tanks. Since entrepreneurs realize that demands depend on this "full price," rather than just the quoted one, they tend to focus their efforts in this manner.

But of course lowering the "full price" implies something radically different than cutting observed prices. Firms can compete with numerous strategies (fighting for better locations for the gas stations, introducing automatic "car-wash" machines, etc.) while maintaining an unchanged quoted price. After all, a better location, and greater density of stations, save more money for a group of customers (as measured by the opportunity cost of their time) than a drop of a cent or two in the price of gasoline. Thus, one should not be surprised if in this particular market (or, in general, for commodities when the quoted price is small relative to the full one) the prices quoted by different companies are the same, there are relatively few price changes, and yet intense competition exists through non-price strategies.[11]

The Bertrand Report

The gasoline industry is a particularly apt illustration of the "full price" argument. This is because the massive "The State of Competition in the Canadian Oil Industry," the so-called Bertrand Report, relied on the static definition of competition and avoided making reference to "full prices." In Volume VI, for example, the Report concentrated all its attention: a) on changes in quoted prices, without making the slightest reference to the history of the industry, or the technological, legal and marketing constraints that shaped it; b) on the words used in some seized documents from the oil companies, forgetting that the interpretation given them by businessmen and managers is different than the one used by economists (see detailed discussion on the Bertrand Report in Brenner and Courville (1982)). This Report provides probably one of the best examples of the dangers posed by the Competition Act in its present form. Section 32 is proposed to be amended by the following subsection:

> (1.2) In a prosecution under subsection (1), the court may infer the existence of a conspiracy, combination, agreement or arrangement from circumstantial evidence, with or without direct evidence of communication between or among the alleged parties thereto, but, for greater certainty, the conspiracy, combination, agreement or arrangement must be proved beyond a reasonable doubt. (p. 24)

If this subsection is taken literally, a firm may be accused of anti-competitive behaviour not only if it charges a monopoly price, but even if it merely attempts to do so. The outcome may be the same as in the U.S. In 1940, the American Supreme Court's statement of the rule against price fixing in the *Madison Oil* case no longer required the demonstration of a probable impact on price. According to Posner (1976) the rule against price fixing had become — erroneously — a part of the law of conspiracy, instead of a part of the law of monopoly. This happened, in Posner's view, because lawyers and judges were more comfortable with conspiracy doctrine than price theory (p. 41). Unfortunately, this seems to be where the new Competition Act is heading.

Other non-pricing strategies and "conscious parallelism"

In the 1960s and 70s, the big seven oil companies in the U.S. started to look for alternative sources of energy, and they all found uranium.[12] Why did all of them look to "uranium?" Why didn't some bet on developing solar power, energy generated by lightning, or from ocean waves (as one French company did)? Wesley Cohen, in his Ph.D. thesis at Yale, examined how this decision was made. Through a request under the Freedom of Information Act, he obtained access to the corporate-planning documents of the seven sisters. He learned that Sohio (Standard Oil of Ohio) in its ''Nuclear Energy Review'' of July, 1969, recommended that the company should venture into the nuclear power business by referring not to the world's future energy demands, but to the strategies of other oil companies. This report had its origins in an earlier examination of the synthetic-fuels industry. ''In that study,'' says the Sohio report, ''a survey of the activities of (our) major domestic competitors indicated heavy involvement by many in one or more aspects of the nuclear industry.''

An internal document of Standard Oil of California dated February 11, 1974 states that the boom in uranium exploration was on the horizon. What were the signals according to which this judgment was made? The document's heading reads: ''Increased activity by majors, Exxon in particular.'' It continues: ''Industry rumors indicate that Exxon Minerals has been proceeding since at least mid-1972 on the basis that uranium prices were going to increase drastically. Conoco, Mobil and Gulf are very active, as shown by the increased hiring of geologists and expansion of staff, including Exxon's recruiting goal of 100 summer students for 1974 v.s. 80 in 1973 for mineral field jobs.'' Cohen concludes that resulting behaviour is ''somewhat akin to noticing that the Joneses next door seem to be putting up a fence, and then putting up your own.'' Such imitative behaviour, however, should not be confused with collusion. Quite the contrary, the behaviour was a result both of the perception that some companies may be getting ahead, and others, if they don't innovate, may fall behind. It took account of the fact that it may be expensive and time-consuming for each company to carry out its own research on future demands. Rather, each can learn from their competitors' behaviour.

Collusion and innovation

As long as firms pursue new and innovative strategies, a finding that pricing and other strategies may be similar should not be interpreted as signs of collusive behaviour. These companies innovate, sometimes imitate, precisely because they are engaged in a competitive struggle, and fear falling behind. The fact that some firms chose to imitate their competitors cannot be condemned. After all, how many people, managers, lawyers or economists in particular, are always entrepreneurial and innovative? The majority in any society merely imitates: this is why the rate of innovation can provide only a necessary, but not sufficient indication of anti-competitive behaviour. In order to infer such behaviour the prosecution should therefore look first at two things: a) at the accused company's relative rate of innovation; b) at whether or not changes in pricing strategies have occurred simultaneously with alterations in production facilities. Only if the accused company had a relatively low rate of innovation and changed its pricing policy *without* any changes in other strategies (investment, R & D, etc.), should one become suspicious of non-competitive behaviour. As to small and medium-sized companies, unless a perverse use of the Competition Act itself prevents them from competing, they can safely be left to their own devices.

The U.S. Congress has recently passed the National Cooperative Research Act, which generally limits the potential antitrust liability of joint research ventures. Even this bill did not prevent the Justice Department from carrying out a 25 month antitrust investigation of MCC, a cooperative research venture in computer technology undertaken by 21 small and medium-sized companies.[13] It is unclear why such an investigation was needed to start with, since neither IBM, nor AT & T participated, and each supports research programs many times the size of MCC. The 25 month delay could have only helped IBM and AT & T. Under the present wording of the Competition Act, small and medium-sized companies in Canada can expect similar delays if they attempt to merge.

V. ABUSE OF DOMINANT POSITION AND COLLUSION

The present Bill (section 50, a-h) does not look at a firm's relative rate of innovation. It fails to ask whether or not changes in pricing policy occurred simultaneously with changes in production facilities and other strategies. Instead, it suggests, at times, that non-competitive behaviour can be inferred from phenomena that can be easily interpreted as competitive.

"Squeezing, by a vertically integrated supplier, of the margin available to an unintegrated customer who competes with the supplier, for the purpose of impeding or preventing the customer's entry into, or expansion in, a market" — is labeled in subsection (a) of section 50 as an "anti-competitive act." But two questions must be raised concerning the view implicit in this statement: first, why would a vertically integrated supplier pursue such a strategy, and second: can it be expected to be successful?

The answer sometimes given to the first question is that somehow the vertically integrated supplier has a monopoly power which it tries to maintain through the "squeezing" strategy, but that this monopoly power is not due to superior performance. This argument seems inaccurate. If the vertically integrated firm does not have an efficiency advantage over its competitors, trying to delay or prevent entry by either "squeezing," "predatory pricing" or by monopolizing distribution must be costly. A business concern cannot pursue it persistently, since all these practices impose losses. As well, a firm's known policy of monopolizing distribution might induce people to start distribution outlets just for the purpose of being bought up (McGee, 1958). Thus, it seems unlikely that any company would pursue such strategies in order to prevent entry and maintain monopoly power. However, companies may pursue such practices under competitive pressures, when adjusting to some unanticipated changes.

The "squeeze"

The accusation of squeezing the unintegrated supplier has been frequently made in the aforementioned Volume VI of the Bertrand Report. In order to understand the changes in the marketing strategies of the oil companies, let us briefly summarize the specific circumstances in which they occurred (an extensive discussion can be found in Brenner and Courville, 1982).

In the early 1950s the oil companies developed an extensive network of low-volume full-service stations in response to consumer demand for frequent servicing of engines, for checking oil, tires, batteries and other accessories. The oil companies experimented with high-volume no-service stations too, but these stations turned out to be unprofitable. During the late 1950s and early 1960s drastic technological changes occurred and the quality of cars changed: lubrication and oil changes were needed less and less frequently, radial tires required less frequent replacement, etc. Also, with increased ownership of cars, specialized facilities such as muffler shops and tire centres developed. Mass merchandisers began selling tires, batteries, motor oil. This led to significant alterations in relative demands: a fall for low-volume full-service stations and a rise for the high-volume no-service gas bars. How did the oil companies respond?

As more drivers could forego service at stations, independent retailers made significant gains in market share. The large firms recognized that in retail gasoline marketing many of their problems were centred around low-volume full-service stations. They realized that they could not continue the high rate of capital investment per gallon for new service stations which had been typical of the industry before.

Self-service

One obstacle to the rapid development of self-serve stations was that such enterprises contravened provincial fire regulations found in gasoline handling laws. In Ontario, for example, gasoline marketing companies had to obtain exemption from the Gasoline Handling Act to establish self-serve outlets. This process took time. The second obstacle was the dealership system. Although the benefits of the dealership system were great in the 1950s, once it is adopted, there are costs of adjustment involved if market conditions suddenly change and marketing strategies must be modified. In the 1960s, when the shift in the structure of demand began to occur, it was common for the major oil companies to give lessee dealers multi-year contracts ranging up to five years. One option open to the oil companies at that time might have been to close a number of full-service outlets and break the contracts. Such an option was never seriously considered because of the damage to the company's reputation among potential future dealers. Instead the companies responded with two strategies: the development of second brands and the provision of subsidies to dealers who continued to operate full-service stations. Both can be viewed in these particular circumstances as strategies to make a graceful — cost minimizing — exit from past commitments and still be able to compete.

"Consignment and commission" was a form of support of the dealer by which the company guaranteed a minimum margin during periods of depressed retail prices. The dealer entered into consignment at his own request, but once the commitment was made, the company established the retail price for gasoline. This arrangement split the risks between the dealer and the oil company. It served as a method of temporarily meeting local competition, without dropping wholesale prices everywhere. During the period that this arrangement held, the company fulfilled part of its previous commitment to the dealer and also had the opportunity to *discover* whether or not a full-service station was still viable in that particular location. This was interpreted in the Bertrand Report as "squeezing" (this would occur under the proposed Competition Act as well); members of the Ontario Royal Commission on Petroleum Products Pricing in July 1976 (see Brenner and Courville, 1982) made a similar determination.

Fighting brands

We then arrive at subsection (d) of section 50, according to which "use of fighting brands introduced selectively on a temporary basis to discipline or eliminate a competitor,'' should be viewed as ''anti-competitive.'' But this is not necessarily the case.

The sale of branded gasoline enables the dealer to use the oil company's trademark and whatever additional services are involved. If the sale of gasoline does not include the use of the refiner's trademark, then it is classified as ''unbranded.'' The second brands introduced by the oil companies were of this type. What is the difference for the customer? Is it not, after all, the ''same'' gasoline that he is buying? The answer is ''no.'' Even without the provision of any service at the pump, a consumer who enters a Shell, or a Texaco, or an Esso station has implicit insurance as to the quality of gasoline. No such assurance exists for unbranded gasoline except, perhaps, after many years of market presence.

The oil companies sold their second brands through the high volume, gas bar stations which were sometimes converted from full-service status. They did not use their trademark on these sales because that would have been a breach of faith with the dealers selling branded gasoline. Internal documents indicate it was the oil companies' intention to follow the second brand strategy only temporarily. But, eventually, when most of the long-term contracts were renegotiated, the high-volume, second brand stations could become branded ones. For, once the companies were free of their past commitments to large numbers of full-service outlets, they could promote an image of providing both self-serve and full-service stations. The development of second ''fighting'' brand stations, used temporarily, can thus be interpreted as a competitive response to the sudden changes in technology and in demand, *taking into account* the constraints of past commitments.

It is interesting to note that in the U.S., I.B.M. was accused of introducing ''fighting machines'' (the 360/90, 360/67 as well as the 360/44). These were alleged to have been ''predatory'' product introductions with prices deliberately set below cost (Fisher et al., 1983, p. 277). As Fisher et al. (1983) point out, such arguments show ''a total misunderstanding of the economic analysis of competition and monopoly; after all, the introduction of new products is usually a sign of competition, not monopoly'' (p. 277).

Thus we see that the new marketing strategies of the oil companies, as well as I.B.M.'s strategy of competing through technological innovations, resulted in acts that were outlawed by some sections in the new Competition Act. The source of the error is the one mentioned earlier: the reliance on static models to understand phenomena in a dynamic world — where innovations, after all, do occur.

Incompatibility

The same error is made in subsection (g) which prohibits the "adoption of product specifications that are incompatible with products produced by any other person and are designed to prevent his entry into, or to eliminate him from, a market." Why such behaviour is viewed as "anti-competitive" is unclear. Consider now the Kodak case. This shows more forcefully than any theoretical discussion why reference to such strategies should be dropped.

In 1972 Kodak introduced a new camera ("Pocket Instamatic") *and* a film (Kodacolor II) that was compatible with it. Berkey, in *Berkey Photo v.s. Eastman Kodak Company* (1979) accused Kodak of attempts to monopolize since it did not reveal its intention to introduce these new products; further, it complained of the fact that only Kodacolor could be used and that this further reinforced Kodak's dominant position. Berkey argued that Kodak had to announce its innovative strategy in advance, so that the competitors could come up with alternative products. While a jury voted in favour of Berkey, the decision was later reversed. Commenting on the first decision, Keith I. Clearwaters (1978), previously with the Justice Department's Antitrust Division wrote:

> It may lead a company with monopoly power (due to previous patents) to hold back on the introduction of new products and processes because of fear that innovations, without advance disclosure, will lead to an antitrust suit by a competitor and the possible break-up of the company. (p. 4)

In the court of appeal, Judge Kaufman reversed the jury's decision stating that

> "the successful competitor having been urged to compete must not be turned upon when he wins ... it would be inherently unfair to condemn success when the Sherman Act mandates competition .... We must always be mindful lest the Sherman Act be involved perversely in favor of those who seek protection against the rigors of competition" (see Jentes, 1980, pp. 937-8, quoting the judge).

McEntee and Kahrl (1980) made similar comments and state:

> ... Berkey, which no longer sells cameras does not advance its predisclosure as part of a demand for equitable relief... Instead, it asks

us to condemn Kodak retrospectively, holding that it violated section 2 and so is liable for damages, because it did not decide on its own initiative to take unusual, self-abnegatory actions as a corrective for unadjudicated prior offenses. This is without justification. (p. 176)

Kodak was not the only company accused of such practice. I.B.M. was also victimized (see detailed discussion in Fisher et al., 1983) and in similar circumstances: when *innovating*. However, instead of being accused of withholding information, I.B.M. was accused of "premature announcements" to delay their competitors from venturing in the new direction it was following. Damned if you do, damned if you don't. But this is exactly the perverse use of the Bill one can expect if this subsection, as well as the previous two (on "fighting brands" and "squeezing") remain in the text, and no reference is made to innovations, technological or managerial. The impact of these subsections seems similar: they could retard innovations and their introduction, as well as adaptations to unanticipated changes, rather than encourage them. And this is completely apart from the costs of lengthy litigations.

Delivered pricing

Another target which has come within the purview of the proposed "Competition Act" is the practice of "delivered pricing" (section 52). This section is written in such tortuous language, that in the absence of the somewhat clearer notes on pp. 24-5 in the "Competition Law Amendments — a Guide" were made, it would have been impossible to be sure of its exact meaning.

A delivered pricing system is one where the price quoted to the buyer includes transport charges.[14] Delivered prices may appear in diverse guises. In one such system, two customers who are located at different distances from the firm are quoted the same price, even if the shipping charges are different. This makes the price independent of the buyer's location, as in the case of Canada Post. In a variant of this system, the firm divides its market in geographical zones. Every customer in a given area is quoted the same price, independent of his distance from the shipping point. Finally, the industry can select either one or several geographic locations as a "basing point." Here, all prices quoted to customers are based on a price fixed at this location plus the shipping cost to the customer. This system disregards the point from which the product is actually shipped. For instance, if Calgary is the basing point then the price quoted would include freight charges from Calgary to the final destination even if the product is actually shipped from Toronto. If all the firms in an industry adopted such a pricing scheme, a buyer's geographic advantage would be eliminated. This pricing system has been compared to others that could be used when customers and firms are far from one another. One example is the FOB (free on board) system. Here, the quoted price equals cost at the factory plus the actual freight charges incurred in shipping the product to the customer. If price was the only characteristic important to customers, and since shipping costs increase with distance, each customer would turn to the closest supplier. This seems to be, at first sight, the best outcome but it is unlikely to occur under a delivered price system. How then can we justify delivered prices? Are prices necessarily higher than if such a system was forbidden by judicial decree?

According to some economists delivered prices may help collusive behaviour since it diminishes the amount of information needed for successful collusion, making it easier to monitor one's competitors prices. If a firm quotes a lower price than its fellows, it would be a *prima facie* evidence of cheating. However, given that (a) clandestine cheating is one of the biggest problems dogging the steps of potential colluders (which would be facilitated by the fact that the competitors are at relatively great distance one from the other) and (b) agreement on prices does not eliminate the possibility of innovating with other strategies (other than price-cutting), one must be skeptical of this explanation for "delivered prices."

Insurance function

Stigler (1949) gave an alternative perspective. Noting that delivered prices were current in industries characterized by *unstable geographic demands*, he suggested that they were a way to provide insurance. If in these circumstances an FOB price system was used, then a factory based in a region of declining demand would have an incentive to "cheat" in order to gain sales from a more fortunate factory based in a region of increasing demand. But a basing point or a delivered price system would insure each firm of some market share in "localized" bad times. According to Stigler, while this was not the ideal way to divide the market, it may have been the best option given that more explicit ways may have run afoul of the antitrust laws.

But there seems to be a more fundamental reason for delivered prices when demands are geographically unstable (as in construction). As pointed out, such a system eliminates geographic advantage in transportation. At the same time, however, it eliminates geographic *disadvantage* when demands are shifting rapidly and in an unpredictable fashion. Assume that the total demand for an industry (plywood used in construction, for example)[15] is stable, but sometimes there is a construction boom in Montreal, two years later in Toronto, which then shifts elsewhere. Under a delivered price system, the buyer in Montreal is indifferent between purchasing from the Montreal based firm, or the one located in Toronto. This *prevents* either firm from going bankrupt in "localized" bad times. In other words, a delivered price system prevents bankruptcies, diminishes the costs of unpredictable reallocation of firms and litigation costs as well. The alternative to such a pricing system in these particular circumstances is merger. But the suggested Competition Act views this with suspicion too. It is thus hard to see how in this case a judicial decree forbidding either delivered prices or merger could lower prices. Quite the contrary should be expected.

The present Bill quite properly consider as mitigating circumstances brandname products and the situation in which a firm is already using its full capacity in a particular locality. These particular circumstance — geographically unstable demands linked with mergers or delivered prices — should be considered in this light as well. Also, as emphasized in the previous section, attention should always be paid to the relative importance of freight costs in the "full price" of the final product when judging whether or not the existence of such a system provides an indication of noncompetitive behaviour. In fact, an even stronger point can be made: because of all these reservations, *no* explicit reference should be made to delivered prices, when no changes in production facilities occur. Indeed, while the U.S. Supreme Court has decided since the 1940s that a basing point system violates the antitrust laws, the testimonies in FTC v.s. Cement Institute et al., 333 U.S. 683 (1948), referred to overt collusion.[16]

VI. CONCLUSION

The conclusion is simple: the framers of the new Competition Act have persistently committed the error of targeting a few aspects of the behaviour and features of enterprises (prices, sizes, etc.). But this has been divorced both from the particular circumstances in which these enterprises found themselves in when unanticipated changes occurred and from the enterprises' other strategies, innovative ones in particular. If indeed the goal of the Act is to promote innovations rather than prevent or delay them, the sections of the Act examined here need a lot of rethinking *and* re-writing.

Notes

1. See Fisher et al. (1983), Brenner and Courville (1982), Brenner (1986).

2. This point is emphasized in Fisher et al. (1983), as well as numerous other writers summarized in Brenner (1986), chapter 3. The fear of "big" corporations may be related *not* to their pricing strategies, but rather to their ability in influencing the political process (see Noonan (1984)). But this is *not* the concern of the present Competition Act.

3. See Sylos-Labini (1984), Brenner (1986), chapter 3.

4. More on this point, on the role of entrepreneurs in particular, can be found in Brenner (1985), chapter 2, and Brenner (1986), chapter 3.

5. This point has been frequently made in the economic literature: see Stigler (1968), Becker (1971), Posner (1976).

6. More on this point can be found in Brenner (1986), chapters 3 and 5.

7. See discussion in Posner (1976).

8. On evidence supporting this view, see Brenner (1986).

9. See elaborate discussion and criticism in Posner (1976).

10. See Becker (1971).

11. This argument should be taken into account not only in the context of "price fixing" and "conscious parallelism," but also for delivered prices and freight costs. For if either freight costs are small relatively to the price of the final product, or the customers are not swayed by tiny variations in price, then it may be advantageous to all parties to charge the same freight costs, and compete through other strategies. Consider the freight costs of Neiman Marcus and L.L.Bean. These are both prestigious houses, which certainly face intense competition from Saks Fifth Avenue, Magnin, Bloomingdales, Lord & Taylor, etc. Carlton (1983) calculates that these two firms use a uniform delivered price system in their catalog orders which represents from 5 to 10 percent of the total cost of the product. These companies have not been prosecuted. Those that have been prosecuted in the U.S. on this ground belonged to industries facing significant fluctuations in demand where freight was an important component in the final price.

12. See Solman and Friedman (1982), pp. 127-30.

13. See Simison (1985).

14. See on delivered prices Scherer (1980), pp. 330-1, Bringham (1985), Carlton (1985), Clark (1938), Haddock (1982).

15. See Johnson (1976) for a description of the plywood case. Haddock (1982) explains delivered pricing in cement, plywood, steel as a possible cost minimizing mechanism in the face of uncertainty, while Carlton (1983) suggests that it could be a way for customers to insure against freight variations.

16. See Haddock (1982).

THE AUTHOR

James C.W. Ahiakpor received his doctorate in economics from the University of Toronto in 1981. Formerly a professor of economics at the University of Ghana, he is now on the staff at St. Mary's University in Halifax. Dr. Ahiakpor's major areas of study are history of economic thought, developmental economics, monetary and micro theory. He has published widely in such periodicals as the *Journal of Development Economics, History of Political Economy, and Economic Bulletin of Ghana.* His first book is due to be published in late 1986, and shall be entitled, *Multinationals and Economic Development.*

Chapter Nine

Regulation and the Consumer Interest

James C.W. Ahiakpor

The competition law amendments bill was launched with the best of intentions. Like previous bills in this genre, it seeks to enhance competition among businesses operating within Canada, promote efficiency and flexibility in the use of resources, fairness of competition between firms and, above all, to confer the benefits of low prices, increased quantity and variety of goods and services on consumers.[1] Few would question the wisdom of pursuing such noble goals. However, the instruments chosen will not promote the overall interests of consumers. The actions proposed under the bill only affect the distribution of income between groups of consumers. There is thus the strong possibility that the interest of *all* consumers may be hurt, even while benefiting some at the greater expense of others. In this chapter, the sources of the bill's errors are explained, and alternative measures to advance the interest of consumers in the economy are put forth.

The chapter is organized as follows. Section I discusses a fundamental error of the bill, namely, its misidentification of welfare-promoting competition with the textbook version of "perfect" competition. Section II examines failures of the proposed bill to enhance consumers' interests. The final section III considers alternative approaches to achieving the good intentions of the bill, along with a summary.

I. COMPETITION

The competition bill does not directly or clearly define that which it presumably desires to promote, namely, competition. However, the meaning of competition to which the bill appears to subscribe may be inferred from those acts listed as ''anti-competitive.'' They include acts whose effects may ''discipline, eliminate or prevent entry of competitors in a market.''[2] And yet the result of fierce competition is to produce the very results the bill lists as indicating ''anti-competitive'' behaviour.[3] Although, on the surface, ''market restrictions,'' ''tied selling'' and ''exclusive dealing,'' also listed in the bill, may appear to be uncompetitive acts, they may well be for the firms involved the most efficient means of conducting competition.[4]

We may appreciate the choice of acts considered ''anti-competitive'' better if we relate them to the notion of perfect competition, as taught in economics textbooks. Perfect competition is characterized by a large number of firms, identical products, perfect information and mobility, zero adjustment costs and many buyers. In this model, no single firm or buyer can affect prices by its actions. Under these conditions the actions listed in the bill would have no chance of sustaining any firm in business for long. Neither would it be possible for a ''supplier (to) extract prices above *competitive levels*,'' or for prices to ''exceed the *competitive norm*'' and ''the free and competitive flow of market forces'' to be blocked by some firms[5] (emphasis added). Also, under perfect competition, there could be no mergers carrying ''the potential of increasing price and/or restricting output at less than *competitive levels*,''[6] an occurrence the bill seeks to prevent (emphasis added). But it is a fact that high prices and mergers may occur in competitive markets. The degree of (sellers') competition is thus not necessarily determined by the number of firms. Such competition (both advertising and price) as we notice in the beverage (beer and soft drinks) or automobile industries, for example, testifies to the fact that the number of firms, their average size or degree of concentration within an industry says little about the rivalrous competitiveness of firms.

Rivalry

Competition, properly defined, means no more than rivalry between two or more actors. Alfred Marshall, generally regarded as the founder of the neoclassical school of economics, from which the so-called perfectly competitive model of economic analysis derives, defined competition as follows:

"The strict meaning of competition seems to be the racing of one person against another, with special reference to bidding for the sale or purchase of anything."[7] Marshall considered the structure of industry, which includes the size and number of firms, secondary to the meaning of competition, arguing

> This kind of racing is no doubt both more intense and more widely extended than it used to be: but it is only a secondary, and one might say, an accidental consequence from the fundamental characteristics of modern industrial life. (*Principles*, p. 4)

And these characteristics include combinations among buyers and sellers. Karl Marx's description of sellers' competition is perhaps even more revealing. Under competition, he wrote:[8]

> The same commodity is offered for sale by various sellers. Whoever sells commodities of the same quality most cheaply, is sure to *drive the other sellers from the field* and secure the greatest market for himself. The sellers therefore fight among themselves for the sales for the market. Each one of them wishes to sell, and sell as much as possible, and *if possible to sell alone*, to the exclusion of all other sellers. Each one sells cheaper than the other. Thus there takes place a competition among the sellers which forces down the price of the commodities offered by them. (emphasis added)

Notice that Marx ended up with more than one seller in the competitive market he described. Only in the case of a single-seller monopoly is there an absence of competition in supply, a situation that is rare.[9] And when a monopoly occurs, it cannot last for any appreciable amount of time unless government grants it exclusive powers. (Otherwise, new competitors would enter the field, attracted by the high profits.) The state could do so by legally limiting entry into the industry, or by preventing foreign competition through tariffs and other such regulations. In the words of John Stuart Mill:[10]

> Governments ... are often chargeable with having attempted, too successfully, to make things dear, than having aimed by wrong means at making them cheap. The usual instrument for producing artificial dearness is monopoly ... The mere exclusion of foreigners, from a branch of industry open to the free competition of every native, has been known ... to render that branch a conspicuous exception to the general industrial energy of the country.

The message should be clear. Rivalry or competition among firms is not necessarily a function of their number. Moreover, monopolistic behaviour of a group of firms cannot long endure unless they have the protection of the state in the form of prohibition of entry into the market, especially of foreigners.[11]

Economic liberty

What is now regarded as "perfect" competition, and generally believed to have been postulated by the classical and early neoclassical economists, must properly be understood as an industrial environment characterized by "perfect liberty" or "free and universal competition,"[12] or "free enterprise."[13] Under the principle of liberty or free enterprise must be included the freedom of sellers or buyers to combine. This point cannot possibly be overemphasized. Alfred Marshall, in his description of the characteristics of free enterprise, made the argument regarding combinations thus:

> (The characteristics include) a certain independence and habit of choosing one's own course for oneself, a self-reliance; a deliberation and yet a promptness of choice and judgement, and a habit of forecasting the future and of shaping one's course with reference to distant aims. They may and often do cause people to compete with one another; but on the other hand they may tend ... in the direction of *cooperation and combination of all kinds* good and evil. But these tendencies toward collective ownership and collective action are quite different from those of earlier times, because they are the result not of custom, not of any passive drifting into association with one's neighbours, but of *free choice* by each individual of that line of conduct which after careful deliberation seems to him the *best suited* for attaining his ends, whether they are selfish or unselfish. (*Principles* pp. 4-5)

Thus the textbook model of perfect competition, which appears to be the standard by which the degree of competition is judged under the competition bill, may be described as a 20th century myth which distorts the meaning of free enterprise. Although its formulators may have intended by it to demonstrate the superiority of free enterprise over a state-regulated economy, the model has produced the exact opposite. It has motivated governments to try to achieve "perfection of markets" through regulation.[14] And yet there is no unique way by which competition may be measured. As pointed out earlier, the number of firms or their size are misleading indicators of the degree of competition.[15] So is a high rate of profits, since this may merely reflect greater risks attending to investment in the industry than elsewhere. Moreover, there may be fierce competition among a small number of firms (auto-makers, for example) who earn high average profits because they have been protected from foreign competition by government. At the firm level, a higher than average rate of profit may be a reflection of greater competitive efficiency and skill.[16]

Of course, the bill recognizes the difficulties involved in measuring competition or ascertaining the intent of acts that might appear, at first glance, to be "anti-competitive." This accounts for the provision of exemption clauses. But the fact is that C-91 nevertheless grants powers to a few bureaucrats. They can make judgments which may turn out to be costly mistakes, especially when the law makes it easier for a competition tribunal to convict.[17] And when they do err, there is no automatic feedback mechanism (such as profits and losses for businessmen) which penalizes this behaviour.

II. CONSUMERS' INTERESTS AND COMPETITION LAW

It is not impossible for government to assist consumers in achieving their preferred choices in the marketplace. Even apart from the cost of interventionism, such "assistance" would be helpful only if government has precise information about consumers' preferences. But it is precisely such information that legislators (or bureaucrats or tribunals) normally do not have. Even if surveys were conducted weekly or daily, the information so gathered may have become obsolete by the time action is about to be taken since consumers' tastes and preferences are far from static.

Instead, it is firms with whom consumers constantly interact in the marketplace which are most capable of ascertaining consumers' preferences. Indeed, competition — through price adjustments, provision of information on product or service characteristics (advertising), introduction of new products — is a reflection of business concern's perceptions of, and attempts to meet, the changing tastes and preferences of consumers. Firms which incorrectly judge consumers' changing desires lose money. They accumulate inventories of unwanted goods, or sell their goods and services at less than profitable prices. Some may even go bankrupt if they are not able to respond to consumers' needs quickly enough.[18] This is the essence of how consumers' sovereignty operates.

In the marketplace, in other words, the dollar votes of the consumers serve as the imprimatur of the actions of firms. If the customers approve of the activities of entrepreneurs, the latter can continue in business; if they do not, bankruptcy must ensue.

Government intervention, then — whether of the anti-combines variety or other sorts of regulation — drives a wedge between firm and consumer. It is basically paternalistic, in that it sets aside and defeats the freely made choices of consumers (and firms as well) on the marketplace. This belief in government intervention into the economy is founded on a dim view of the thoughtfulness (or rationality) of consumer behaviour. It reflects the perception that consumers do not know what satisfies them and cannot choose among alternative goods and services in order to obtain their own highest preferences. If consumers are so inept, then perhaps regulatory legislation to protect them is proper. (Of course, such an assumption leads to a contradiction. For it implies that such foolish consumers can magically turn into voters skillful enough to elect wise legislators who will then turn around and restrain them in their role of consumer.) But if consumers are acknowledged to be constantly and rationally pursuing their own self-determined interests, then the case for competition legislation vanishes.

Limits of knowledge

In this regard Adam Smith gave the following warning to legislators:

> The statesman, who should attempt to direct private people in what manner they ought to employ their capital, would not only load himself with a most unnecessary attention, but assume an authority which could safely be trusted, not only to no single person but to no council or senate whatever, and which would no-where be so dangerous as in the hands of a man who had folly and presumption enough to fancy himself fit to exercise it. (*Wealth of Nations*, 1, p. 478)

Of course, Smith's warning is regularly ignored because, in their noble desire to be helpful, legislators easily lose sight of the limits to their knowledge. Moreover, they underestimate the thoughtfulness of consumers. But occasional reminders about the limited knowledge of others in the marketplace may yet temper the zeal to interfere in their activities.[19]

That "consumers benefit directly from increased competition" or "consumers and small business are among the prime beneficiaries of an effective competition policy" seems to be the fundamental premise of the competition bill.[20] It is true that increased competition may confer the benefits of low prices, increased variety and quantity of goods and services to consumers. But it is a mistake to believe that legislation to restrict freedom of competition, by whichever means firms consider efficient, is the best way to achieve this goal.

For economic freedom does not operate only in a perfectly competitive market, if one indeed exists in reality. On the contrary, the free enterprise system exists wherever there is rivalry or competition. And this obtains provided only that the potential for competition is not legislated away by the creation of artificial barriers to entry.

Consultation

There were "lengthy, thorough, and valuable consultations with the provincial governments as well as the business, consumer, legal and labour communities and other interested parties" on the merits of the competition bill. [21] It is a fact that the Consumers' Association of Canada, among other private groups, did not strongly oppose the restrictive measures in the competition bill. Does this indicate that consumer choice is irrational? Certainly not. For one thing, the C.A.C. might not have represented the true beliefs of its constituents. But let us assume, for the sake of argument, that this is not the case. Then,it would be perfectly consistent for consumers to act or believe themselves to be acting rationally, and yet to support a bill that *promises* lower prices, larger quantity and variety of goods and services. It rather would have been contrary to their interests if they said "no" to the question: "would you like the government to prohibit firms from engaging in "anti-competitive" acts, including mergers, that raise prices and limit the quantity of goods and services you would like to purchase?"

Even if consumers were assured of a fall in other prices that would leave their real incomes unchanged, they would still be acting rationally in agreeing to accept a bill that would prevent such changes in relative prices. For there are costs to collecting information on relative prices and adjusting consumption habits to them. The apparent acquiescence to the competition bill by consumer groups may possibly be justified by consumers' desire to avoid these additional search and adjustment costs.

Moreover, evaluation of the same information is bound to differ between business people and bureaucrats, perhaps even more than opinions differ among investors. This is a phenomenon that produces daily variations on the stock and foreign exchange markets.

Furthermore, most individuals are aware that by themselves they have little effect on market prices. This is why they may, individually, seek the protection of government against sellers. This phenomenon is what explains the popularity of such regulations as rent control, minimum or maximum price laws, and anti-combines acts. [22] But if the question were asked: ''do you think government or its agencies know your tastes and preferences well enough for them to have the power to determine which goods and services are to be available to you in the marketplace?'' the answer would readily be ''no''! [23] The same argument applies to producers' groups. [24]

Dichotomy

Another important error in the bill is its dichotomy between the benefits to consumers and to producers. In a more complete understanding of the marketplace, everyone is a consumer! Some people receive wages only, while others earn their incomes from capital (real or financial) and land. Still others benefit from gifts or transfer payments. Thus government intervention to lower or prevent price changes in some markets can be viewed as an attempt to intervene in the distribution of income between those who earn their wage, interest, rental or profit incomes from the affected industry and those who earn their incomes elsewhere. The effect of such intervention is to discriminate against income earners in the affected industry, but it is not at all clear this is the intention of the bill. [25]

Similarly, the attempt to favour small firms within an industry amounts to discrimination against those who earn their incomes from large firms. And yet there is no overwhelming evidence that large firms are necessarily more profitable, or less ''worthy,'' than small firms. Nor is there any indication that the rich tend to be dependent on the earnings of large firms and the poor (or less rich) on that of small firms. The point is that firms are merely representatives of consumers. Not *all* consumers suffer welfare loss, even if some do, from an increase in the price of some goods and services. Price changes cause incomes to be distributed among consumers differently from that which would have occurred in their absence. The ''losses'' of one group of consumers may be the ''gains'' of another. And since higher prices do not necessarily increase the income of firms, it is not even clear that those who earn their incomes from such businesses gain at the expense of those who earn theirs from other industries.

Inflation

However, all consumers may lose from increases in *all* prices, especially when this leads to the enjoyment of a constant smaller quantity of goods and services, that is, in a period of inflation. [26] But individual firms do not have the power to cause inflation, or raise all prices. To be that successful, they would need government to protect them against competition, especially from foreigners, or restrictions on the movement of resources to other industries. The most potent source of inflation is growth in the quantity of money beyond the growth of real goods and services. Only the government holds the key to the money printing press, through the operations of the Bank of Canada. Others who attempt to print money face the criminal charge of counterfeiting and time in jail, on conviction. Thus, the most important sources of injury to *all* consumers lie in the hands of government itself, namely its trade, tariff, tax, and monetary policies, not in the activities of private firms.

Finally, the bill would allow government to constantly monitor, or meddle in, the investment decisions of firms. This may well prevent or delay introduction of goods and services that otherwise would have resulted if entrepreneurs were allowed the freedom to act according to their own best judgments. This includes pre-notification of mergers and exemption clauses that require the Tribunal to ascertain whether mergers lessen competition or have "the potential of increasing price and/or restricting output at less than competitive levels."[27] Considerable time and resources will have to be spent trying to ascertain and interpret the relevant facts. The historical background has been one of previous failures of tribunals to obtain conviction of firms charged with anti-competitive behaviour. Given the unseemly eagerness to successfully convict under the new bill, the likelihood of potentially beneficial mergers being halted looms large.[28] Even if mergers are not halted, *all* consumers lose. For fewer goods and services will be produced as a result of this diversion of productive resources into the investigation process. Such a use of resources constitute a dead-weight loss to the community, of the type, paradoxically, associated with the monopolization of industry by the perfectly competitive model.

III. SUMMARY AND IMPLICATIONS

(a) The competition bill is correct in identifying as its goal increased benefits to consumers, stimulating economic growth, and the promotion of increased competition in the Canadian economy;

(b) Competition which is beneficial, however, is not the textbook version of "perfect" competition; it is rather rivalry among firms, which can be achieved only by eliminating all legal barriers to entry.

(c) The degree of competition is hard to measure — neither the rate of profits among firms or the size of firms nor the number of firms in an industry are any necessary indication of rivalrous competition;

(d) It is a mistake to attempt to "protect" consumers through competition legislation;
(e) It is misleading to contrast the interests of consumers and producers since everyone is a consumer; and
(f) The Competition Tribunal has almost an impossible task, the pursuit of which threatens losses for all consumers by limiting the supplies of goods and services below that which would have been available otherwise.

These arguments have clear implications for government policy. In the first place, we must recognize the inherent inconsistency of attempting to improve upon competition by legislating competitive behaviour. As even the bill itself acknowledges, it may take a combination of firms to become effective competitors both at home and abroad. There are thus great dangers in granting the kind of supervisory roles to bureaucrats envisaged under the bill. This ought to be made clear. Tribunal decisions are superfluous and wasteful of economic resources when they turn out to be consistent with business decisions. They may be even more wasteful and harmful to the interest of consumers when they do not.

Imports

Great good would be done for consumers by allowing into this country as many Japanese cars, and foreign-made clothes and shoes as Canadians would like to purchase. This would far better serve consumer interests than competition laws affecting the automobile, clothing and shoe industries. Protective tariffs and non-tariff barriers lower real income by diverting resources into less productive enterprises which would not have survived without them.[29] As observed by the Economic Council of Canada (1969 Report, p. 24), "Canadian competition policy has represented an attempt to provide a partial substitute for the greater intensity of competition that would have prevailed in the absence of tariffs."[30] The inconsistency and futility of such a policy for enhancing the interest of consumers needs to be recognized. Free enterprise means just that: absence of legal inducements or impediments to the pursuit of income-earning opportunities by entrepreneurs, opportunities that centre on satisfying the *revealed* tastes and preferences of consumers. Said Smith:

All systems either of preference or of restraint, therefore, being thus completely taken away, the obvious and simple system of natural liberty establishes itself of its own accord. Every man ... is left perfectly free to pursue his own interest his own way, and to bring both his industry and capital into competition with those of any other man, or order of men. The sovereign is completely discharged from a duty, in the attempting to perform which he must always be exposed to innumerable delusions, and for the proper performance of which no human wisdom or knowledge could ever be sufficient; the duty of superintending the industry of private people, and of directing it towards the employment most suitable to the interest of the society. (*Wealth of Nations*, 2, p. 208).

Consider the profits record of Canadian state enterprises or crown corporations and the results of such schemes as the National Energy Program or wage and price control. They reflect the good intentions of government to direct the economy towards certain ends, but they also bear out Smith's views rather accurately. The best way to promote the interest of consumers is to leave firms free to respond to the dictates of consumers in the marketplace.

Notes

1. See, Consumer and Corporate Affairs Canada, *Competition Law Amendments: A Guide* (henceforth, *Guide*), Supply and Services Canada, 1985, p. 1 and passim.

2. They also include squeezing of profit margins of vertically integrated customers, use of fighting brands, freight equalization and "unique" specification of products. See Bill C-91, especially section 50.

3. Somewhat ironically, the government does recognize that undercutting competitors, for example, an act which also squeezes the profits of others, does help consumers. Thus it is observed: "If competitors fall from the market because a dominant competitor is more effective in meeting (sic) consumers needs, this is not an abuse of market power, but rather a natural consequence of the competitive process." *Guide*, op. cit., pp. 22-23. For some illuminating examples of the use of market power or dominant positions in the competitive world of

politics and sports, see Block, W. *A Response to the Framework Document, for Amending the Combines Investigation Act*, Fraser Institute Technical Document 82-01, January 1982, pp. 4-5.

4. See Block, op.cit., pp. 25-31, for illustrations.

5. *Guide*, pp. 24 and 26.

6. *Guide*, p. 19.

7. Marshall, A., *Principles of Economics*, (8th edition), London: MacMillan, 1964, p. 4. In fact, the textbook version of "perfect" competition is an early 20th century analytical device by mathematical economists in their quest to demonstrate the validity of some comparative statics versions of Marshallian economic principles. It is not quite what the classical economists had in mind, as is made clear below. For a history of the "perfect competition" fable, see Stigler, G.J., "Perfect Competition, Historically Contemplated," *Journal of Political Economy*, Vol. 54 (February 1957), pp. 1-17.

8. Marx K., *Wage-Labour and Capital/Value, Price and Profit*, New York: International Publishers, 1976, p. 21. Marx also argued that the rise of market price may be caused not by lack of competition among sellers, but by a greater degree of competition among buyers (ibid., pp. 21-22).

9. The same is true in Canada. According to official opinion, "there are very few industries in Canada in which only one firm controls the market," *Guide*, p. 22.

10. John Stuart Mill, *Collected Works*, Robson, J.M., (ed.), Vol. 3, London: Routledge & Kegan Paul, 1965, pp. 927-28.

11. This is a point not lost on the government. The *Guide* (pp. 4, 9, and 16) acknowledges the role of tariffs and other institutional barriers in limiting competition in Canada.

12. Smith, Adam, *The Wealth of Nations*, (Canan Ed.), Chicago: University of Chicago Press, 1976, Vol. 1, especially pp. 63 and 165.

13. Marshall, A., op.cit., especially p.8.

14. See, for example, Stigler, G.J., *The Citizen and the State: Essays on Regulation*, Chicago: University of Chicago Press, 1975, especially pp. 103-113.

15. See, for example, Caves, R.E. and Pugel, T.A., "Intra-industry Differences in Conduct and Performance: Viable Strategies in U.S. Manufacturing Industries," Harvard Institute of Economic Research, Discussion Paper No. 734, 1979. They found that "most industries display no demonstrable systematic relation between profit rate and size of firm" (p. 10). Also see Williamson, J.H., "Profit, growth and sales maximization," in *The Theory of the Firm*, Archibald, G.C. (ed.), Harmondsworth, England: Penguin, 1971, pp. 328-51, for a demonstration of the point that "there is no more reason to expect profitability to decline with size than there is evidence to suggest that it does."

16. For more supportive empirical studies, see Green, Christopher, *Canadian Industrial Organization and Policy*, (2nd ed.), Toronto: McGraw-Hill Ryerson, 1985, especially chapter 6.

17. See *Guide*, pp. 3, 17.

18. For example, the troubles of North American automobile industry in the late 1970s partly reflect their inadequate response to changed consumer preferences towards large gas-inefficient vehicles, Chrysler being the best example.

19. According to T.W. Hutchison, "to promote clarification of the extent and limits of economic knowledge and ignorance may well do much more to reduce dissatisfaction with current economic policies and their results, than do many or most of the contributions to confused and undisciplined wrangles and debates on particular policy problems." *Knowledge and Ignorance in Economics*, Chicago: University of Chicago Press, 1977, p. 5.

20. E.g. *Guide*, pp. 1, 4, 8, 21, 22, and 34.

21. *Guide*, p. 6.

22. See, for example, Block, W.E. and Olsen, E.O., *Rent Control: Myths and Realities*, The Fraser Institute, 1981; Walker, M.A., *The Illusion of Wage and Price Control*, The Fraser Institute, 1976. On the dangers of rejecting (causal) scientific principles with apparently contradictory evidence, see, for example, John Stuart Mill, *Essays on Some Unsettled Questions of Political Economy*, (2nd Ed.), New York: Augustus M. Kelly, 1968, especially pp. 161-163. He warned: "With regard to *exceptions*; in any tolerably advanced science there is properly no such thing as an exception. What is thought to be an exception to a principle is always some other and distinct principle cutting into the former; some other force which impinges against the first force, and deflects it from its direction. There is not a *law* and an *exception* to that law," (p. 162).

23. The continued violation of drug and prostitution laws is an illustration of this point.

24. Competition is costly to both winners and losers. This is one reason domestic producers favour import tariffs — to keep out foreign competition. Even within the domestic market some of the winners may desire the restrictions entailed in the legislation in order to preserve their current gains. Losers, if they are not sure of the outcome of future competitive struggle, may prefer to keep their present diminished positions. In any case, the bill is directed more at restraining winners from extending their gains. Thus, it should not be surprising that vehement opposition was not expressed against the bill by firms consulted. In the words of Alfred Marshall, "In many cases the 'regulation of competition' is a misleading term, that veils the formation of a privileged class of producers, who often use their combined force to frustrate the attempts of an able man to rise from a lower class than their own. Under the pretext of repressing anti-

social competition, they deprive him of the liberty of carving out for himself a new career, where the services rendered by him to the consumers of the commodity would be greater than the injuries, that he inflicts on the relatively small group which objects to his competition,'' *Principles*, p. 7.

25. It is quite a different matter when government, acting on its sense of society's moral judgment, seeks to restrain income-earning opportunities in industries declared illegal, e.g. prostitution and recreational drugs. But pursuit of the preference for ''equitable distribution of income,'' a goal some economists cite for favouring state intervention in the marketplace does not justify actions under this bill either. We typically do not know how the revenue in an industry is distributed among individuals although it may be easy to determine its distribution into wages, rent, interest and profits. ''Equitable distribution of income,'' if it were worthy of pursuit, may better be achieved through direct taxation.

26. With a growing population, even constant output implies that everyone has less to consume over time.

27. *Guide*, p. 19. Without a measure of competition this is almost an impossible task.

28. See, *Guide*, pp. 3, 17.

29. For a good, clear and non-technical exposition of this argument, see Hazlitt, H., *Economics in One Lesson*, Westport: Arlington House, 1978, especially, pp. 74-84.

30. It may be worth pointing out that the existence of tariffs *per se* does not constitute an impediment to free trade, according to the classical exposition of the doctrine. Rather it is the use of tariffs to discriminate against or in favour of domestic production. See, for example, Adam Smith, op. cit., 2, pp. 190-191, 255 or Alfred Marshall, ''Memorandum on Fiscal Policy of International Trade (1903)'' in Keynes, J.M., ed., *Official Papers by Alfred Marshall*, London: MacMillan, 1926, pp. 365-420. Thus remedy of this policy does not require abolition of all tariffs.

THE AUTHOR

Donald N. Thompson is Professor of Administrative Studies at York University in Toronto. He has also taught at Harvard University, the London School of Economics, and the University of Alberta. He was Chief Economist and Director of Research for the Royal Commission on Corporate Concentration.

He has authored or edited seven books and about fifty articles in the areas of marketing, competition policy, and strategic planning. His books and monographs relating to competition policy are *Franchise Operations and Antitrust* (1971), and *Conglomerate Mergers in Canada* (with Donald J. Lecraw) (1978). He was editor of *Contractual Marketing Systems* (1971).

Chapter Ten

The "Abuse of Dominant Position" Provision

Donald N. Thompson

On December 17, 1984, the Honourable Michel Côté, Minister of Consumer and Corporate Affairs, tabled for First Reading in the House of Commons a Bill C-91, to amend the Combines Investigation Act.[1] One of the principal proposals in the Bill is replacing the criminal offense of monopoly in Section 33 of the existing legislation, with a civil "abuse of dominant position" provision. The new provision employs a behavioural rather than a structural test of illegality, focusing on anti-competitive conduct rather than the notion of monopoly.

The underlying philosophy of the change was stated by Mr. Côté in his press conference introducing the legislation as recognizing "that high levels of concentration may be necessary to make Canadian industry world competitive, to the benefit of consumers and business."[2] This underlies the approach in the merger and specialization agreement provisions, as well as in the "abuse of dominant position" clause.

Indeed in recognizing "Canada as a trading nation," and citing the Macdonald Commission Report's emphasis on industrial restructuring and competitivenesss, Mr. Côté if anything understates the changes which have occurred from the benevolent competitive environment of the 1950s and 1960s. Today Japanese multinational companies carve out dominant shares of Canadian and other western markets; European cartels build strong positions in sectors such as fine chemicals and heavy machinery; newly industrialized countries such as Brazil and Israel create government-subsidized, export oriented aerospace and defense industries; and Pacific Rim and Eastern European countries produce a wide range of goods for the low end of the market.

I. A NEW ENVIRONMENT

The Japanese government's response to the new competitive environment has been to restrict domestic competition through MITI-formulated cartels and import protection, to subsidize industrial restructuring, and to finance research into the next generation of technology. In the U.S., the Reagan administration has pushed forward proposals to remove antitrust as an obstacle to industrial restructuring. Not only is there now a wide tolerance for mergers, but the administration has sought the power to exempt from prosecution even price-raising acquisitions in industries hurt by import competition. The U.S. is encouraging research joint ventures, and is seeking repeal of antitrust treble-damage remedies except in cases of overcharges or underpayments. The Reagan administration has in the past few years allowed a joint venture between the world's two largest automobile companies, General Motors and Toyota; allowed the LTV Corporation, the third largest steel producer, to acquire fourth-largest Republic Steel; allowed the merger of the third and fourth largest tire manufacturers, B.F. Goodrich and Uniroyal; and ignored all the ''aggregate power'' concerns of three decades in permitting the conglomerate merger of two giant companies, General Electric and RCA. It has been argued that this represents an American triumph of ideology over economics, or a confusion of laissez-faire with efficiency. It would be hard however to argue that Canada should be taking a negative view of industrial restructuring, or even a neutral one, when our dominant trading partner is embarked on so dramatic a course.

II. THE ''ABUSE OF DOMINANCE'' PROVISIONS

The proposed sections 50 and 51 of Bill C-91 would replace the monopoly offense in section 33 of the present Act. The offense of ''abuse of dominant position'' creates a civil reviewable matter, providing for remedies when dominant firms are engaging in anti-competitive conduct. The elements to be proved (sec.51) are as follows.

1. ''One or more persons'' must ''substantially or completely control, throughout Canada or any area thereof, a class or species of business.'' This is based on the definition of monopoly in the present Act. By retaining the words ''one or more,'' the Bill applies to single suppliers.

But because there are few situations in Canada where one firm substantially controls its market, the more usual application will be to "joint dominance" situations between nonaffiliated persons. The emphasis is on "dominance," in terms of control, and not on "joint"; the logic is apparently that if the test for dominance is close to "virtual monopoly," then the test for "joint" must be very permissive.

2. The firms or firms must engage in "a practice of anti-competitive acts."[3]

The Bill (sec.50) provides a list of "illustrative" anti-competitive acts:

(a) squeezing, by a vertically integrated supplier, of the margin available to an unintegrated customer who competes with the supplier, for the purpose of impeding or preventing the customer's entry into, or expansion in, a market;

(b) acquisition by a supplier of a customer who would otherwise be available to a competitor of the supplier, or acquisition by a customer of a supplier who would otherwise be available to a competitor of the customer, for the purpose of impeding or preventing the competitor's entry into, or eliminating him from, a market;

(c) freight equalization on the plant of a competitor for the purpose of impeding or preventing his entry into, or eliminating him from, a market;

(d) use of fighting brands introduced selectively on a temporary basis to discipline or eliminate a competitor;

(e) pre-emption of scarce facilities or resources required by a competitor for the operation of a business, with the object of withholding the facilities or resources from a market;

(f) buying up of product to prevent the erosion of existing price levels;

(g) adoption of product specifications that are incompatible with products produced by any other person and are designed to prevent his entry into, or to eliminate him from, a market; and

(h) acquiring or inducing a supplier to sell only or primarily to certain customers, or to refrain from selling to a competitor, with the object of preventing a competitor's entry into, or expansion in, a market.

The list is non-exhaustive so that acts of similar character can be held to be anti-competitive.

3. There must not only be an anti-competitive act, but the "object of the practice" must be to lessen competition. All of the listed anti-competitive acts, and acts of similar character, include consideration of the purpose, object or design of the dominant firm, in evaluating whether the conduct in question is reasonable competitive behaviour. In addition to the purpose or intent of the dominant firm, there is another condition;

4. The anti-competitive practice must have, or be likely to have, "the effect of preventing or lessening competition substantially in a market." This "substantial" test is also found in the new merger proposal and elsewhere in the Bill. The test appears to be an "on balance" weighing that will permit an offset of pro-competitive and anti-competitive factors.

   Can one infer "likely effect" from "purpose or intent?" Probably not, as they are drafted as separate sections. Each of the provisions must probably be met separately: substantial or complete control of a class of business; *and* anti-competitive acts; *and* an object to lessen competition; *and* the effect of preventing or lessening competition substantially.

5. The Bill provides a defence (sec.51(4)), where it is found that competition has been lessened as a result of the superior competitive performance of the firm. C-91 speaks in terms of "performance," not "efficiency." This means that the Tribunal will have to decide whether a lessening of competition resulted from anti-competitive conduct, or from superior competitive performance. The Bill gives no suggestion as to how superior competitive performance is to be measured, thus creating considerable uncertainty in the application of the law. Certainly defences such as experience-curve based "lowest cost producer" strategies can likely now be introduced by an accused firm.

III. RELATED PROVISIONS OF BILL C-91

In looking at the meaning of the new provision on "Abuse of Dominance," it is necessary to also consider three other aspects of Bill C-91; the new adjudicative tribunal, the treatment of conspiracy, and the new provisions on mergers.

Bill C-91 no longer deals with monopolies and mergers as criminal matters. These areas are to be adjudicated under a civil law framework by a specialized Competition Tribunal, which it is hoped will permit more sophisticated judgment and a more flexible process. The Competition Tribunal will be composed of judges from the Trial Division of the Federal

Court, and lay members. A judge will chair the Tribunal. The Tribunal's functions will be strictly adjudicative, with no role in supervising the investigative powers of the Director. Judges alone will determine questions of law, and judges and lay members together will determine factual matters, and questions of mixed fact and law. Only the Director can bring a case before The Tribunal. Appeals from decisions of the Tribunal will be heard by the Appeal Division of the Federal Court.

In discussing the Tribunal, commentators have drawn an analogy between its structure and that of the Australian Trade Practices Tribunal, or the Restrictive Practices Court of the United Kingdom. While there are similarities with both, perhaps a better analogy might be the function of an Administrative Law Judge in hearing section 5 cases under the Federal Trade Commission Act in the United States. A series of FTC cases on "indirect collusion" suggest much as to how the proposed Tribunal might function in hearing "abuse of dominance" cases.[4]

Stemming uncertainty

Unlike merger and monopolization provisions, conspiracy in restraint of trade (sec.32) is retained as criminal law. Two sections are added by Bill C-91. First the uncertainty stemming from the 1980 decision of the Supreme Court of Canada in *Atlantic Sugar* is remedied. This is done by restating the common law standard that the existence of an agreement can be proven from circumstantial evidence with or without direct evidence of communication among the parties. Second, the issue of intent left unclear by the *Atlantic Sugar* and *Aetna Insurance*[5] decisions, is addressed by imposing a "single intent" requirement. It must be proven that the parties intended to and did enter into a conspiracy, but not that the parties intended the conspiracy to lessen competition unduly.

But the important issue here is that the conspiracy provisions, which interact with the "Abuse of Dominance" section, remains under criminal law, and requires a criminal burden of proof. In contrast, "Abuse of Dominance" provisions are civil. Bill C-91 specifically prohibits (in sec.51(7)(a) and 32.01) proceedings being commenced both under Section 32 and 51 on the basis of the same facts; the Department must choose either the criminal or the civil route.

Sections 63 to 72 of the Bill create a civil merger provision, with the test of whether a merger substantially lessens competition. Criteria to be considered include the extent of foreign competition in the market, a "failing firm" test for the acquired company, the availability of substitutes, and barriers to entry. There is also an "efficiency gains" test based on the results of the merger. Because these are relatively easy tests, it is likely that few mergers will be deterred by the provision. Thus, more onus will be placed on policing possible anti-competitive conduct of the merged firms under the "Abuse of Dominance" provisions, and less on preventing the merger in the first place.

The Bill specifically prohibits simultaneous proceedings (in sec.51(7)(b) and 70(b)) under the merger provisions, where an order is also sought under the "Abuse of Dominance" provisions.

Remedies

There are several sections of Bill C-91 which deal with remedies available in "Abuse of Dominant Position" cases. Most important, sec.51 states that on finding anti-competitive acts which meet the tests of "Abuse of Dominant Position," the Tribunal can make an order prohibiting the practice or act. If that is not likely to restore competition in the market, the Tribunal may in addition order any other action, including the divestiture of assets or shares. There is a "Charter of Rights" proviso in the section which states that an order can be made which interferes with the rights of the firm involved only to the extent necessary to achieve the purpose intended — that is, the order can only be remedial, not punitive. Section 28 of the Bill suggests a specific penalty, that the Governor in Council may by order, remove or reduce customs duties where lessening of competition is facilitated by the existence of duties.[6] However no fines or other criminal remedies are provided—only conduct or structural remedies.

There is a provision in Section 76 for the Director of Investigation and Research to apply to the Tribunal for an interim order relating to the anti-competitive practice, but only where an application for a permanent order has already been filed. The process for obtaining an interim order is analogous to that in seeking injunctive relief from a superior court, and is the only answer provided, aside from a concern for future civil damages, to the "why not do it until you get caught" argument.[7]

There is a specific provision (in sec.78) allowing the Tribunal to vary an existing order, or to rescind it, on application by the Director or by the firm, where the circumstances that led to the making of the order have changed, either making the existing order ineffective, or making it unnecessary.

Negotiations

Finally, there is a provision (sec.77) which will undoubtedly find much use, permitting the Director to negotiate an order with the dominant firm, on consent, and to have the Tribunal accept that order without hearing evidence as they would if the order were contested. The negotiated consents may be for original orders or for changes to existing orders of the Tribunal.

Under what conditions may the ultimate remedy, divestiture of assets or shares, be undertaken? Once the Tribunal came to an understanding of the ways in which structure and conduct interrelate to sustain market power and permit anti-competitive acts, it might alter both in order to create change. However under our current legal doctrine of remedies, divestitures are highly unlikely to occur. Indeed the best histories we have to go on are the Section 2 Sherman Act cases involving anti-competitive actions in monopolistic settings, and those cases show that even in the U.S., divestiture is virtually never used.[8] In the earliest important case, the holding company through which Standard Oil exercised control over the oil industry was dissolved, but the holdings were simply conveyed pro-rata to the shareholders, and a national monopoly was replaced by a series of regional monopolies under common control.[9] The 1938 *Alcoa* case ended with an order for divestiture of the Canadian subsidiary, but no dissolution of the U.S. parent.[10] Even in the 1953 *United Shoe Machinery* case, the initial decree provided no structural remedy. It was not until 1968 that the Supreme Court agreed that further relief was necessary, but even then it only worked out a divestiture of assets reducing USM's market share to a still-controlling one-third.[11]

Application to joint monopoly situations

It is clear from the Bill and from the list of anti-competitive acts in Section 50 that the "abuse of dominant position" provision reaches single firm monopolization behaviour. But Section 51(1) makes it clear that the "abuse" can be carried on by more than one firm, and that so long as the several firms involved have substantial or complete control of a business, there is no requirement that there be overt agreement. The Director might bring an Application before the Tribunal based on parallel behaviour, but with no allegation of communication whatsoever, so long as all the members of the control group follow the same practices.

Put simply, oligopoly theory argues that the "joint-monopolist" firms in an industry with few members face two tasks: to establish a mutual consensus regarding the correct price and/or division of market, and to develop some mutual understanding that there will be adherence to the consensus— that there will not be any cheating.[12]

In some industries, interdependent competitors find it easy to "think alike," and an initial consensus and understanding is reached through a "meeting of minds," with no communication or signalling other than the mutual awareness of their interdependence. But this situation is uncommon. Most oligopolies because of the number of size distribution of firms, product differentiation, or cost characteristics of the product, require some mechanism greater than a simple "meeting of minds" to arrive at a stable consensus. This is so-called conscious parallelism plus activity, some of which is clearly intended to be reachable under "abuse of dominant position."

At the other extreme, there are industries where competitors appear to require formal collusion, through direct communication and sometimes with written agreements as to price and markets.

The case of formal collusion would almost always be dealt with under the Section 32 conspiracy provisions, with criminal law sanctions.[13] The other extreme is consensus through a meeting of minds with no communication or signalling. This would certainly not be considered conspiracy, and would likely not be successfully attacked under the "dominant position" provisions either because "purpose or intent of lessening competition" could not be established, or because the "superior competitive performance" defence in sec.51(4) would prevail.

How might "abuse of dominant position" provisions be applied to joint monopolists involved in oligopoly practices such as basing point pricing formulas, information exchange, augmented price leadership, or price protection agreements?

Basing-points

The first of these, basing point pricing, is the most straightforward.[14] Joint monopolists sometimes seek to avoid price competition in markets such as cement, which feature homogeneous products and high shipping costs. They find a complication when customers and are suppliers geographically dispersed, because a different delivered price exists for each customer from each supplier. The problem is simplified if all adopt a convention that the delivered price equals list price at the plant site, plus the published shipping tariff from one or two agreed upon "basing points" to the customer. A further protection against error or uncertainty comes from distributing the published shipping rate-lists to all.

In such an arrangement, the adoption of delivered-pricing-only arrangements by all firms (plus perhaps the distribution of shipping rates) becomes the "plus" factor in "conscious parallelism plus" behaviour. Delivered pricing arrangements are traditionally attacked under conspiracy provisions, because they imply a tacit agreement that customers near a firm's own plant will not receive any reduction in price reflecting the lower transportation costs of servicing.[15] However Bill C-91 specifically lists (sec.50(c)) freight equalization as an example of an anti-competitive act that will be attacked under "abuse of dominant position," rather than under conspiracy. This may either be an attempt to add importance to the "abuse of dominance" provision, or may reflect a strong lack of confidence in the conspiracy provision.

Information exchange

Exchanges of information among joint monopolists may be used as a coordinating mechanism in an oligopoly situation.[16] Where sales information is not public, data on recent selling prices signals to competitors that movement in the price has occurred, and permits competitors to follow quickly. If price changes are communicated before they take effect, the result may be identical to that of direct collusion. Information about competitor's actual sales volume changes is an indicator of the use or non-use of secret discounts. Often, not all firms in an industry exchange such information. But signalling purposes may be fulfilled even if only a few firms unilaterally provide such information about their own activities. The extreme case is actual exchange of invoices or sales volume printouts to permit monitoring of price or volume changes.

In such extreme cases, exchange of information might certainly be attacked under the "abuse of dominant position" provision. There will be problems however in non-extreme cases given the existence of a "superior competitive performance" defence. It can be argued that information exchanges to have a pro-competitive effect because they provide firms with a better understanding of market conditions. Information exchanges might also be considered as simply more efficient ways of obtaining data that could be obtained independently—for example supermarket chains exchanging computer price printouts, in lieu of each doing manual store price checks on all others.

Price leadership

Augmented price leadership, or "leadership plus," takes place in an industry where having a non-competitive price even for a short period of time may result in a substantial loss of volume. The usual oligopoly situation where one firm changes its price, others observe the price change and decide whether to match the first price or post some other price, may in this type of industry prove unsatisfactory.

A common result is a price setting situation in which one firm publishes a new price list to take effect weeks after the publication date. Competitors see the new prices and publish their own revised prices, either matching the first list or modifying it. The originator may withdraw its original list and substitute a new one as several rounds of proposals and counterproposals occur. Rival firms become aware of all aspects of the consensus price, and signal through their price lists that they will adhere to the new consensus. Such "leadership plus" can have effects identical to those of direct communication and agreement among competitors.

Does such behaviour violate the "abuse of dominant position" provisions? In most cases, probably not. Even if the "leadership plus" is interpreted as an anti-competitive act, it would be difficult to establish that the object of the practice is to lessen competition. Rather, the conduct might be considered reasonably competitive behaviour in an oligopoly situation. To establish lessening of competition, there might have to be an additional factor such as the price leader lowering prices for a period of time to discipline those who did not follow the new price.

Price protection

Price protection contracts are guarantees by sellers to their customers, that the price they receive will be the lowest granted to any customer for a specified future period. Thus a customer will receive a rebate if someone else negotiates a lower price within that period. Any but the least risk-adverse buyers will seek and accept such a guarantee, because it protects them from an inability to bargain as well as rivals.

Sellers like to see price protection contracts offered by their competitors. This is because such contracts inhibit selective price cutting by reducing margins on all sales rather than on incremental ones. Sellers might not wish to enter into such a contract with their own customers, but may be forced to do so by competitive pressure when such contracts are the industry standard. Of course the firm may voluntarily enter into such a contract to constrain its own future actions, by providing assurances to competitors that it will not cut price.

Is a price protection contract an anti-competitive act under the "abuse of dominant position" provision? Again, probably not. The first firm to offer such a contract may invoke the "reasonable competitive behaviour." It may argue that it is differentiating its offering to secure business. The second and subsequent firms may claim they are forced to follow suit for competitive purposes. The net result of such contracts may be "lessening competition sustantially," but the "object of the practice" for each individual firm is benign.

IV. CONCLUSION

Without much doubt, the provisions in C-91 which deal with "abuse of dominant position" are a considerable improvement over the monopoly provisions found in Section 33 of the Combines Investigation Act. The changes reflect the less benevolent competitive environment faced by Canadian industry in the 1980s, as well as evolving approaches to competition policy in the U.S. and elsewhere, and treat as a civil reviewable matter practices which are not generally considered to be criminal behaviour.

The new provisions appear to be effective in dealing with anti-competitive actions by single-firm monopolists, but arguably less effective applied to joint-monopolist situations. The combination of having to meet separate tests of substantial or complete control of a class of business, *and* anti-competitive acts, *and* an object of lessening competition; *and* the effect of preventing or lessening competition substantially, *plus* the need to overcome the "superior competitive performance" defence, will probably eliminate most of the "conscious parallelism plus" situations found in oligopolistic industries. Those situations which are caught, such as basing-point pricing systems, could arguably be attacked equally well using the conspiracy provision.

Notes

1. Bill C-91, "An Act to establish the Competition Tribunal and to amend the Combines Investigation Act and the Bank Act and other Acts in consequence thereof," 1st Session, Thirty-third Parliament, 33-34 Elizabeth II, 1984-85. The Combines Investigation Act is R.S.C. 1970, c.C-23, as amended.

2. *Remarks to the Press* Regarding Competition Law Amendments By The Honourable Michel Côté, Minister of Consumer and Corporate Affairs Canada, Ottawa, December 17, 1985, Speech S-85-28.

3. The wording of 51(1)(b) is "That person or *those* persons have engaged in or are engaging in a practice of anti-competitive acts...," implying that *all* persons must be engaging in the practice.

4. Early cases of interest are *FTC v. Cement Institute*, 333 U.S. 683 (1948), and *Triangle Conduit & Cable Co. v. FTC*, 168 F.2d. 175 (7th Cir. 1948). Later cases which indicate the evolution of thought are *Boise Cascade Corp. v. Federal Trade Commission*, 637 F. 2d 573 (9th Cir. 1980), and most importantly, the "indirect collusion" approach of the FTC in *Ethyl Corp.*, No.9128 (F.T.C. Aug.5, 1981).

5. *Atlantic Sugar Refineries Co. Ltd. et al v. The Queen*, 2 S.C.R. 644 (1980); *Aetna Insurance Co. et al v. The Queen*, 75 D.L.R. (3d) 332 (1977).

6. The likelihood of removal or reduction of customs duties should not be overstated. Since 1948 there have been 14 references re tariff reduction, but only one which was implemented. That involved plate glass in 1953-54, and was granted in conjunction with a Tariff Board request for the same reduction.

7. An application to the Tribunal on abuse of dominant position must be made not more than three years after the practice has ceased (sec.51(6)). But given that fines are not available, what remedy would the Director ask, several years after cessation of the practice? Only an order that the practice not be used in the future.

8. Indeed the lack of divestiture in the U.S. cases occurred in spite of the existence there of the so-called "fruits doctrine." This asserted that the structural remedy of divestiture was appropriate even when it was not needed to deal with the defendant's conduct. Divestiture was warranted simply where the defendant had acquired something he would not have acquired without anti-competitive behaviour. The fruits doctrine could not be adopted by the proposed Tribunal because of the "Charter of Rights" proviso discussed in the text.

9. *Standard Oil Co. of New Jersey v. United States*, 221 U.S. 1, (1911), Page 17.

10. *United States v. Aluminum Co. of America*, 91 F. Supp.333 (S.D.N.Y. 1950).

11. *United States v. United Shoe Machinery Corp.*, 110 F. Supp. 295 (D.Mass. 1953), affd per curiam 347 U.S. 521 (1954); and 391 U.S. 244 (1968).

12. Discussions of joint monopoly, oligopoly theory and competition policy may be found in H. Goldshmid, H. Mann and J. Weston, eds. *Industrial Concentration: The New Learning* (1974); Turner, "Definition of Agreement Under The Sherman Act; Conscious Parallelism and Refusals to Deal, *Harvard Law Review* 75 (1962) at 655; Posner, "Oligopoly and the Antitrust Laws: A Sug-

gested Approach, *Stanford Law Review* 21 (1969) at 1562; Posner, *Antitrust Law: An Economic Perspective* (1976). Discussions of signalling theory are Blechman, "Conscious Parallelism, Signalling and Facilitating Devices: The Problem of Tacit Collusion Under the Antitrust Laws," *New York Law School Law Review* 24 (1979) at 881; or G.A. Hay, "Oligopoly, Shared Monopoly and Antitrust Law," *Cornell Law Review* 67 (1982) at 439. The most complete overview of the Canadian cases is W.T. Stanbury and G.B. Reschenthaler, "Oligopoly and Conscious Parallelism: Theory, Policy and The Canadian Cases," *Osgoode Hall Law Journal* 15 (1977), at 617.

13. Written communication was central to the conviction for conspiracy by Mr. Justice Pennell of Canadian General Electric, Westinghouse Canada and GTE Sylvania Canada under the old section 32(1)(c). Mr. Justice Pennell cited eight pieces of documentary evidence, including letters to competitors discussing "inadvertent breaches" of list prices. *R. v. Canadian General Electric et al*, 29 C.P.R. (2d)(1976).

14. See "Note, Conscious Parallelism in the Use of Delivered Pricing Systems: A Modified Per Se Standard of Review Under the Federal Trade Commission Act," *Cornell Law Review* 66 (1981) at 1194; Kaysen, "Basing Point Pricing and Public Policy," *Quarterly Journal of Economics* 63 (1949), at 289.

15. If the basing point system is far from the supplier's plant, nearby customers may pay a much higher price than distant ones. The joint refusal of competitors to reward nearby customers with lower prices has served as circumstantial evidence of conspiracy in U.S. cases.

16. The classic information exchange case is *United States v. Container Corp.*, 393 U.S. 333 (1969). See also Posner, "Information and Antitrust: Reflections on the Gypsum and Engineers Decisions," *Georgetown Law Journal* 67 (1979), at 1193.

THE AUTHOR

Donald J. Lecraw is Professor, Centre for International Business Studies, School of Business Administration, The University of Western Ontario. He received a B.S. in physics from Stanford, an M.B.A. from Harvard Business School, and a Ph.D. in Business Economics from Harvard University. He has published widely on the multi-national enterprise, industrial organization and competitive policy, choice of technology, economic development, and international trade. He was Chief Economist for the Royal Commission on Corporate Concentration and a member of the Advisory Board on Industrial Structure for the Macdonald Royal Commission. He has done work for the Economic Council of Canada, the Institute for Research on Public Policy, and the U.N. Centre on Transnational Corporations.

Chapter Eleven

Industry Structure and Competition Policy*

Donald J. Lecraw

I. INTRODUCTION AND APOLOGIA

Competition policy in Canada must be formulated and administered in relation to Canada's basic economic structure. This, in turn, is largely determined by Canada's natural resource base, its relatively small population and large geographic size, and its proximity to the large U.S. market. Current technology in many industries also dictates that to achieve scale efficiency, operating units and firms be of a size which is large relative to Canada's small domestic markets. Scale efficiency implies high concentration in many industries. Yet high industry concentration potentially allows firms to engage in noncompetitive behaviour. If so, the efficiency gains from achieving economies of scale are not passed on to the consumer, but rather accrue to the firm's owners, managers, and workers or are wasted through X-inefficiency. The high level of foreign ownership in Canada sharpens this problem to the extent that efficiency gains leading to supranormal profits may accrue to the foreign shareholders in the corporation.

*The research for this paper was partially funded by the Centre for International Business Studies, School of Business Administration, The University of Western Ontario.

The goals of any competition policy should be to foster efficiency and dynamism by corporations. In many industries large scale operations at the plant and firm level may be necessary to achieve these goals. Firms can achieve efficiency goals through internal growth, mergers and acquisitions, joint ventures, specialization agreements, export consortia, etc. These activities are necessary if Canadian industry is to be globally competitive and to improve on its dismal record of productivity growth. Yet competition policy must also try to ensure that these efficiency gains accrue to the Canadian consumer. These twin goals are recognized in Bill C-91 (p.7, "Purpose"):

> The purpose of this Act is to maintain and encourage competition in Canada in order to promote the efficiency and adaptability of the Canadian economy, in order to expand opportunities for Canadian participation in world markets while at the same time recognizing the role of foreign competition in Canada, in order to ensure that small and medium sized enterprises have an equitable opportunity to participate in the Canadian economy and in order to provide consumers with competitive prices and product choices.

These will be difficult goals to attain at best for any competition policy. They will be especially hard to achieve in Canada given its basic market structure.

The next section of this paper presents a brief review of the theoretical and empirical basis of industrial organization, with particular reference to Canada. This serves as the background for the formulation of Competition Policy. Section III provides a summary of the structural aspects of recent attempts to formulate a competition policy in this country, and Section IV briefly reviews one aspect of Bill C-91 related to industry structure.

II. INDUSTRIAL ORGANIZATION: THEORY AND EVIDENCE

The structure-conduct-performance (SCP) paradigm is one of the most fundamental and widely used methods of analysis in industrial organization. It forms the theoretical basis for many of the sections of Bill C-91, especially those dealing with mergers and acquisitions, joint ventures, specialization agreements, and "abuse of dominant position." These sections are designed to improve industry performance in Canada by altering the conduct of firms and by influencing the structure of some industries and markets.

The SCP paradigm posits relationships between "basic conditions" in an industry, its structure, conduct, and performance in terms of allocational, technical, and dynamic efficiencies. It also has implications for the distribution of income between suppliers, producers and consumers.[1] The SCP paradigm has been used, developed, and tested empirically since it was first introduced by Mason (1959).[2] Empirical tests of the SCP paradigm have been carried out in all industrialized countries and in several less developed nations as well.[3] These studies have usually found a statistical link between industry structure variables and industry performance as measured by profitability, price cost margins, or various other efficiency measures. In general they support the conclusion that as industry concentration and barriers to entry rise and as exposure to international trade decreases, performance in terms of efficiency and equity declines. Taken together these studies provide support for government action via competition. In this view economic performance can be improved by using the SCP paradigm to identify industries in which undesirable performance is likely to exist. As well, basic industry conditions, structure, conduct, and even industry performance can be altered directly.

Government policy

This can be done by changing supply and demand conditions through trade, tariff, and public sector procurement policies. Government can alter industry structure through its merger, research and development, advertising and foreign ownership policies. Small and medium-sized firms can be enhanced through direct government investment, or incentives. Industry can be regulated via laws that prohibit certain types of conduct — price fixing, market sharing, retail price maintenance, delivered pricing, etc. Finally, government can try to affect performance directly through such means as regulation of prices, profits and investment, or through public ownership (Crown Corporations).

Governments in Canada and other high income countries have used some combination of all of these initiatives to try to increase the allocative, technical, dynamic, and X-efficiencies of their economies to improve the equity of the distribution of income for groups and regions, to increase economic stability and growth, as well as to address a host of non-economic concerns such as national security, national unity, etc.

There seems to be a growing consensus in Canada and abroad, however, that many of these initiatives both have not achieved their goals and have had undesirable side-effects on other areas of national concern. As a consequence, industry deregulation and the privatization of government operations and government-owned firms have become increasingly used.[4]

In competition policy there has also been a re-thinking, both in Canada and abroad, away from an activist stance by government. There are now fewer attempts to influence industry structure through merger policies. The move has been toward a more laissez-faire approach that relies to a greater degree on market dynamics and less on government intervention. This trend toward a less interventionist competition policy may have been fostered by four factors:

1. Increased evidence has been uncovered that large firm size in many industries is necessary for efficient operations. I.e., there are economies of scale out to very large plant and firm sizes, and mergers are often undertaken to achieve these economies of scale rather than to enhance market power.
2. Industry structure as it affects performance has been found to be far more complicated than was described in the original formulation and testing of the SCP paradigm (see, for example, Bain, 1956). Attempts to change industry structure directed solely or even primarily against concentration have not had the results envisioned. In fact, there have been many unforseen, and even perverse, consequences.
3. There has been increased awareness and concern over the competitive position of national firms in a globally competitive world trade, production and investment environment. In the face of large national and multi-national enterprises abroad, highly mobile capital and technology, and falling tariff and non-tariff barriers to trade, there has been a re-ordering of anti-combines policy.
4. Starting in the late 1970s, there has been a movement toward the election of more conservative governments. They are more predisposed toward allowing the market determine economic outcomes rather than use government intervention in the micro economy as a means of determining those outcomes.

We shall take these points in order:

Efficiency

The linchpin in the SCP paradigm has been the positive relationship between industry concentration and industry profitability. The relationship has been demonstrated statistically in a host of studies over the past few decades. The increased profitability that was found to accompany high concentration, however, could arise from two sources: greater efficiency of the large firms that usually populate concentrated markets, or the market power of firms in concentrated industries (Williamson, 1968). Up to and through the mid-1970s, although there was vigorous debate, probably most industrial organization (I/O) economists believe the second explanation for the profit-concentration relationship.[5]

Since that time, however, a number of studies have concluded that first, economies of scale are available to large firms even in such markets as the United States; and second, that accessing these economies of scale may be the major motivation for horizontal and vertical mergers. For example, Buzzell (1981, pp.47-48) found that in the United States total costs as a percentage of price adjusted sales were 96.8 percent for firms with small market shares compared to 92.7 percent for firms with large market shares. In other words, profits/price-adjusted sales were 2.9 times higher for firms with large market shares than for those with small shares. Spence (1981) concluded that not only are there economies of scale, but that as production volume increases (both in terms of output/time and total accumulated output) firms in many industries move down a learning curve and achieve lower costs per unit of output. Spence (1981, p. 68) concluded: "An attempt to enforce competition by deconcentration, implemented through explicit or implicit limits on market share, runs the risk of reducing the technical efficiency of industries with moderate learning curves."

Recent evidence

Recent studies of the scale problem for Canadian industry by Baldwin and Gorecki (1983a,1985b) used previously unavailable, highly disaggregated, plant level data. They reached several strong and important conclusions. The scale problem for Canadian manufacturing industries is far more severe than had previously been found on two dimensions: average plant size in Canada was much smaller than that in the United States, and the penalties in terms of lower value added per worker arising from sub-minimum efficient scale operations are large.[6] Their studies also showed that average relative plant size had increased in Canada relative to that in the United States over the period 1970-1979 (Baldwin and Gorecki, 1983a). The major determinant of subscale operation in this country was the size of the Canadian market, particularly in concentrated, tariff-protected industries. Baldwin and Gorecki (1985a, p.435) concluded:

Two policy implications can be drawn. First, a competition policy that aims, as a matter of policy, at reducing the degree of concentration as a way of increasing competition will have to incur, as a cost, increased small plant market share and its attendant suboptional capacity.

Beyond the (low) growth rate of markets in Canada, firms can increase their size by exporting (if they are producing internationally tradable products), internal growth, or merger. The first two routes to increased scale efficiency are difficult to pursue. To grow via exports requires the firm to be (at least) cost competitive on an international basis. Yet this in turn requires at least minimum efficient scale to start with. Internal growth faster than the increase of the entire market implies growth at the expense of competitors, a difficult, risky, costly and time consuming process at best. Hence Globerman's (1977, p.44) conclusion that:

> ... we interpret the evidence for Canada as being more supportive of an economies-of-scale motive [for mergers]. We are inclined to reject the hypothesis that mergers are primarily motivated by the desire to restrict competition.

Industrial concentration

Despite this sanguine conclusion, it must be firmly borne in mind that Canadian industry is highly concentrated. However, there are many problems with any given measure of industry concentration. In general, the more aggregate the measure of an "industry" using the SIC classifications, the more heterogeneous the products assigned to that industry and the lower the measure of industry concentration (Green, 1985, pp. 57-72). Ideally, products that compete directly with each other (i.e., for which the cross elasticity of demand is high) should be classified as belonging to the same industry. No statistics are publically (or privately?) available on the concentration of Canadian industry on this theoretically correct basis. Whatever level of industry aggregation is used, however, it is safe to say that Canadian concentration ratios are significantly higher than those in the United States, even when adjustment is made for international trade exposure (Baldwin, Gorecki, 1983a).[7] Khemani (1985) reported that concentration levels in Canada fell continuously in highly concentrated industries and rose in low concentration industries from 1948 to 1980. When manufacturing industries are disaggregated into individual product categories (the 5-digit level) concentration levels are seen to be generally very high in Canada with over 95 percent of a products (representing 75 percent of shipments value) with

C_4* greater than 50 percent. If international trade and interproduct competition were factored into these figures, C_4 would drop dramatically, but the effects of regional industries would push C_4 higher (Khemani, 1985). A word of caution is in order here. At present, market structure is measured only very simplistically by concentration ratios. Any analysis of this data is difficult and open to a wide variety of interpretations. Under Bill C-91, it will be up to the Tribunal to disentangle this complicated maze. It will have to decide the appropriate trade off between the increased industry concentration and firm market share and the increased scale of efficiencies that may arise from increased firm size. And this is no simple task.

Complexity

Over the past ten years, our knowledge of industrial organization and industrial dynamics has increased tremendously, although there is, of course, still much more to learn. One of the most important conclusions of this work is that use of the SCP paradigm is often overly simplistic and in many instances leads to incorrect conclusions. It is beyond the scope and space limitations of this paper to give a thorough and complete summary and evaluation of this important literature. It has been reviewed by Caves (1980) and presented in book-length form by Porter (1980, 1984). Several studies, however, should be mentioned as they are of direct relevance to the formulation and implementation of competition policy in Canada.

Kwoka (1979) found that in the United States industry profits rose above the competitive level as the market shares of the two largest firms in an industry increased, but fell to the competitive level as the market share of the third largest firm increased. Hence a merger that would increase the market share of the third largest firm in an industry would tend to increase industry performance even though industry concentration as measured by C_4 increased. Stonebreaker (1976) found that low profitability among small firms in an industry increased the perceived risk of entry and hence acted as a barrier to entry. Baldwin and Gorecki (1983b) came to a similar conclusion for firms in Canada: poor performance among small firms in an industry was the single most powerful and consistent barrier to new entry in industries in Canada from 1970 to 1979. Hence a merger between a large

---

*C_4 is the four-firm concentration ratio: the percentage of sales (revenues, output, etc.) accounted for by the 4 largest firms in the industry — ed.

firm and a smaller, less profitable business, although it would increase industry concentration, would also tend to *lower* barriers to entry and arguably *increase* the level of industry competition and hence performance. Porter (1979, p.226) concluded:

> ... important differences exist in the structural features that explain profit levels for differently situated firms in an industry ... this test does add support for the view that the structure within industries has an important influence on firm profitability.

Similarly Dalton and Esposito (1981) concluded:

> The important implication of this broader approach to industry analysis is that size may not be the primary determinant of competitive behavior and performance .... Thus, the difference between the traditional [SCP] model and the strategy formulation model is not merely one of emphasis, but one of substance ... the public policy implications of each model can be quite different.

Empirical studies in Canada

Khemani (1985) replicated Shepherd's (1982) U.S. study using data on Canadian industries. He divided industries within the major sectors of the economy into three groups: Oligopolistic Industries, Government Supervised or Regulated Industries, and Effectively Competitive Industries. The assignment to "oligopolistic industries" was based primarily upon C_4, but import exposure, trends in the number of enterprises, ease of entry, market share stability, and history or evidence of anti-competitive practices were also factored in. Two results of this analysis stand out: a) government supervised or regulated industries comprise a higher proportion of the Canadian economy than of the U.S. economy; b) in general, Canadian industries are less effectively competitive than those in the United States. Despite these conclusions, Khemani (1985, p.33) concluded:

> ... based on the observations that (i) industry concentration levels have decreased generally and also in highly oligopolistic industries over the 1970-80 period, (ii) there has been entry by firms in virtually all industries, (iii) there has been turnover among the ranks of leading firms in the great majority of industries and (iv) there has also been an increase in import penetration; one may conclude that the structural con-

ditions in the manufacturing industries of Canada are changing such as to result in increased competition.

This is an encouraging conclusion (particularly coming from a member of the Bureau of Competition Policy) and one that should be investigated for other sectors of the economy.

Another development in industrial organization economics is also germane to competition policy in Canada. This is the theory of "contestable markets" of Baumol, Panzar, and Willig (1982). A perfectly contestable market is one in which: a) all producers have access to the same technology; b) scale economies, but no sunk costs exist; c) incumbents cannot change prices instantly; and d) consumers respond to price differences. If a market is perfectly contestable, then post-entry oligopoly is irrelevant, strategic entry deterrence is impossible, and performance will approximate the competitive norm.

As Dixit (1982, p. 16) concluded:

> This theory has important normative features. Equilibrium in an "as if contestable" market, when one exists, provides a much better benchmark for social policy than an unrealistic "as if competitive" standard under natural monopoly or oligopoly. This serves to focus regulatory policy towards removing barriers to contestability. [Yet] as a positive theory of market structure, it needs careful handling.

Similarly, Schmalensee (1982, p.27) concluded:

> As in macroeconomics, increased uncertainty about the consequence of intervention argues against attempts to fine-tune performance [via anti-trust policy]. Attempts to make marginal changes in inherently imperfect markets are certain to be expensive and may not increase efficiency even if successful ... enforcement agencies should thus concentrate their efforts in areas (like price fixing) ... [but] in other areas of the law (like monopolization), they should at least hesitate to bring cases....

The theory of contestable markets has served to focus attention on entry and exit barriers and firm mobility in and out of industries. Shapiro and Kheman (1985, pp. 22-23) concluded:

> We observe a high positive correlation between entry and exit across industries because barriers to entry restrict the amount of displacement

and exit ... our results suggest that *de novo* entry is unlikely to be a source of significant short-term de-concentration.

Khemani and Shapiro (1985, p. 16) reached similar conclusions:

> Domestic *de novo* firms stand last in the queue of potential entrants ... Foreign and incumbent firms face no significant barriers to mobility ... Firms which enter by diversification are not deterred by structural barriers to entry, but are deterred by high levels of concentration and specialization.

The theory of contestable markets then is highly relevant to the concerns of Canadian competition policy and should be used as a tool for analyzing the effects of mergers, joint ventures, speculation agreements, etc., on the Canadian economy. This task will not be easy since markets are highly complex and there are few simple rules for structural analysis. This conclusion should lend caution to the Tribunal whenever its decision may effect industry structure and serve to focus its attention on anti-competitive conduct of firms in Canada's concentrated industries.

Foreign trade

Global competition has become one of the buzzwords of the 1980s. As a consequence of falling tariff and non-tariff barriers to trade, enhanced international mobility of capital, increasingly rapid international diffusion of technology, and the growth of multinational enterprises based in many countries, exports and imports as a percent of GNP have increased significantly for most countries. As well, the more rapid growth of several European countries and Japan relative to the United States has led both to an increase in the number of large firms internationally and to an increase in the number of large, non-American firms.

The rise in international competition between nations and between large firms in many industries has important implications for national competition policy. In such global industries, if a firm does not have the size and capabilities to compete worldwide through investment, research and development, production, and sales, it may be doomed to failure over the long run. Hence a competition policy that limits firm size will have an adverse effect on the national economy. This evolution toward global competition has led even economists such as Thurow (1980, 1983) to change their minds about the efficacy of government's use of competition laws to restrain firm size.

Thurow now sees large firm size as a necessity for competitive survival in many industries. In such cases, international competitive pressures can serve as a check on anti-competitive behaviour and supranormal profits that might previously have accompanied large size and highly concentrated industries. This conclusion would seem to hold with even greater force in Canada given its much higher levels of import penetration and export dependence and the relatively small size of its firms.

Bill C-91 seems to recognize the imperatives of global competition. It is filled with references to being or becoming competitive on export markets and competing more effectively with imports via mergers, specialization agreements, and joint ventures. In fact the Bill (and the background papers distributed with it) read as if they were introduced during some sort of "National Export Week."

To this point, the knowledgeable reader might question why this paper has at best been fighting victories already won and at worst beating a dead horse. If the industry structure components of Bill C-91 had incorporated the major features of "Proposals for Amending the Combines Investigation Act, A Framework for Discussion" (Department of Consumer and Corporate Affairs, 1981), this discussion of economies of scale, the complexity of industrial markets, and the imperatives of global competition might be necessary, and even beneficial, once again. But the industry structure components of Bill C-91 would seem to be almost entirely dissimilar (even opposite) of those in the previous "Proposals." In fact, the Bill explicitly recognizes the importance of economies of scale, factors other than concentration in industrial structure, and the importance of being competitive on export markets and in competing with imports.

However, Bill C-91 as it currently stands is flawed in two respects: 1) It does not give sufficient recognition to the three points outlined above in its sections on mergers and acquisitions and "abuse of dominant position"; 2) in several instances its guidelines for the Tribunal are too broad (i.e., leave the Tribunal with too little direction and too much discretion), too restrictive (i.e., leave the Tribunal too little leeway to take into consideration all the aspects of the effects of a merger), non-operational, or just plain incorrect and counterproductive.

III. STRUCTURAL ASPECTS OF PAST COMPETITION BILLS

Before analyzing the industry structure aspects of Bill C-91, a very brief review of the industry structure aspects of previous proposed laws might be useful. Various bodies in Canada have been studying how Canadian competition policy could be reformed since the 1960s. The Economic Council of Canada (1969) made sweeping recommendations for change in Canada's competition policy. This report viewed competition essentially as a means toward achieving the goal of economic efficiency. To this end, it recommended dividing combines laws into two parts: one to prohibit collusive agreements to fix prices and allocate markets, resale price maintenance, and misleading advertising; the other to set up a "Competitive Practices Tribunal" to determine when mergers, specialization agreements and "restrictive trade practices" are not in the public interest. These recommendations were incorporated in Bill C-256, but there was substantial resistance to many of its sections. In response, the government split the Bill into two "stages." The first clarified "unduly," prohibited bid rigging, extended the Act to services, and changed the misleading advertising sections; the second stage included the more controversial sections on mergers, monopolization, specialization agreements, etc. Stage I was passed in 1975; Stage II was delayed to be studied further. This review was completed by Sheock and McDonald (1976) who recommended the formation of a Board to evaluate mergers and some anti-competitive practices. The Director could bring proposed or past mergers to the Board for review and possible prohibition (for a proposed merger) or dissolution (for a past merger). If the Board found the merger would have (or had) "with reasonable probability" the "effect of creating or enhancing artificial restraints in a market to a significant extent" and this effect was not "on balance offset by real-cost economies or by diminution of other artificial restraints," then the Board could dissolve or prohibit the merger. These and other recommendations (on joint monopolization and price differentiation) were incorporated in Stage II (Bill C-13) introduced in 1977. This Bill also met with extreme and widespread opposition and was ultimately dropped.

In 1981, Andre Ouellet, Minister of Consumer and Corporate Affairs, circulated "Proposals for Amending the Combines Investigation Act: a Framework for Discussion." Instead of a Tribunal, the civil courts were to be used. Mergers and "joint monopoly" were to be ruled *per se* illegal (with no efficiency defense) if the combined market share of the merged firm were above some uniform threshold for all industries. These proposals met a storm of protest and were not introduced as law in Parliament. This was fortunate since the uniform threshold would have had terrible structural effects on the Canadian economy. For example, Khemani (1985) calculated that at the 5-digit SIC level in 1980, 2,324 of the 4,131 products had a C_4 of 100 percent (and Khemani has told me verbally that for the majority of these products C_1 and C_2 were 100 percent), while 3,378 (82 percent) had a C_4 greater than 80 percent. Given that many (most) firms produce in multiple product categories, a *per se* ban on mergers based on a market share threshold (and if market share was defined to be at the 5-digit level, apparently a real possibility), would have prohibited most mergers in Canada. Yet the Economic Council of Canada (1969, p. 86) found that between 1945 and 1961 only 8 percent of all mergers "might have qualified for a public interest examination" (see also in this regard Block, 1982).

The threshold

In April, 1983, Bill C-29 was introduced. It retained the civil courts provision of Ouellet's Proposal, but dropped the *per se* illegality of mergers with a market share above some threshold level. Mergers could have been prohibited or dissolved if they prevented or lessened competition and did not bring about efficiency gains that would result in a "substantial real net savings of resources for the Canadian economy." This Bill also failed to be passed into law.

Finally, on December 17, 1985, Bill C-91 was given its first reading. Bill C-91 once again places the Stage II sections of competition policy, including the mergers section, under a Tribunal and changes the criteria for action against a merger to one that (Sec. 64[2]) "prevents or lessens, or is likely to prevent or lessen, competition substantially" unless there are "gains in efficiency that will be greater than, and will offset the effects of any prevention or lessening of competition" (Sec. 68[1]). The industry coverage is (Sec. 64[1]): "in a trade, industry or profession" and their sources and outlets, excluding firms falling under the Bank Act and those in regulated industries. Crown Corporations are now included within the jurisdiction of the Tribunal, but with an override provision by the Prime Minister. Note the evolution of criteria for rejecting mergers from "not in the public interest" (C-256), to "enhancing artificial restraints" (Skeoch, McDonald, C-13), to a *per se* market share threshold (Proposals) to "preventing or lessening competition" (C-29 and C-91). The mitigating factors have changed from "net benefits" (C-256), to "offsetting real cost economies" (C-13), to no offsetting factors (Proposals) to "real net savings of resources" to "gains in efficiency" (C-29 and C-91). These represent successive attempts to wrestle with the fundamental structural dilemma of the Canadian economy posed at the start of this paper: to achieve efficient operations in many industries requires large size and (in Canada) concentrated industries which in turn may lead to undesirable effects on competition, and most importantly, on performance.

IV. INDUSTRY STRUCTURE AND BILL C-91

With this background we can briefly examine one structural aspect of Bill C-91 in more detail. The general criterion in C-91 for evaluating a merger is "preventing or lessening competition." C-91 defines what is meant by this in Sec. 64(2):

> For the purpose of this section, the Tribunal shall not find that a merger or proposed merger prevents or lessens, or is likely to prevent or lessen, competition substantially *solely* on the basis of concentration or market share [emphasis added].

In commenting on the Ouellet Proposals, Lecraw (1981, p. 487) wrote:

> ...the use of concentration ratios and market shares as the *sole* structural variables toward which attention and actions are directed may lead to inappropriate actions [emphasis added].

C-91 seems to have taken this statement into account. Although the Tribunal will have discretion in defining "solely," nonetheless it presumably will operate using the wording of the Bill as a guide. But "solely" implies at least "primarily" and perhaps "overridingly." If this were the *de facto* definition, then C-91 would feature some of the worst effects on mergers of the Proposals. As C-91 presently stands we will have to wait until the Tribunal's decisions are handed down. This would place heavy onus on the members of the Tribunal and shows the importance to be placed on its composition.

Bill C-91, Sec. 68(2) defines the efficiency basis for allowing a merger as:

> In considering whether a merger or proposed merger is likely to bring about gains in efficiency described in Subsection (1), the Tribunal shall consider whether such gains will result in:
>
> a) a significant increase in the real value of exports, or
> b) a significant substitution of domestic products for imported goods.

This is all the guidance given the Tribunal in determining if a merger would lead to increased efficiency. This format may cause problems for three reasons: 1) There is the possibility that these two measures of efficiency would be interpreted to be the only valid evidence for efficiency gains; 2) even if this were not to happen, undue attention might be focused on trade gains from increased efficiency, while efficiency gains in non trade exposed industries might not be taken into account or given due attention; 3) increased exports or decreased imports are not necessarily evidence of efficiency gains or evidence that these gains, if any, would accrue to Canada. Finally, a few words about the composition of the Tribunal. Under Sec. 3(2), the Tribunal shall consist of four members selected from among the judges of the Federal Court-Trial Division and eight "other members" appointed by the Governor in Council, possibly with the advice of an advisory council, "representatives of the business communities, the legal community, consumer groups and labour." It would be highly unfortunate if the lay members of the Tribunal were selected to give coverage of various interest groups (as is common in Canada): labour, business, government, the West, the East, francophones, anglophones, etc. The Tribunal does not need advocacy, it needs balance and expertise.

Notes

1. See Sherer (1980) for a complete exposition of the SCP paradigm.

2. See also E.H. Chamberlin, (1933), Joan Robinson (1961).

3. See Scherer (1980) for a review and evaluation of this literature and Green (1985) for a similar, if less exhaustive, review of the SCP literature for Canada.

4. See the many papers and the Interim and Final Reports of the Economic Council of Canada, Regulation Reference on these points.

5. A group of I/O economists loosely known as the Chicago School actively supported the efficiency explanation, however. The two sides of the controversy are presented in Goldschmid *et al.* (1974).

6. Depending on the measure used, average Canadian plant size was between 60 percent and 71 percent of that in the United States. If Canadian plants were to expand in size to those in their counterpart industry in the United States, output per worker would increase by 10-15 percent (Baldwin and Gorecki, 1983a, 1985b).

7. See Green (1985) and Khemani (1985) for comparative statistics.

THE AUTHOR

Edwin G. West received his Ph.D. in economics from London University. A member of the economics department at Carleton University, he has been a visiting professor at Oxford, Berkeley, Virginia Polytechnic Institute, Emory and the University of Chicago. A prolific writer, Dr. West is author of over a dozen books and no fewer than one hundred articles in scholarly journals. His main areas of interest include the economics of education, public choice, minimum wages, history of economic thought, and particularly the work of Adam Smith.

Chapter Twelve

Canada's Competition Act in the Light of U.S. Experience: A Cautionary Tale

Edwin G. West*

INTRODUCTION

Although more common in the U.S., the word ''antitrust'' summarizes legislative-cum-judicial attempts to reduce anti-competitive behaviour in the marketplace. Since this is indeed the announced purpose of the Competition Act proposed for Canada, and since it is a briefer expression, the term ''antitrust'' will be used throughout this essay. Antitrust discussion, experience, and activity in the U.S. is undoubtedly more ''mature,'' more analyzed, and more thoroughly documented than it is in Canada. It is accordingly appropriate to draw upon salient aspects of the ongoing American debate especially where they have an obvious bearing upon Canadian proposals.

To a large extent the suggested Canadian Competition Law Amendments are general in their scope and are being introduced with proportionately more expressions of aspiration than of details of specific content. Consider for example the Minister of Consumer and Corporate Affairs' statement that

*I have benefited from discussion on this subject with Fred McChesney, David Haddock and Peter Aranson of the Economics Department, Emory University, Atlanta.

an effective competition law should improve the efficiency of the Canadian economy, enhance our international competitiveness, and ensure fairness in the marketplace for small business and consumers. This initiative will reduce the need for direct government intervention, and place greater reliance on market forces and the private sector for economic renewal.[1]

The desirable effect of the proposed legislation is conditioned on the competition law being "effective." But this remains to be seen. Much depends on who is appointed to offices in the proposed Tribunal and on the members' particular philosophies and adopted analytics. Things could move in alternate directions. To take one example: the probability of the reduction in the need for government intervention (see the previous quotation) depends on the nature, size, and rate of growth of the antitrust bureaucracy that eventually emerges. Experience in the U.S. is not very encouraging. The FTC is, after all, one of the largest and least monitored of American administrations.

II. INTELLECTUAL STATUS OF ANTITRUST

Many of the intellectual foundations of antitrust in the U.S. appear to have been steadily crumbling. In particular, the traditional use of structuralist models of the economy to assess efficiency has been under considerable attack for many years. This is true especially of the employment of concentration ratios as a measure of market dominance by particular firms. Despite the fact that the U.S. Department of Justice still relies on guidelines containing an index of market concentration (the Herfindahl Index) that measures the proportion of total industry output accounted for by a particular firm, empirical work by Brozen and Demsetz remains a serious challenge to their relevance. As early as 1970 Brozen argued that if collusion is an increasing function of market concentration the above-average profits stemming from it should persist over time.[2] His research findings, however, were consistent with the view that the above-average profits were short-lived. Such profits appeared to encourage industry entry, after which there was the eventual decline of prices as well as profits.

Demsetz, meanwhile, concentrated on other reasons (besides collusion) for any relationship between concentration and profitability.[3] His data indicated that larger firms in concentrated industries operated at a lower cost than their competitors. The biggest firms in industries with concentration ratios in excess of 50 percent produced at below average cost. The higher rates of return experienced by these firms were attributed by Demsetz to their superior performance rather than to collusive practices.

Counter-productivity

Obviously, legal judgment based on simple concentration ratios as an indicator of undesirable monopoly power can, if Demsetz's findings are general, result in a *decrease* in national efficiency. This point is relevant to Canada. Depending on the types of models used and the nature of the quantity of evidence employed, several features in its new Competition Act *could* be counter-productive of its own stated objectives. Although it is provided that the proposed Tribunal in Canada "would not be permitted to find that a merger substantially lessens competition *solely* on the basis of evidence of market share or concentration,"[4] concentration ratios, nevertheless, will obviously continue to have *some* weight.

The nature of the outcome of the activities of the proposed Tribunal will depend also upon the economic training of its members. To those educated in neoclassical economics monopoly will be viewed primarily as the polar opposite to the now familiar "perfect competition" of the textbooks. Others, with a different training, will emphasize that "perfect competition" implies perfect decentralization wherein exchange costs happen to be zero. Yet in the real world, they will insist, exchange is not costless so that competition can be consistent with a wide variety of institutions that are employed to accommodate time, uncertainty, and the costs of transacting.[5] Such arrangements include, for example, tie-in sales, vertical integration and manufacturer-sponsored resale price maintenance. Such price-making behaviour follows from the fact that in the real world decentralization is imperfect.

III. MONOPOLY AND WELFARE

The neoclassicists will regard as important a well-known empirical methodology that measures the social costs of monopoly in terms of a comparison with its supposed polar opposite market structure of perfect competition. The most influential study of this type to date has been that of the Chicago economist Harberger.[6] It will be useful to produce a summary of his analysis here since it can be used at various points in our discussion as a bench mark or point of comparison.

Harberger's basic argument can be summarized in terms of Figure 1. Assume that long-run average costs are constant for both firm and industry and are represented by the line $M_c = A_c$. The perfectly competitive output would be at Q_c where M_c intersects the demand curve DD. If a monopolist were substituted he could maximize profits by producing Q_m at price P. His monopoly profit, u, would be represented by the rectangle ABCP. The loss of consumers' surplus is measured by the trapezoid AECP. The part of this area represented by ABCP, however, is not destroyed welfare but simply a transfer of wealth from consumers to the monopolist. The net loss to society as a whole from the monopoly is given by the "welfare triangle" ABE denoted in Figure 1 by w.

After making some heroic assumptions, in particular that marginal cost (M_c) was constant for all industries and that the price elasticity of demand was unity everywhere, Harberger estimated an annual welfare loss of $59 million for the U.S. manufacturing sector in the 1920s. To many people this figure was surprisingly small since it represented only one tenth of one percent of the U.S. national income for that period. Subsequent writers have argued that Harberger's measure was a serious underestimate for statistical and other reasons. But all such criticisms have been of a technical nature and implicitly accept Harberger's basic methodology.

Price discrimination

Consider next another type of qualification. In the frictionless world of the neoclassical model where all exchange costs are zero, it would be profitable for the monopolist to produce more than Q_m in Figure 1. This would be the case, for example, with the institution of a two-part tariff where a second price is charged for all purchases in excess of Q_m. If this price were located exactly halfway between P and C it could be shown that the triangle of welfare loss would shrink to one quarter of the existing size of w. An extension of such multi-part pricing, of course, would reduce the welfare triangle of loss still further. With the presence of zero exchange costs, which is assumed in the neoclassical world, *perfect* price discrimination is possible. This implies the fullest kind of multi-part pricing wherein the number of prices reaches infinity. In this case the whole of the trapezoid CPAE would consist of transferred wealth from consumers to producers. Deadweight welfare loss from monopoly would be zero.

If the neoclassical analyst objects that perfect price discrimination does not exist in the real world, he has to offer reasons. It is difficult, meanwhile, to conceive of any practical explanation that could be couched in terms of anything else than significant costs of exchange, such as, for instance, positive information costs and risk. But such explanation undermines

Figure 1

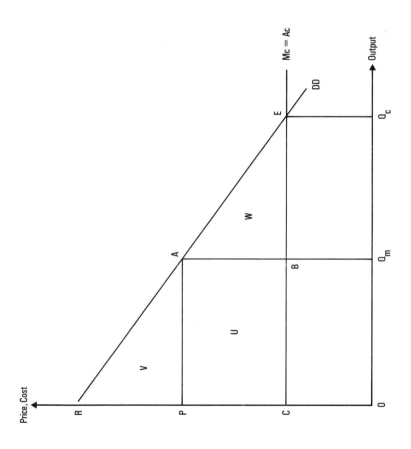

the "purity" of the neoclassical model and returns us in the direction of the classical world of *imperfect* decentralization featuring real world limitations on knowledge, and the existence of dynamic change under uncertainty.

An alternative view

Consider next the attitude and approach of members of an imagined antitrust tribunal who have received a *classical* training. Again we may employ Figure 1. But first recall that, instead of the notion of perfect competition as a static long-term equilibrium (as in neoclassical economics), they will start with the view of competition espoused by Adam Smith and his successors, as a process of rivalry within a time dimension. In the setting of the classical dynamic economy, it is the possibility of profit that drives the innovating entrepreneur. But once profits are obtained by a successful pioneer, his operation is immediately copied by others so that there is a constant tendency for entrepreneurial profit to be competed away. It is this focus on a continual series of short runs that distinguishes this analysis from that of "perfect competition" which is always expressed in terms of the very long run.

Assume then the discovery of a new product, call it X, by an entrepreneur who proceeds to offer Q_m of it at price P (see Figure 1). It is only academically true that he is restricting output compared with what potential rivals would produce if they possessed his knowledge and business acumen. But since, in reality, they do not, the only alternative to Q_m supply of product X is some positive quantity of conventional products that the factors were previously producing (the supply of X being zero). The result of his activity in producing X, therefore, is pure social gain, and this is measured in Figure 1 by the profit plus the consumer surplus v (APR). The welfare triangle of social loss (w) does not exist.

Rivalrous competition

It can be expected, of course, that the entrepreneur's action will lead to the eventual entry of rivals. At this stage competition will lead to a lowering of price towards cost. This process will then involve a transfer of wealth from the original entrepreneur to consumers. *But the latter's original and temporary profit is necessary to induce him to introduce the product, and at an earlier time than otherwise.* It is this earlier introduction that indeed produces the social gains. So while such temporary profit may be viewed as proceeding from the market structure of "imperfect competition," nevertheless, according to this "classical" analysis, the monopolies so described are necessary institutions since economic growth would be much weaker without them. Indeed, society recognizes such logic when it grants temporary legal monopolies in the form of patents.

In the past, the type of economics that has been informing U.S. antitrust bodies has, in large, been that of a neoclassical (static) kind. But, to be consistent, the neoclassicists should have long ago examined typical antitrust practice to see whether it conforms to their theory in terms of Figure 1. Yet research based on this approach has only recently been conducted (and by outside analysts). It suggests, in fact, that the U.S. government's selection of antitrust cases has *not* been based primarily on considerations of consumer welfare (as measured by the welfare triangle ABE in Figure 1).[7] Other research concludes, meanwhile, that the real issues concern politics more than economics.[8]

IV. POLITICS

Since antitrust rules are legislated, their association with politics is, of course, inevitable. But the political dimension may be viewed at several levels. Some observers believe that antitrust rules originate, at least ideally, at the constitution making level rather than at the post-constitutional day-to-day political stage. To some, the purest ideal would envisage citizens deciding on optimum laws from behind a "veil of ignorance" from where they produce the basic social contract. They would be doing this from the perspective of individuals who have yet no precise knowledge of their own fortunes in society, not knowing, for instance, whether they will be rich, poor, workers, businessmen, or government officials. While not necessarily going back this far, many people in the U.S. believe in fact that the antitrust laws are "our competitive constitution," and that the Sherman Act, in particular, is the "Magna Carta" of free enterprise. "Born in that gilded era of "robber barons" and their "greedy trusts," the Sherman Act put the government in the business of saving consumers from the higher prices and restricted outputs that, supposedly, would characterize the untrammeled operation of free enterprise."[9]

In a similar vein the Minister of Consumer and Corporate Affairs Canada has introduced his new Bill with the observation: "Competition law is like a constitution — a Charter for the marketplace."[10] But such a statement is much more difficult to accept in this country, and for several reasons. First it seems incongruous to speak of a "charter for the marketplace" in a nation like Canada that has recently and explicitly adopted a new basic constitution wherein recognition of individual property rights has been deliberately excluded. Second, the method proposed for establishing the Competition Act engages a political process that is altogether different from that of constitution-making (which involves, for instance, some form of special constitutional convention). Third, there is evidence that the proposed legislation is that of a post-constitutional day-to-day government which depends upon the voter loyalty of interest groups to secure a simple majority (rather than a near unanimous vote). This is contained in the emphasis by the Minister that "We have consulted extensively, listening not only to business interests, small and large, but to the provinces, to consumers, and to organized labour."[11] But "organized labour" is itself a monopoly and one that is beyond the reach of antitrust. A labour union will politically support a product monopoly if it belongs to its own employer, for then union members may share with the entrepreneur the monopoly rents obtained from consumers. The latter will normally be too dispersed to have much political influence. On the other hand, the union will oppose a product monopoly that supplies its employer with inputs.

A paradox

More important still, competition may be far from adequate in the (post-constitutional) *political* process. Indeed some economics literature in the U.S. now contains sophisticated analysis suggesting that in most democracies the very institution of government is usually a monopoly.[12] If this is true, we face a highly paradoxical situation. Public policy prescription described in the textbooks is, after all, a process whereby monopoly in general is policed or controlled by an institution that is itself a monopoly, and one that openly consults other monopolies about the appropriate modification of its antitrust laws. To the innocent neoclassical prescriber of "optimum" competition policy, the real world outcome in such circumstances is likely to be untidy, perplexing, unpredictable, and often counter-productive.

Those in the U.S. who still see some specially profound dimension in their original Sherman Act of 1890 are on the intellectual defensive. They must concede that it is not usual to expect pure constitutional outcomes (as described above) to proceed from special interest group politics that surround the normal 50 percent majority voting process. It is perhaps surprising that research into this paradox has for a long time been neglected. But in 1985 DiLorenzo produced evidence challenging the presumption that the original intent of the Sherman Act was to promote competition in an increasingly monopolized economy.[13] It is generally agreed that the main targets of the Act were the late nineteenth century trusts. In retrospect, however, DiLorenzo found that, far from causing output to fall (as would follow, for instance, in the monopolistic action in Figure 1 where quantity falls from Q_c to Q_m and price increases from OC to OP), the trusts caused output to expand faster than the rest of the economy and, in some cases, more than ten times faster, for decades at a time. As a result, moreover, their prices were *falling*. The latter phenomenon was not only recognized by Congressional opponents of the trusts, but it was the subject of their complaint that falling prices drove less efficient "honest men" out of business. DiLorenzo concludes:

> There was relatively little enforcement of the Sherman Act for at least ten years after it was passed, but it did serve to immediately divert attention from a more certain source of monopoly, tariffs, which were sharply increased just three months after passage of the Sherman Act by a bill sponsored by Senator Sherman himself.

V. THE ANTITRUST INDUSTRY

Robert Reich now argues that, in the U.S., antitrust has become an industry on its own, serving its own interest groups and exhibiting a stubborn capacity for survival.[14] There is, he argues, a demand and supply for antitrust. In their purchases and sales within this market, buyers and sellers very often seek to profit from antitrust in ways that are not conducive to the public welfare. The interests of consumers tend to become neglected because they are too disorganized to purchase antitrust at all. Smaller firms, on the other hand, have more incentives to use the industry. They can, for instance, utilize antitrust to ward off an unfriendly tender offer or to obtain protection against discounting. Larger firms, meanwhile, might purchase antitrust immunity. They can often do this, for instance, by buying enough antitrust defence to deter a plaintiff from initiating an action against them.

Part of the industry, Reich argues, consists of the government antitrust bureaucracies. Predictably, these strive for high budgets and look for the maximum amount of work to do. To this end, government enforcers are apt to sell sheer numbers of cases regardless of their social benefit. And, as always, lawyers are at work in *their* own self-interest. Plaintiffs' counsel are apt to link defendants and plaintiffs according to the likely return on the time and effort involved in counselling. The result is that: "Outside defence counsel are apt to overprescribe their antitrust services."[15]

VI. COSTS AND BENEFITS

All the above considerations raise the crucial question whether antitrust is worth the expense. The information package on Canada's new Competition Act put out by Consumer and Corporate Affairs speaks only of potential benefit and not at all about the potential costs. It will now be obvious that the costs are not confined to the stipends of tribunal members and the salaries of the administrators of the antitrust structure. They include, in addition, all the payments made to legal counsels, the opportunity costs of business personnel in reading briefs or attending court, and the vast quantity of expensive consultancy advice to the defence and/or prosecution. If the objective of the Competition Law is to restore the consumers' surpluses contained in triangles such as ABE in our Figure 1, the total costs of doing this, just specified, may be well in excess of the benefits.

Another important cost associated with the failures of American antitrust is associated with its rigid adherence to *per se* rules. The U.S. Supreme Court, for instance, appears intransigent in its insistence on such a rule against vertical price fixing.[16] In the words of McChesney (1986),

> Everyone knows the decision is wrong as a matter of economics, and no political or social rationale is offered to justify the rule either. Yet the Supreme Court continues to adhere to its *per se* rule against maximum price fixing and treble-damage suits against newspaper publishers for price fixing continue to succeed. What is remarkable is not that the Courts have got it wrong — to err is human — but that everyone knows that it is wrong, and yet no change is forthcoming.

Another example of unyielding adherence by the Court to *per se* rules is that of tie-ins. These are viewed as invariably anti-competitive despite logical demonstration that tying can be a useful way of protecting a firm's brandname, ensuring quality and promoting safety.[17]

Traditional hostility

Consider also the Federal Courts' traditional hostility to collusive price fixing and information exchanges. Such a stance is now under open challenge from analysts. Donald Dewey, for instance, argues that, provided there is free entry, economic welfare will be greater under a legal system that permits collusion than under one that effectively suppresses or restrains it.[18] The effects of legalizing collusion, according to Dewey, will include the reduction in uncertainty and will therefore lead to lower costs of investment and fewer marketing mistakes. By reducing uncertainty the fraction of national income invested will increase. The case is different where entry is not free; but such barriers are typically attributable to government legislation, including tax laws, franchise requirements, safety standards, and import quotas.

Some of the announced prior conditions in Canada's Competition Act suggest a similar tendency towards *per se* rules. Consider especially the new civil provision designed to cover delivered pricing. The Ministry's *Guide* (p. 24) complains that the present legislation does not contain a specific provision that can deal with the competition problems associated with delivered pricing arrangements. It is concerned with the practice of a supplier charging freight rates in different zones at levels higher than the actual cost so that price is not uniform and some prices are above competitive levels. As Haddock (1983) has shown, however, this reasoning neglects the possibility that the supplier may be operating where average cost is higher than marginal cost and average costs are above the demand curve at all points. In this situation no uniform price charged to all consumers will allow the firm to survive. Somebody must pay the overhead costs of the firm and one way is for some buyers to pay more of the overhead than others. If the firm is not allowed to do this it will fail and this will be to the detriment of customers as well as of shareholders.[19]

The point of all these observations is that because phenomena such as price-fixing, tie-ins, collusion and delivered pricing have been demonstrated to promote market efficiency, at least in many circumstances, then where these same arrangements have been suppressed indiscriminantly by antitrust action, it must reduce potential national income. To this extent it must impose serious costs on society, costs that should enter into any comprehensive cost/benefit analysis.

VII. COMPETITION AND FAIRNESS

It has been argued in the U.S. that, in its original antitrust design, Congress had a preference for small businesses on political grounds.[20] Yet if small businesses cannot survive because of the greater competitive edge of larger organizations, the use of antitrust to protect the former occurs at the cost of a significant efficiency loss. There is, in other words, a trade-off between "fairness" and efficiency. If these two objectives do underlie the legislation, then the outcome of most court cases is likely to be much less predictable. Even on its own terms, however, the concept of "fairness" is questionable. If, by protecting small but less efficient businesses, the general price level is higher than otherwise, this situation would appear to be grossly *unfair* to consumers. And some consumers have incomes below the official poverty level. In any case, even if there is a political desire to redistribute income on the grounds of "fairness," however defined, there are other more traditional and more appropriate mechanisms for effecting it. The antitrust machinery is, in other words, too clumsy an instrument for this purpose.

Advocates of the Canadian Competition Law Amendments appear not to be entirely clear on this issue. On the one hand they explain that "if competitors fall from the market because a dominant competitor is more effective in meeting consumers' needs, this is not an abuse of market power, but rather a natural consequence of the competitive process."[21] On the other hand they observe "there is a clear need to strengthen the legislation to ensure *fairness* in the marketplace and maintain the drive and initiative of the small business sector which has enormous potential for job creation."[22] It is interesting that the economics of politics predicts that governments will be prejudiced towards small businesses. This is so (a) because, collectively, they have more votes than large businesses, (b) because of the lower costs of organizing and the more concentrated benefits, the small businesses will have a greater incentive to undertake political lobbying than consumers, who are costly to organize and to whom the benefits are more widely diffused. And we have seen that work by DiLorenzo (above) suggests that the smaller business interests enjoyed disproportionate influence in the passing of the U.S. Sherman Act.

Consider now the Ministry of Consumer and Corporate Affair's statement, produced in the previous quotation, to the effect that the small business sector has "enormous potential for job creation." This raises the question whether full employment is appropriately the responsibility of an antitrust tribunal or whether such policy is better implemented through the traditional channels. In any case the claim that small businesses create more jobs is ultimately empirical and the source of the evidence for it is not mentioned in the *Guide*. It is interesting to note, meanwhile, that recently completed U.S. research on the relation between antitrust enforcement and employment finds that antitrust has had *adverse* consequences.[23]

Conclusion

What of the new enthusiasm shown by the Ministry of Consumer and Corporate Affairs Canada for the potential that it believes a revised Combines

Investigation Act will have in promoting competition? It comes at a time when belief in the effectiveness and purposes of antitrust in the U.S. are increasingly under attack, and this for all the reasons set out above. Falling confidence is found especially among the economics profession, as any sampling of the learned journals will demonstrate. But even outside the sphere of systematic analysis the disenchantment appears widespread. Indeed it covers the ideological spectrum from left to right. On the left, John Kenneth Galbraith describes antitrust as a "charade" and calls it the "last eruption of the exhausted mind."[24] Lester Thurow concludes "antitrust has been a failure. The costs it imposes far exceed any benefit it brings."[25] Rather than amend the present antitrust law, Thurow would prefer to abolish it altogether because it is standing in the way of America, Inc.[26] On the right the libertarian economist Dominick Armentano would repeal antitrust as a "fraud" and a "hoax" since even Court-decreed bans on collusion impede efficiency.[27]

Experience in the U.S. shows that antitrust courts make errors which they often refuse to correct. In addition, Robert Reich and others have demonstrated the ways in which special interest groups abuse antitrust law for personal gain. The costs involved in this latter phenomenon, as with those connected with the errors of judicial decision-making, are far from trivial. It is not to be expected that Canada is so far different from the U.S. that such costs are not likely to be present here also. This being the case it may well be that a new Competition Act which sharpens the teeth of the Canadian antitrust system will result in a *reduction* in efficiency, despite the claims of its advocates to the contrary.

Notes

1. Letter from Michel Côté, for public circulation, Ministry of Consumer and Corporate Affairs, December 17, 1985.

2. Y. Brozen, "The Antitrust Task Force Deconcentration Recommendation," *Journal of Law and Economics,* 1970.

3. H. Demsetz, "Industrial Structure, Market Rivalry and Public Policy," *Journal of Law and Economics* 1973.

4. *Competition Law Amendments: A Guide* (hereafter Guide), Consumer and Corporate Affairs, Canada, December 1985, p. 17 (my italics).

5. Harold Demsetz, *Economic, Legal, and Political Dimensions of Competition*, Professor Dr. F. DeVries *Lectures in Economics* No. 4, North Holland, Amsterdam, 1982.

6. A.C. Harberger, "Monopoly and Resource Allocation," *American Economic Review, Proceedings*, Vol. 44, (May), pp. 73-87, 1954.

7. Long, Schramm and Tollison, "The Determinants of Antitrust Activity," *Journal of Law and Economics* 16 (1973); Siegfried, "The Determinants of Antitrust Activity," *Journal of Law and Economics* 17 (1975).

8. Faith, Leavens and Tollison, "Antitrust Pork Barrel," *Journal of Law and Economics* 25 (1982).

9. Fred S. McChesney, "Law's Honour Lost: The Plight of Antitrust," forthcoming 1986, *Antitrust Bulletin*.

10. Remarks to the Press Regarding Competition Law Amendments by Michel Côté, Minister of Consumer and Corporate Affairs Canada, Ottawa, December 17, 1985.

11. Remarks to the Press, December 1985.

12. Geoffrey Brennan and James Buchanan, *The Power to Tax*, Cambridge University Press, 1980.

13. T.J. DiLorenzo, "The Origins of Antitrust: An Interest Group Perspective." *International Review of Law and Economics*, 5, (1985).

14. Robert Reich, "The Antitrust Industry," *Georgetown Law Journal*, 68 (1980).

15. Reich, p. 1070. For a general survey of findings similar to those in Reich, and including accounts of systematic positive economic research, see W.F. Shughart and Robert D. Tollison, "The Positive Economics of Antitrust Policy: A Survey Article," *International Review of Law and Economics*, 5, (1985). In this piece the authors argue that "the antitrust bureaucracy operates much like regulatory bureaucracy in general."

16. The key case has been *Albrecht v Harold Company* 390US 145(1968). The most recent instance has been *Northwest Publications, Inc. v. Crumb* 752F. 2d 473 (9 Cir. 1985).

17. See Eisenach, Higgins and Shughart, "Warranties, Tie-ins, and Efficient Insurance Contracts: A Theory and Three Case Studies," *Research in Law and Economics* 6, (1984).

18. Donald Dewey, "Information, Entry and Welfare: The Case for Collusion" *American Economic Review* 69, 1979.

19. David D. Haddock, "Basing-point Pricing: Competitive vs Collusion Theories," *American Economic Review* 72, June 1983.

20. G. Pitofsky, "The Political Content of Antitrust," *University of Pennsylvania Law Review* 127 (1979).

21. *Guide,* pp. 22, 23.

22. *Guide,* p. 34, (italics supplied).

23. Shughart and Tollison, "The Employment Consequences of the Sherman and Clayton Acts" (Manuscript 1985). Quoted in McChesney above.

24. Quoted in Eleanor M. Fox and James T. Helverson (eds.) *Antitrust Policy in Transition: The Convergence of Law and Economics* ABA Press, 1984, p. 23.

25. Lester Thurow, *The Zero-Sum Society* (1980).

26. The New York Times, October 19th 1980.

27. D. Armentano, *Antitrust and Monopoly: Anatomy of a Policy Failure* (1982).

Bibliography

Armentano, Dominick. *Antitrust and Monopoly: Anatomy of a Policy Failure* (1982).

Armentano, Dominick. *The Myth of Antitrust.* New Rochelle, New York: Arlington House, 1972.

Armstrong, Donald E. *Competition versus Monopoly.* Vancouver: The Fraser Institute, 1982.

Bain, J. *Barriers to New Competition.* Cambridge, Mass.: Harvard University Press, 1956.

Baldwin, J. and Gorecki. "Trade, Tariffs, and Relative Plant Scale in Canadian Manufacturing Industries: 1970-1979." Economic Council of Canada, Discussion Paper No. 232, 1983.

Baldwin, J. and P. Gorecki. "Entry and Exit to the Canadian Manufacturing Sector: 1970-1979." Economic Council of Canada, Discussion Paper No. 225, 1983b.

Baldwin, J. and P. Gorecki. "The Determinants of Small Plant Market Share in Canadian Manufacturing Industries in the 1970s." *Review of Economics and Statistics,* Vol. 67, No. 1, 1985a.

Baldwin, J.R. and P.K. Gorecki. *The Role of Scale in Canada-U.S. Productivity Differences.* Royal Commission on the Economic Union and Development Prospects for Canada, Vol.6 (Ottawa: Queen's Printer, 1985b).

Baumol, William J. "Contestable Markets: An Uprising in the Theory of Industry Structure." *American Economic Review,* March 1982, Vol. 72, pp. 1-15.

Baumol, William J. and James A. Ordover. "Use of Antitrust to Subvert Competition." *Journal of Law and Economics,* Vol. 28, No 2, May 1985, pp. 247-65.

Baumol, W.J., J.Panzar, and R.D.Willig. *Contestable Markets and the Theory of Industry Structure.* San Diego: Harcourt Brace Jovanovich, 1982.

Becker, Gary S. *Economic Theory.* New York: Alfred A. Knopf, 1971.

Bertrand, Robert J. "The Marketing of Gasoline" in *The State of Competition in the Canadian Oil Industry.* Ottawa: Ministry of Supply and Services, 1981.

Bingham, Robert H. "The Uniform Delivered Pricing Method in the Grocery Manufacturing Industry." *Journal of Marketing,* Vol. 14, 1950, pp. 594-600.

Block, Walter. *A Response to the Framework Document for Amending the Combines Investigation Act.* Vancouver: The Fraser Institute, 1982.

Block, Walter. "Austrian Monopoly Theory—A Critique." *Journal of Libertarian Studies,* Vol. 1, No. 4, 1977.

Bork, Robert H. *The Antitrust Paradox: A Policy at War with Itself.* New York: Basic Books, 1978.

Brenner, Reuven. *Betting on Ideas: Wars, Invention, Inflation.* Chicago: University of Chicago Press, 1985.

Brenner, Reuven. *Competition: The Leapfrogging Game.* Forthcoming, Cambridge: Cambridge University Press, 1987.

Brenner, Reuven and Léon Courville. *Gasoline Marketing.* Shell Canada Ltd., 1982.

Brozen, Yale. "The Antitrust Task Force Deconcentration Recommendation." *Journal of Law and Economics,* 1970.

Brozen, Yale. *The Competitive Economy: Selected Readings.* Morristown, New Jersey: General Learning Press, 1975.

Carlton, Dennis W. "A Reexamination of Delivered Pricing Systems." *Journal of Law and Economics,* Vol. 26, April 1983, pp. 51-71.

Caves, R.E. "Corporate Strategy and Structure." *Journal of Economic Literature,* Vol.18, No.1, 1980.

Caves, R.E., M.E. Porter, A.M. Spence and J. Scott. *Competition in an Open Economy.* Cambridge, Mass.: Harvard University Press, 1980.

Chamberlin, E.H. *The Theory of Monopolistic Competition.* 1933, 7th ed.; Cambridge: Harvard University Press. 1956.

Choffray, Jean-Marie and Gary L. Lilien. *Market Planning for New Industrial Product.* New York: John Wiley and Sons, 1980.

Clark, J.M. "Basing Point Methods of Price Quoting." *Canadian Journal of Economics and Political Science,* Vol. 4, November 1938, pp. 477-89.

Clearwaters, Keith I. Quoted in "Innovations, Competition and Antitrust Laws." *Research Management,* Vol. 21, No 3, May 1978, p. 4.

Demsetz, Harold. "Industrial Structure, Market Rivalry and Public Policy." *Journal of Law and Economics* 1973.

Demsetz, Harold. *Economic, Legal, and Political Dimensions of Competition*: Professor Dr. F. DeVries *Lectures in Economics* No. 4, North Holland, Amsterdam, 1982.

Department of Consumer and Corporate Affairs. "Proposals for Amending the Combines Investigation Act." mimeo, Ottawa, 1981.

Dewey, Donald. "Information, Entry and Welfare: The Case for Collusion." *American Economic Review* 69, 1979.

DiLorenzo, T.J. "The Origins of Antitrust: An Interest Group Perspective." *International Review of Law and Economics,* 5, (1985).

Dixit, A.K. "Recent Developments in Oligopoly Theory." *American Economic Review,* Vol.72, No.2, May 1982.

Economic Council of Canada. *Interim Report on Competition Policy.* Ottawa: Queen's Printer, 1969.

Faith, Leavens and Tollison. "Antitrust Pork Barrel." *Journal of Law and Economics* 25 (1982).

Fisher, Franklin M., John J. McGowan and John E. Greenwood. *Folded, Spindled and Mutilated: Economic Analysis and U.S. v.s. I.B.M.* Cambridge, Mass.: M.I.T. Press, 1983.

Fox, Eleanor M. and James T. Helverson (eds.). *Antitrust Policy in Transition: The Convergence of Law and Economics.* ABA Press, 1984, p.23.

Gee, Edwin A. and Ch. Tyler. *Managing Innovation.* New York: John Wiley and Sons, 1976.

Globerman, Steven. *Mergers and Acquisitions in Canada.* Ottawa: Supply and Services Canada, 1972.

Globerman, Steven. "The Consistency of the Foreign Investment Review Act: A Temporal Analysis." *Journal of International Business Studies,* Summer 1984.

Globerman, Steven. *U.S. Ownership of Firms in Canada.* Montreal: C.D. Howe Research Institute, 1979, pp.86-94.

Globerman, Steven. "The Report of the Royal Commission on Corporate Concentration and Its Implications for Competition Policy," in J.R.S. Prichard, W.T. Stanbury and T.A. Wilson, *Canadian Competition Policy: Essays in Law and Economics.* Toronto: Butterworths, 1979.

Goldschmid, H., H.M. Mann and J.F. Weston. *Industrial Concentration: The New Learning.* Boston: Little Brown, 1974.

Green, C. *Canadian Industrial Organization and Policy.* Toronto: McGraw-Hill Ryerson, 1985.

Haddock, David D. "Basing-Point Pricing: Competitive vs. Collusive Theories." *American Economic Review,* Vol. 72, June 1982, pp. 289-306.

Hammond, D.L. "R & D in the Electronics Industry," in W.N. Smith et al. (eds), *Industrial R & D Management.* New York: Marcel Decker Inc., 1982.

Harberger, A.C. "Monopoly and Resource Allocation." *American Economic Review, Proceedings,* Vol. 44, (May), pp.73-87, 1954.

Ijiri, Yuje and Herbert A. Simon. "Business Firm Growth and Size." *American Economic Review,* Vol. 54, March 1964, pp. 77-89.

Jensen, M.C. "Takeovers: Folklore and Science." *Harvard Business Review,* Nov.-Dec. 1984.

Jentes, William R. "Assessing Recent Efforts to Challenge Aggressive Competition as an 'Attempt to Monopolize." *Antitrust Law Journal,* Vol. 49, No 3, pp. 937-52.

Johnson, James C. "How Competitive Is Delivered Pricing?" *Journal of Purchasing and Material Management,* Summer 1976, pp. 26-30.

Khemani, R.S. and D.M. Shapiro. "On Entry and Mobility Barriers." mimeo, Bureau of Competition Policy, Department of Consumer and Corporate Affairs, Ottawa, March 1985.

Khemani, R.S. "The Extent and Evolution of Competition in the Canadian Economy," in McFetridge (ed), *Canadian Industry in Transition.* Royal Commission on the Economic Union and Development Prospects for Canada, Vol.2, Ottawa: Queen's Printer, 1985.

Kirzner, Israel. *Competition Entrepreneurship.* Chicago: University of Chicago Press, 1973.

Kolko, Gabriel. *The Triumph of Conservatism.* Chicago: Quadrangle, 1967.

Lecraw, Donald J. and Donald N. Thompson. *Conglomerate Mergers in Canada.* Ottawa: Supply and Services Canada, 1977.BB

Lecraw, D.J. "Proposals for Amending the Combines Investigation Act — a Business Economist's View." *Canadian Business Law Journal,* Vol.5, 1981.

Lecraw, D.J. et al. *Economics of Industrial Policy and Strategy,* Royal Commission on the Economic Union and Development Prospects for Canada, Vol.5, Ottawa: Queen's Printer, 1985.

Long, Schramm and Tollison. "The Determinants of Antitrust Activity." *Journal of Law and Economics* 16 (1973); Siegfried, "The Determinants of Antitrust Activity." *Journal of Law and Economics* 17 (1975).

Mason, E. *Economic Concentration and the Monopoly Problem.* Cambridge, Mass.: Harvard University Press, 1959.

McEntee, Joseph L. and Robert C. Kahrl. "Damages Caused by the Acquisition and Use of Monopoly Power." *Antitrust Law Journal,* Vol. 49, No 1, pp. 165-200.

McGee, John S. "Predatory Price Cutting: The Standard Oil (N.J.) Case." *Journal of Law and Economics,* October, 1958.

Noonan, John T. Jr. *Bribes.* New York: MacMillan, 1984.

Pearson, John W. "Organizing the R & D/Manufacturing/Marketing Interface in a Large Diverse Product Line Company," in W.N. Smith et al. (eds), *Industrial R & D Management.* New York: Marcel Decker Inc., 1982.

Peltzman, Sam. "Issues in Vertical Integration Policy." in J.F. Weston and S. Peltzman, eds. *Public Policy Toward Merger.* Pacific Palisades: Goodyear Publishing Company, 1969.

Pitofsky, G. "The Political Content of Antitrust." *University of Pennsylvania Law Review* 127 (1979).

Plouffe, Alain. "Le recours aux lois antimonopoles afin d'éliminer la compétition." Rapport de recherche présenté à la Faculté des études supérieures, Université de Montréal, December 1985.

Porter, M.E. *Competitive Advantage.* New York: Free Press, 1985.

Porter, M.E. *Competitive Strategy.* New York: Free Press, 1980.

Posner, Richard A. *Antitrust Law.* Chicago: University of Chicago Press, 1976.

Robinson, Joan. *The Theory of Imperfect Competition.* 2nd ed.; New York: St. Martin's Press, 1961.

Rothbard, Murray. *Man, Economy and State.* Los Angeles: Nash, 1970, chapter 10.

Scherer, F.M. *Industrial Market Structure and Economic Performance.* Chicago: Rand McNally College Publishing Co., 1980.

Schmalensee, R. "Antitrust and the New Industrial Economics." *American Economic Review,* Vol. 72, No. 2, May 1982.

Shapiro, D.M. and R.S. Khemani. "The Determinants of Entry and Exit Reconsidered." mimeo, Bureau of Competition Policy, Department of Consumer and Corporate Affairs, Ottawa, October 1985.

Shepherd, W.G. "Causes of Increased Competition in U.S. Economy, 1939-1980." *Review of Economics and Statistics,* November 1982.

Shughart, W.F. and Robert D. Tollison. "The Positive Economics of Antitrust Policy: A Survey Article." *International Review of Law and Economics,* 5, (1985).

Simison, Robert L. "Quiet War Rages on Technology's Front Line." *The Wall Street Journal,* December 24, 1985.

Simon, Herbert A. and Charles P. Bonini. "The Size Distribution of Business Firms." *American Economic Review,* September 1958, Vol. 48, pp. 607-17.

Skeoch, L.A. and B.C. McDonald. *Dynamic Change and Accountability in a Canadian Market Economy.* Ottawa: Department of Consumer and Corporate Affairs, 1976).

Solman, Paul and Thomas Friedman. Life and Death on the Corporate Battlefield. New York: Simon and Schuster, 1982.

Stigler, George J. *The Organization of Industry.* Homewood, Ill.: Richard D. Irwin Inc., 1968.

Stigler, George J. "A Theory of Delivered Price System." *American Economic Review,* Vol. 39, December 1949; reprinted in *The Organization of Industry,* Homewood, Ill.: Richard D. Irwin Inc., 1968.

Stonebreaker, R.J. "Corporate Profits and the Risk of Entry." *Review of Economics and Statistics,* February 1976.

Sylos-Labini, Paolo. *The Forces of Economic Growth.* Cambridge: Mass., M.I.T. Press, 1984.

Thurow, L. *Dangerous Currents: the State of Economics.* New York: Vintage Books, 1984.

Thurow, L. *The Zero Sum Society.* New York: Basic Books, 1980.

Utterback, James M. "The Process of Technical Innovation in Instrument Firms." Ph.D. dissertation, M.I.T., January 1969.

Williamson, O. "Economies as an Antitrust Defense." *American Economic Review,* March 1968.